The Art Institute of Chicago
From 1879 to the Modern Wing

ART SPACES

Erin Hogan

SCALA

D0637593

The Art Institute of Chicago

T he Art Institute of Chicago has always been a modern museum. Founded in 1879 as a repository of objects for students to copy—in the fine tradition of nineteenth-century art education—it was built on the belief in Chicago as a major international metropolis, a hub of modern transportation systems, the crossroads of a burgeoning and united nation. The earliest benefactors of the Art Institute invested heavily in the idea that an emerging world-class city needed a world-class museum, and they filled its galleries with the leading avant-garde art of the era, the paintings of Manet and Monet and Seurat and Renoir, the works that are now the basis of one of the leading Impressionist and Post-Impressionist collections in the world. One hundred and thirty years later, with the addition of the Renzo Piano–designed Modern Wing, the Art Institute still looks forward, embracing the new and fueled by the relentless civic optimism for which Chicago is known. The name of the building reflecting not the founding donors but the celebration of the moment, the

> The Art Institute's second building (far right) at Michigan Avenue and Van Buren Street, next to the Fine Arts Building and the Auditorium Building, c. 1890.

Modern Wing features state-of-the-art "green" technology and showcases a twentieth- and twenty-first-century art collection as immersed in the new as some of the museum's original gifts. The building is the latest embodiment of the ethos that has always guided the institution.

The Art Institute spent the first decade and a half of its existence roaming the streets of the bustling downtown. Incorporated under the name **The Chicago Academy of Fine Arts**, it rented space in 1879 in a commercial building on the southwest corner of State and Monroe streets. Three years later, in 1882, the Academy changed its name to **The Art Institute of Chicago**, and the institution leased and then purchased land at Michigan Avenue and Van Buren Street, not far from the entrance of the museum today. To the commercial building then occupying the site an addition designed by Burnham and Root was grafted. Five years later, in 1887, Burnham and Root designed an entirely new structure for this same site,

> The Art Institute of Chicago's building on Michigan Avenue at Van Buren Street, 1882.

> The Art Institute's permanent building under construction, 1892/93.

the entire complex occupying a (now demolished) building next to the (still standing) Fine Arts Building and Auditorium Building. This facility too would be quickly outgrown.

By 1890 the founding trustees, including Charles L. Hutchinson, the first president of the Board of Trustees, and Director William M. R. French had their eyes on more permanent quarters. Taking advantage of the upcoming World's Columbian Exposition, they struck a deal with the fair's organizers to share the cost of a structure that would hold events during the fair and then be turned over to the

Art Institute. On land filled with rubble from the Great Fire of 1871 and donated by the Chicago Park District Board, construction began in 1891 on a narrow stretch of property between Michigan Avenue and the railroad tracks that lined the shore of Lake Michigan. By November 1, 1893, after its use during the Exposition, the building became the home of the Art Institute. Designed by Shepley, Rutan and Coolidge, the successor firm to the office established by the great Boston architect H. H. Richardson, this structure—later named for trustee Robert Allerton—was designed in the reigning Beaux-Arts idiom, replete with loggia,

◄ View of the north façade of the Michigan Avenue building, showing artists' names on the architrave; photograph 1991.

classical columns, and the names of eminent artists, few of whom were actually represented in the museum's holdings, inscribed on the building's architrave.

The building's guardian lions—long among Chicago's favorite icons—were commissioned by Mrs. Henry Field (in memory of her husband), created by sculptor Edward Kemeys, and installed in 1894. Photographs of the young Art Institute depict a stolid edifice surrounded on three sides by vast, empty space, the lions isolated sentinels guarding the building as if it were a frontier outpost. While today the museum is a central hub—connected to the Loop on the west and the ecosystem of Grant and Millennium parks to the north, east, and south—the original building seemed to colonize a terra incognita of railroad yards, tracts of empty lands, and a decidedly unglamorous lakefront. The building was U shaped, with the longest face running down Michigan Avenue, flanked to the north and south by smaller

▲ The Art Institute of Chicago, c. 1900.

▲ Fullerton Hall,
1898; photo-
graph 2008.

wings. It retained this basic form for less than two years and was to undergo significant changes in rapid succession.

By 1895 the original U shape of the building was filled in with a one-story addition (later demolished) for the School of the Art Institute, built along the railroad tracks that separated the museum from the lakeshore. Three years later, Fullerton Hall—with its stained-glass dome designed by Louis Comfort Tiffany—was completed, and in 1901 its "pendant" space, the Ryerson Library, was finished as well. Both of these rooms, which were restored in 2001 and 1991, respectively, were designed by the original architects of the building, Shepley, Rutan and Coolidge.

Within less than a decade, then, the Art Institute was undergoing constant change. A new wing had been added, and the two open courts in the original plan had been filled in with a 425-seat

◄ View of the
    second-floor gal-
    leries, c. 1905, at
    the top of the
    original staircase
    in the Michigan
    Avenue building.

➤ Ryerson Library, 1901;
    photograph c. 1991.

auditorium and a library. The museum's collection at this time was dominated by a large gift from the government of France of hundreds of plaster casts of the great works of Greek and Roman art. Visitors entering the lobby in 1900 were greeted by a spatially dominant cast by the eminent American artist Daniel Chester French, the brother of the Art Institute's director. This plaster sculpture was a study for an even more imposing version of its subject, *The*

> A portion of the plaster-cast collection of Classical sculpture, c. 1910.

> The Michigan Avenue lobby with a plaster-cast study for Daniel Chester French's *The Republic* (1893); photograph c. 1900.

Republic, which, gilded and 65 feet tall, had welcomed visitors to the Court of Honor at the World's Columbian Exposition. A reduced replica stands today in Jackson Park on the city's South Side. In the gallery south of the lobby visitors found a cacophony of Roman casts; to the north, galleries of Renaissance casts. The second floor was largely devoted to paintings, the galleries carefully divided according to the earliest gifts—among them, the Henry Field Memorial Collection, the A. A. Munger Collection, and the Mr. and Mrs. Samuel M. Nickerson Collection—while other rooms even then recognized distinguished benefactors such as Elizabeth Hammond Stickney and Charles L. Hutchinson.

As the collections grew, so did the original Allerton Building. A mere ten years after its completion, a two-story-high gallery, named Blackstone Hall, replaced the 1895 one-story addition for the School. An enormous space, Blackstone Hall held more than 150 plaster casts as well as formidable architectural fragments, including a section of the portal of the Cathedral of St. Etienne, from Limoges, France, treated as a massive sculpture. The sheer mass and density of the works contained in Blackstone Hall were counterbalanced by intricate architectural ornamentation and

▲ Hutchinson Gallery,
December 1907.

A drawing class of the School of the Art Institute in Blackstone Hall (1895), c. 1908.

Blackstone Hall, c. 1905.

delicate balconies and balustrades, set off even further by the light that poured in from windows along the gallery's east wall.

For the next ten years, additional galleries and improvements, all designed by Shepley, Rutan and Coolidge, sprouted like buds from the Allerton stem: galleries for prints and drawings, second-floor galleries atop the double-height Blackstone Hall, a bridge from the Allerton Building to Blackstone Hall, an administrative wing, and in 1910, the Grand Staircase. The top of the Grand Staircase was crowned with a cast of *Winged Victory*. Then and now the central intersection of the original building, the Grand Staircase, more than a century later, remains without the dome that was intended to cover it. Meanwhile, that same year, on the exterior, a spacious terrace and balustrade wrapped around three sides of the

◄ The Art Institute of
Chicago following the
addition of terraces
and balustrades,
c. 1910.

► The Grand
Staircase, c. 1910.

building (the first and only time that the position of the guardian lions has changed).

The Art Institute, by 1911, had filled in its originally empty central court, expanded to the north and the south, and reworked its "front yard" in concert with the 1908 widening of Michigan Avenue. Its Neoclassical façade blackened by soot from the adjacent railroad tracks and dirt from the constant gritty bustle of the ever-expanding downtown, the museum placed itself, with a bold stroke, in the forefront of modern art by hosting the infamous 1913 Armory Show, known as the *International Exhibition of Modern Art*. This exhibition, one of the most scandalous presentations of contemporary art, had originated in New York. Filled with work excoriated in the New York press as radical, degenerate, and dangerous, this exhibition found a home in Chicago at the Art Institute, under the auspices of the Association of American Painters and Sculptors. Some students from the School of the Art

◄ Students from the
School of the Art
Institute protesting
the Armory Show on
the steps of the
museum, 1913.

Institute, however, took to the streets to protest the paintings of Cézanne, Duchamp, Van Gogh, Matisse, and Picasso.

The galleries of the Art Institute in the early years of the twentieth century were radically different from what is now considered standard display space. Patterned rugs and mosaics covered the floors; walls were painted in rich, deep colors; and billowing ferns and other plants further shaped the space. As it did with the Armory Show, the Art Institute often worked in conjunction with many organizations to mount exhibitions, including the Women's National Farm and Garden Association, which sponsored what were essentially garden shows within the museum's galleries.

Its halls filled and its temporary exhibition galleries on constant rotation, the Art Institute by 1916

> The Antiquarian Society Galleries of the Art Institute, 1914.

> The Henry Field Memorial Collection Gallery of the Art Institute, c. 1916, with an art-glass ceiling (now removed) designed by Tiffany and Co.

> Lorado Taft's
  *Fountain of the
  Great Lakes*
  (1907–13), seen
  just after its
  installation in
  1913 adjacent to
  the south terrace
  of the museum.

> > Aerial view
    showing
    Gunsaulus
    Hall, at right,
    extending east
    across the
    tracks of the
    Illinois Central
    Railroad,
    c. 1920.

was looking again to expand and began to eye the landfill to the east. To the building's eastern façade was added Gunsaulus Hall, which, spanning the tracks of the Illinois Central Railroad, remains the principal east-west artery of the Art Institute. This long, narrow structure consisted of two floors of galleries, the lower level originally daylit with generous floor-to-ceiling windows running the length of the space. Again, Shepley, Rutan and Coolidge (and then Coolidge and Hodgdon) were called upon for this phase of expansion. Four years later, in 1920, the Burnham Library of Architecture—the outgrowth of a bequest from the great Chicago architect and city planner Daniel H. Burnham—was designed by Howard Van Doren Shaw and constructed south of the Ryerson Library.

Gunsaulus Hall provided the Art Institute much needed gallery space, but it would not be connected to further major expansion for nearly ten years, when, between 1924 and 1925, the Charles L. Hutchinson Wing, the George Alexander McKinlock, Jr., Memorial Court, and the Kenneth Sawyer Goodman Memorial Theatre (designed by Howard Van Doren Shaw) were added. These structures were all an emphatic claim to

the land across the tracks. Coolidge and Hodgdon designed the Hutchinson Wing and the McKinlock Court, the latter, with its *Fountain of the Tritons* by Carl Milles (installed in 1931), still a central gathering point for visitors. Then, as now, this quiet courtyard, sheltered from the nearby train tracks and filled with towering trees and the sound of trickling water, is a place of respite from the dense limestone and energized galleries of the rest of the museum.

Named in honor of the institution's first president, who served from 1882 until his death in 1924, the Hutchinson Wing consisted of a phalanx of galleries that followed the north and south boundaries of the Art Institute footprint on the western side of the tracks. The interaction of McKinlock Court and the Hutchinson Wing is an early indication of how Art Institute leaders envisioned their eastward expansion, particularly given the extent to which the lakefront had been built up with landfill. The narrow strip of land originally east of the rail yard had grown by the 1920s into a sizeable tract. The Hutchinson Wing with its adjacent courtyard would eventually develop

▲ The George Alexander McKinlock, Jr., Memorial Court, 1924.

➤ McKinlock Court, following the 1931 installation of Carl Milles's *Fountain of the Tritons* (1926); photograph 1936.

into a prototype for a series of additions along that eastern front, with more galleries and neighboring courtyards providing light and circulation planned in stages or units—an expansion plan that could proceed over time as funding became available, not contingent on one great sum or one massive project. One step was made in this direction in 1927 with the construction of the Agnes Allerton Wing for the Department of Textiles, south of the Hutchinson Wing, designed by Coolidge and Hodgdon.

Another step, the most significant addition built from this prototype, was taken in 1939 with the completion of the Robert Allerton Wing (the original building having not yet been renamed for him). Designed as part of a grand scheme by Holabird and Root, it consisted of yet another suite of galleries surrounding two interior courtyards, similar in intent, if not sophistication, to McKinlock Court.

From the 1920s through the completion of this Allerton Wing, activities in other areas of the Art Institute did not cease as the "eastern front" was developed. In 1926, for example, an addition on the

ground level of the original building provided space for in-house needs and amenities for visitors such as a Members' Room, restaurant, and tea room. The following year, a link between the Goodman Theatre and McKinlock Court was built for the School. In 1929 the Burnham Library of Architecture was combined with the Ryerson Library and relocated in galleries adjacent to the Ryerson. The Goodman Theatre also expanded, adding a studio theater in 1929 (designed by Howard Van Doren Shaw) and offices and storage in 1938 (designed by Holabird and Root).

The pace of these expansions was vigorous. From the time of its initial occupation of the Michigan Avenue building following the close of the World's Fair, very few years had passed in which museum leaders were not planning, fund-raising, or overseeing the construction of these myriad additions. In the nearly five decades since 1893, the size of the museum more than doubled—the growth of its collections continuing to outpace its physical expansion—and the museum kept reaching new milestones. In 1933–34 the Century of Progress Exposition created an influx of visitors to Chicago, just as the Columbian Exposition had fifty years earlier. The museum hosted an *Exhibition of Painting and Sculpture* as its contribution to the fair, and even today the single-day attendance record for that exhibition of 44,442 still stands.

The year 1939 can be seen, then, as the culmination of the Art Institute's early and ambitious plans, those that saw the construction of everything the institution had become: a building straddling the Illinois Central tracks, with packed rectangular blocks of spacious galleries interspersed with peaceful courtyards, along with space for the School as well. The Century of Progress exhibition showcased the vitality of the museum and its role as a cultural hub in a city that had come into its own. And thus in 1939, while the city faced other challenges and responsibilities brought about by the onset of World War II, the museum settled into a brief period of dormancy.

Although the Art Institute had plans already drawn for continued growth on the east side, following the Holabird and Root plan, when it regrouped and began to expand again in the postwar period, its first project was the B. F. Ferguson Memorial Building

◄ Aerial view of the Art Institute, c. 1930.

of 1958. The galleries and physical plant had evolved constantly through the decades, yet the administrative work of the museum had been confined to the same space it had occupied since the 1920s. Thus museum leaders decided that office space was the first priority. The Ferguson Building (designed by Holabird and Root and Burgee), then as now, held offices for executives and curators, museum education, conservation, and museum photography, as well as packing and shipping facilities. Set against the highly articulated façade of the 1893 building, the plain face of Ferguson—unadorned and silent—would establish the language for the exteriors of the expansions to follow.

Through 1958 and 1959, several spaces were renovated or reconstructed, including the ground and main floors of Blackstone Hall, which included the addition of Morton Auditorium, and the main floor of the central building, refitted to include the first Glore Print Study Room.

With the construction of the Ferguson Building, it was finally acknowledged that the Art Institute could not continue to expand in terms of individual galleries and accompanying courtyards. Far more ambitious plans were required as the collections of the museum grew and enrollment in the School increased. The Ferguson Building was the first step of what might be called the second phase of the museum's evolution, one in which wings—not halls or galleries—were constructed, and previous additions were necessarily demolished rather than expanded. The pace of change slowed, but the additions themselves became grander, more comprehensive, and more enduring. The Art Institute of today reflects this second phase, which began its entrance into postwar Modernism in the austere lines and bureaucratic solidity of the Ferguson Building.

The second building of this phase, completed in 1962, was the Sterling Morton Wing, designed by Shaw, Metz and Associates. Emerging from the south side of the original building, the wing provided a symmetrical counterpoint to the Ferguson Building on the north. Featuring a stunning, freestanding spiral staircase and connected to the central complex by a two-story, glass-walled atrium flooded on sunny days with light, the Morton Wing provided two levels of galleries and

Within the image: ICONS OF DIVINITY FROM SOUTH AND SOUTHEAST ASIA

THE T.T.

▲ Staircase within the atrium of the Sterling Morton Wing; photograph 2008.

◄ The South Stanley McCormick Memorial Court (1965) and the exterior of the Morton Wing (1962), showing Lorado Taft's *Fountain of the Great Lakes* (1907–13) installed against the building's west façade; photograph 1994.

► Since its installation in 1965, the South Garden, with its planters of cockspur hawthorn trees, has remained essentially unchanged; photograph 2007.

In 1974, behind this stolid frontage, Gunsaulus Hall was still reaching across the tracks but many of the eastern additions from earlier in the century were destroyed to make room for the most ambitious project in the School's history, the construction of the Columbus Drive studios, classrooms, galleries, and auditorium, which also included, for the first time, an east entry to the museum. The architects of this East Wing project were Skidmore, Owings and Merrill. By the time the building was dedicated in 1976, the entire east face of the Art Institute had completely changed. Eschewing the solid rectangular bulk of the Ferguson and Morton wings, architect Walter Netsch of SOM instead created a rhythmic series of angular forms culminating in the stepped and tilted planes of the east entrance and the dramatically pitched roof of Rubloff Auditorium, still the largest auditorium of the Art Institute campus. While earlier additions were in

▲ Aerial view of the East Wing and School of the Art Institute under construction, c. 1975.

keeping with the tone and mass of the original building, the East Wing struck a decidedly different note, still clad in limestone but fronted with reflective glass and composed of forceful, acute angles. The complex was considered complete with the installation of Isamu Noguchi's commissioned sculpture, *Celebration of the 200th Anniversary of the Founding of the Republic*, dedicated November 30, 1976.

Filling out the interior of the new East Wing was one of the most remarkable projects undertaken by the museum: the reconstruction of a portion of Adler and Sullivan's original Chicago Stock Exchange Building. Built the same year as the Beaux-Arts home of the museum, 1893, the edifice was demolished in 1972, but the appointments of its Trading Room and the entrance arch to the building were saved by architectural preservationists. Overseen by Vinci-Kenny Architects and completed in 1977, the Stock Exchange Trading Room today exhibits some of the most richly patterned stenciling of Louis Sullivan's entire career, one composition alone requiring fifty-two colors. His

◄ View of Isamu Noguchi's fountain *Celebration of the 200th Anniversary of the Founding of the Republic* outside the East Wing, dedicated in November 1976.

► The Chicago Stock Exchange Trading Room, designed by Adler and Sullivan, reconstructed within the Art Institute, c. 1975–77; photograph 1983.

brilliant canvas-covered walls and ceiling, illuminated by decidedly modern light fixtures, are as vivid as when they first framed the frantic floor trading that made Chicago an economic force in the nation.

With the addition of the Morton Wing and the East Wing, the Art Institute had expanded on a scale unprecedented in its history. But there was still, as ever, a desire for growth. Over the next decade, Marc Chagall's *America Windows* would be commissioned and installed; the Department of Textiles would be rebuilt; and the ground floor of the main building would be reconfigured to create galleries, storage, a conservation laboratory, and offices for the Department of Photography. New spaces for the display

◄ The Roger McCormick Memorial Court within the Daniel F. and Ada L. Rice Building (1988); photograph 1998.

▲ Galleries of European painting and sculpture on the second floor of the Allerton Building following the 1985–87 renovation.

The Modern Wing

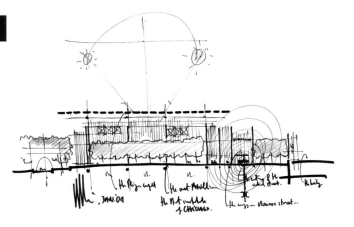

If the only constant is change, then the Art Institute was ready to change again. In 1999, the museum, under Director James N. Wood, selected Renzo Piano as the architect of its largest expansion to date. Piano, with offices in Genoa and Paris, where he directs the Renzo Piano Building Workshop, was already well known as the designer of Paris's Centre Georges Pompidou (1977; with Richard Rogers) and of both the Menil Collection (1987) and the Cy Twombly Gallery (1995) in Houston, but he had yet to be commissioned for the projects for which he is now perhaps best known: the Nasher Sculpture Center in Dallas (2003); the High Museum of Art in Atlanta (2005); and the California Academy of Sciences in San Francisco (2008). With his place as the foremost museum architect of our time assured, Piano's practice is defined by his belief in transparency, his commitment to materials and sustainable practices, and the ethereal quality he imparts to these cultural repositories.

Piano drew his ideas for what was then being called the New North Wing from the rectilinearity and flatness of Chicago and from the movement of the sun across the unmoving regularity of the city's street plan. Piano's design represented at once a continuation of and a radical departure from the museum's

▲ Renzo Piano's sketch of the Monroe Street elevation of the Modern Wing, 2004.

▲ Former Art Institute Director James N. Wood with Joost Moolhuijzen of the Renzo Piano Building Workshop.

▶ Renzo Piano's sketch of the "flying carpet" above the Modern Wing, 2004.

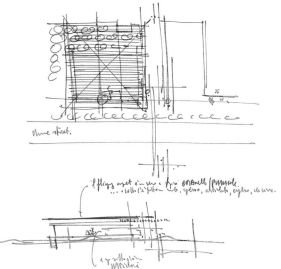

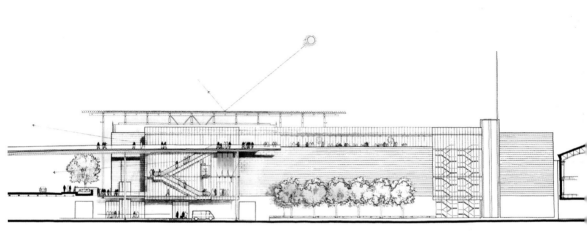

existing architecture. Like his predecessors, he favored natural light and a sense of circulation—critical to some of the Art Institute's earliest expansions designed around interior courtyards and carried through via the use of skylights or laylights in the Grand Staircase, Allerton Building, and Rice Building. Also like his predecessors, Piano proposed a building clad in Indiana limestone, keeping in character with the existing complex.

But Piano's design for the wing also represented a very different architectural voice for the Art Institute, not the bass notes of the prior additions, but a soaring soprano. His limestone cladding works in concert with a façade of glass and thin steel mullions

▲ Rendering of the preliminary design of the west façade of the Modern Wing, with a portion of the Nichols Bridgeway.

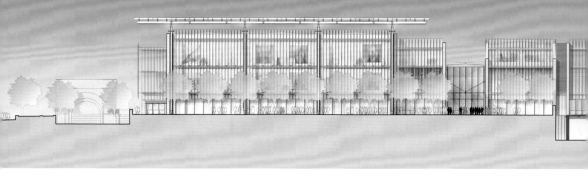

▲ Rendering of the Monroe Street elevation.

to impart an emphatic verticality set against the horizontality of Ferguson, Morton, Rice, and even the railroad tracks that still run under Gunsaulus Hall. His proposed building took the museum in a new direction, up instead of out. The steel mullions referenced and echoed the history of modern architecture for which the city of Chicago is known, but at the same time, with their thin frames and soft white color, they updated structural steel for a new century.

The plan for the building changed very little from the proposal stage to the actual construction. Piano conceived two "pavilions" for the building, connected by a main artery that would form a north-south intersection to the east-west trajectory of

Gunsaulus Hall. Both pavilions have three levels of galleries and associated spaces, with a full sublevel for storage and mechanical functions. In the east, and larger, pavilion, Piano planned an education center double the size of the existing facility housed in the 1893 building, with a separate entrance for students arriving in school buses; a second floor devoted to contemporary art; and a third floor devoted to twentieth-century European painting and sculpture. Inside the museum's second "front door" on Monroe Street, the building's "main street" would house ticketing, information, and member services; a "black box" gallery for new media; photography galleries; and an entry into the existing building. Also connected to the east pavilion would be a ground-level garden between the New North Wing and Rubloff Auditorium to the south.

The west pavilion, at street level, would hold a museum shop, more visitors' services, and a special exhibition hall. The second floor would contain, along with another link to the existing building, galleries for the museum's Department of Architecture and Design and a meeting room for the institution's Board of Trustees. The third floor, overlooking the Ferguson

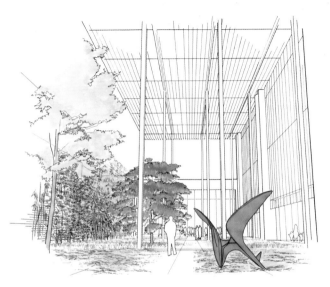

▲ Rendering of a preliminary design of the garden court between the east pavilion of the Modern Wing and Rubloff Auditorium.

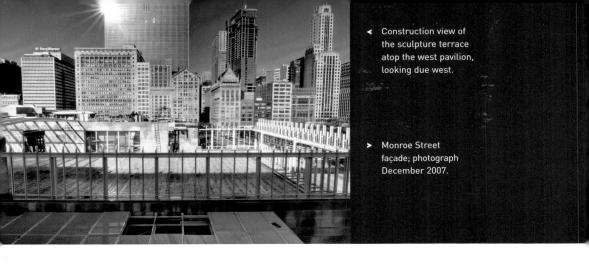

Construction view of
the sculpture terrace
atop the west pavilion,
looking due west.

Monroe Street
façade; photograph
December 2007.

Building to the "cliff wall" of Michigan Avenue sky-scrapers, includes a dining facility and a sculpture terrace with a vantage of Millennium Park and the sweeping forms of Frank Gehry's Jay Pritzker Pavilion across the street.

Piano has said that "architecture must fly: it is made of emotions, tensions, transparency." All of his projects have taken this most firmly rooted of the arts—architecture—and transformed it into something that soars. The proposed New North Wing did indeed fly, with a dominating sense of lightness and air. Reflected in the north-facing façade are the towering

◄ Detail of the Monroe Street facade.

skyscrapers that form the northern edge of Millennium Park. The double glass curtain wall—manufactured in Germany because no American plant could fabricate such large sheets of glass—works as a trap for the outside air, warming it or cooling it as a protective measure for the works of art inside and conserving the energy usually required to maintain ideal gallery conditions.

Entering the building, visitors are enveloped in the double-height Anne D. and Kenneth C. Griffin Court, the main circulation space of the wing. Here the verticality of the façade is carried through in the

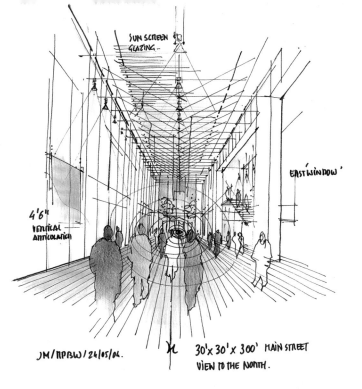

> Perspective sketch of "main street," or
> Griffin Court, looking north, 2004.

Labels within sketch:

SUN SCREEN GLAZING

EAST WINDOW

4'6" VERTICAL ANTICOLARIA

JM/RPBW/24/05/04.

30'x 30'x 300' MAIN STREET
VIEW TO THE NORTH.

first impression of the building by the delicate frames and trusses—inspired by Piano's passion for sailing—that support the skylight atop this main artery. A suspended staircase provides access to the galleries above, set against a sheer wall that separates the building from the garden on Columbus Drive and gives visitors a view of the south façade of the east pavilion, which echoes the insistent upward momentum of the north face with its mullions and slender anchoring piers.

Driven by the challenge of working with light while controlling it sufficiently to protect the works of

◄ ◄ Construction view of "main street" or Griffin Court, looking north.

◄ Construction view of the suspended staircase adjacent to Griffin Court.

► Construction view of the 300-foot-long Griffin Court, looking southeast.

◄ Construction view of the "flying carpet" over the east pavilion and the site of the garden between the new addition and Rubloff Auditorium.

▼ Construction view of the assembly of the "flying carpet," looking northeast.

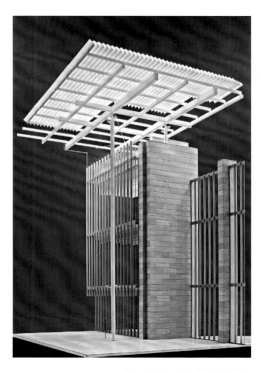

> Model showing limestone wall, glass curtain wall, and "flying carpet" roof.

art, Piano devised a floating canopy, a "flying carpet" of shaped blades that bring light into the galleries from the north and shield them from the harsh light of the east, south, and west. Caught by these curved blades, light is filtered into the top-floor galleries through a skylight and velum scrim, transforming the sun's rays, season by season and minute by minute, into a functioning property of the building. This flying carpet is surely one of the most distinctive features of the entire structure. By floating above the roof of the east pavilion, it embodies the soaring quality that Piano speaks of, protecting the galleries beneath and shading the garden to the south. Aesthetically, it

takes the Art Institute from its foundation in Indiana limestone in the opposite direction, toward the skyline of the city and the sky above, while also resonating, in its broad, flat sweep, with the lake to the east.

Composed of 2,656 blades or fins, engineered precisely for the Art Institute's location, the flying carpet is Piano's "soft machine," filtering light as do the tree canopies in the neighboring parks. This "soft machine," somewhat paradoxically, is made possible by the city's rigid urban grid. "All this is made easier in a city that is built on precise north-south and east-west axes, perfectly in tune with the cycle of the sun," Piano has said. "The shelter will give the museum what it needs in terms of light, much as the open lattice of the Pritzker Pavilion gives shelter to the Great Lawn in terms of sound."

◄ View of the "flying carpet" above the east pavilion of the Modern Wing, looking northeast.

▼ Construction view, looking north from the roof
of the Modern Wing toward the Pritzker
Pavilion, Great Lawn, and Lurie Garden in
Millennium Park.

Piano's references to Millennium Park are no
mere nods to the Art Institute's neighbor to the north.
Completed in 2004, Millennium Park is one of
Chicago's most ambitious civic projects. Here monu-
mental public art—including Jaume Plensa's *Crown
Fountain* and Anish Kapoor's magical *Cloud Gate*—is
set amidst carefully tended gardens and walkways
that surround the Park's central feature: the Frank
Gehry–designed Pritzker Pavilion, a daring bandshell
of fractured and curled ribbons that glow red at night
like an enormous hearth for the city. The Pavilion is
the centerpiece of a park that draws millions of visitors every year.

The vitality and energy of the Park, just across
Monroe Street from the Art Institute site, became a
catalyst for the only major modification to the build-

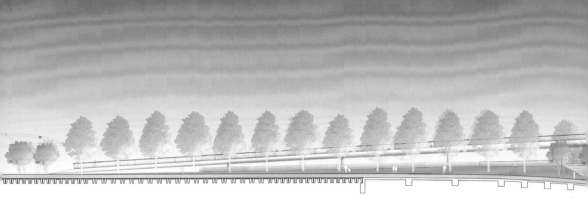

ing since its original plan: the addition of the Alexandra C. and John D. Nichols Bridgeway in 2004. A 620-foot-long pedestrian bridge, it runs deep into the Park, landing near the edge of the Great Lawn and connecting on the other end to the third floor of Piano's west pavilion. Thin and graceful—described alternately as a blade or the hull of a ship—the bridge draws together these two hubs of civic life, the Park and the Art Institute. It certainly provides

visitors with commanding views, but it also, perhaps more critically, increases circulation around the entire lakefront, bringing Millennium Park to the Art Institute and thus into the wider Grant Park and lakefront campuses.

The Nichols Bridgeway represents the final feature of an Art Institute addition that embodies the ethos of the museum since its founding: constantly seeking the new and the best, striving for growth,

and placing itself emphatically at the center of civic life. It is in this spirit that the building was named by its anonymous founding donors in 2005, nearly ten years after Piano was selected to design it: the Modern Wing.

Modern in name, in orientation, and in its collections, it is also modern in making use of the most up-to-date technologies and sustainable practices, both of which are hallmarks of Piano's practice as an architect. The façade of double glass increases the building's energy efficiency by forming a buffer against cold and warm air, lessening the load on the cooling and heating systems. The interior layer of glass is covered by a screen of photovoltaic cells that protect the art from direct sunlight; light sensors in the galleries adjust the artificial light according to the brightness of the day or time of day. This unique system makes it possible to maintain consistent light

▲ Rendering of the final design of the west façade and the Alexandra C. and John D. Nichols Bridgeway.

levels in the Modern Wing, while maximizing the amount of daylight used to illuminate the galleries.

These ingenious systems—the double curtain wall, the calibrated lighting systems, the use of as much natural light as safe and possible—make Piano's one of the most energy efficient museum buildings in the United States. While the museum has made attempts in the past to incorporate sustainable practices—most notably the solar array installed in 2002 atop the Rice Building, which provides enough energy to light the upper-level east galleries—never before has it made such a commitment to "green" technology. Only now, reaping the benefits of modern engineering, could museums, with their strict requirements for light, temperature, and humidity levels, even dream of ceding some of that control to the elements. The Art Institute will be applying for one of the highest ratings—silver—granted by the U.S. Green

◄ Perspective sketch, looking north, of the Nichols Bridgeway.

◄ Construction view of the Nichols Bridgeway, looking south.

◄ Rendering of a third-floor gallery of modern European art in the east pavilion of the Modern Wing.

► Art Institute Director James Cuno, Joost Moolhuijzen, Renzo Piano and Dominique Rat of the Renzo Piano Building Workshop, and Bob Larsen of Interactive Design Architects.

Building Council as part of its Leadership in Energy and Environmental Design (LEED) program.

With the evolution of the Modern Wing, the most ambitious expansion in the museum's history, current Director James Cuno thought it only fitting that the project be accompanied by the most ambitious reinstallation program of the existing buildings in the museum's history. The Modern Wing, with its 264,000 square feet, increases the museum's total size by nearly 35 percent, allowing every one of its ten curatorial departments to display more of their permanent holdings. It represents a rare opportunity to step back from, examine, and reshape the story of artistic production that has been told through the 130 years of the museum's existence. Thus, three teams—Renzo Piano Building Workshop, Chicago's Vinci Hamp Architects, and the young firm of Workshop Hakomori Yantrasast (wHY) in Los Angeles—are renovating existing galleries, building new ones, and working with curators to reinstall their collections.

The changes will be sweeping and dramatic, nowhere more so than in the long arm of Gunsaulus Hall, its windows bricked over since the 1930s, which in 2008 was transformed into the light-filled Alsdorf

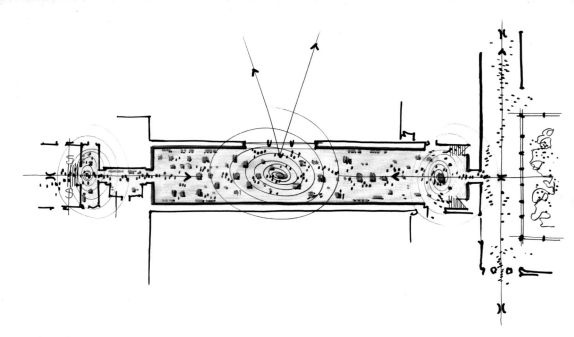

▲ Renzo Piano's 2006 sketch for the
renovation of Gunsaulus Hall.

Galleries of Indian, Himalayan, Southeast Asian, and Islamic Art. With a new plan by Piano, some of its original windows have been uncovered and restored, allowing daylight into the gallery for the first time in more than 70 years and affording visitors the chance to look directly out over the railroad tracks and toward Millennium Park.

Such changes will affect every department as well: in June 2008 the Department of Prints and Drawings dedicated new galleries designed by Kulapat Yantrasast of wHY; the former home of contemporary art, Morton Wing, will be refitted on the lower level to house the museum's collection of African art and Indian art of the Americas; the upper

▲ View from the newly renovated Gunsaulus Hall, looking north, 2008.

> Monroe Street elevation of the Modern Wing, as seen from the Lurie Garden in Millennium Park, fall 2008.

level of the Morton Wing will afford the museum the space to fold European decorative arts, textiles, and the Harding Collection of Arms and Armor into the painting and sculpture galleries devoted to art of the same period. In the upper level of the Allerton Building and upper Gunsaulus Hall, Vinci Hamp is overseeing the design and construction of the expanded space for the museum's renowned collection of European, and particularly Impressionist and Post-Impressionist, painting.

A suite of galleries dedicated to the art of design from Europe and the United States is planned for the lower level of the Rice Building, uniting, for the first time, European decorative arts with twentieth-century and contemporary design. And galleries formerly dedicated to architecture—their location atop the Ryerson Library a legacy of the era when the Department of Architecture was an extension of that library—will be filled with the museum's collection of American folk art when the Department of Architecture and Design moves their principal galleries into the Modern Wing.

No other museum has attempted such a reinstallation program while remaining open with a full slate of exhibitions and programs, further evidence of the Art Institute's dual commitment to serving its visitors in the present while looking constantly to the future. The character of the museum is mirrored in Piano's description of building sites as "wonderful places, where everything is in movement . . . a great human adventure . . . a place of extraordinary discoveries." Here at the leading edge of the twenty-first century, the Art Institute of Chicago, with the completion of the Modern Wing and the renovation of buildings that date from nearly every decade since 1893, is not preparing for the moment when everything is finished and complete; instead it recognizes that art, culture, and civic life are constantly changing, always "in movement." It is the character of the museum to reflect that fluidity by embracing the new and seeking growth in every opportunity. This fluidity is writ large in the architectural history of the museum, and with the addition of the Modern Wing, thrown open to the sky, the lakefront, the parks, and the city.

Copyright © 2009 The Art Institute of Chicago

First published in 2009 by
Scala Publishers Limited
Northburgh House
10 Northburgh Street
London EC1V 0AT
www.scalapublishers.com

Produced in collaboration with
The Art Institute of Chicago
111 South Michigan Avenue
Chicago, Illinois 60603-6404
www.artic.edu

Distributed outside The Art Institute of Chicago
in the book trade by
Antique Collectors' Club Limited
Eastworks
116 Pleasant Street, Suite 60B
Easthampton, MA 01027
United States of America

ISBN 978-1-85759-580-2

All rights reserved.

No part of the contents of this book may be reproduced, stored in a retrieval system, or transmitted in
any form or by any means, electronic, mechanical,
photocopying, recording, or otherwise, without the
written permission of The Art Institute of Chicago
and Scala Publishers.

Designed by Pooja Bakri
Edited by Robert V. Sharp, Director of Publications,
The Art Institute of Chicago
Production assistance by Sarah Guernsey, Associate
Director of Publications, and Kate Kotan,
Production Assistant
Photography editing by Joseph Mohan,
Photography Editor
Project Management by Amanda Freymann

Except where credited below, all photographs were
produced by the Department of Imaging, Christopher
Gallagher, Associate Director.

Historic Architecture and Landscape Image
Collection, Ryerson and Burnham Archives, the Art
Institute of Chicago (image 77205): 2
Judith Bromley: 35R
Chicago History Museum: 5
James Iska: 43, 59
Joseph Mohan: 29
Renzo Piano Building Workshop: 37, 38R, 39, 40, 41,
45, 49, 54–55, 57, 58, 60
Bob Thall: 33
Tigerhill Studio: 30
Charles G. Young, Interactive Design Architects: Front
cover, 42, 44, 46, 47, 48, 50, 51, 52, 53, 56, 63, 64

Every effort has been made to acknowledge copyright of images where applicable. Any errors or omis-
sions are unintentional and should be brought to the
attention of the publishers.

PARTY PIECES

10570775

PARTY PIECES
COCKTAIL FOOD WITH A DIFFERENCE

POLLY TYRER

Macdonald Orbis

A Macdonald Orbis BOOK
© Polly Tyrer 1986

First published in Great Britain in 1986 by Macdonald & Co (Publishers) Ltd
London & Sydney
A member of BPCC plc

Reprinted 1987

All rights reserved
No part of this publication may be reproduced, stored in a retrieval system, or
transmitted, in any form or by any means without the prior permission in writing
of the publisher, nor be otherwise circulated in any form of binding or cover
other than that in which it is published and without a similar condition including
this condition being imposed on the subsequent purchaser.

British Library Cataloguing in Publication Data
Tyrer, Polly
    Party pieces: cocktail food with a
    difference.
    1. Snack foods   2. Entertaining
    I. Title
    641.5'68   TX740

    ISBN 0-356-12569-6

Filmset by SX Composing Ltd, Rayleigh.
Printed in Spain

Produced, designed and edited by Shuckburgh Reynolds Ltd,
289 Westbourne Grove, London W11 2QA

Editor: Gila Falkus
Designer: Clare Clements
Photographer: Martin Brigdale
Home Economist: Polly Tyrer

Macdonald & Co (Publishers) Ltd, Greater London House,
Hampstead Road, London NW1 7QX

FOR JENNY

ACKNOWLEDGEMENTS

Thanks to Gila Falkus for her painstaking work editing this book; to Jenny Kieldsen for help with the home economy and generally getting things right; to Leith's Good Food Ltd, especially Anne Renowden and Robert Kelso; to Prue Leith and Cynthia Vivian for the loan of their cookery libraries; and, for general help and good ideas, to Seemah Joshua, Annie Langford and those at Springfield Farm.

Contents

INTRODUCTION

In the 1920s and 30s cocktail parties with their dry martinis, aspic toasts and ladies in chic black dresses, were considered the height of style. But, for over forty years, the idea of a drinks party became as stale as the dried up canapés that were usually served. Now cocktail parties are once again in vogue, hard on the heels of today's fashionable cocktail bars. Gone is the austere image of the 1920s – cocktails are bright and exotic-looking; cocktail food is fresh and varied.

It is hardly surprising that the cocktail party has survived – they certainly have a lot to recommend them. You can pay back all those social debts in one go. The menu can be adapted for weddings, christenings, birthdays, 'just drinks' or even barbecues (see the menu suggestions on pages 152-3). You can also have a lot of fun creating delicious-tasting and irresistible looking food. The only rules to remember are that the food must be small enough to be eaten in one or two bites and not too messy to be picked up with the fingers. But although most people know how to cook a meal for their family and friends, they have no idea how to tackle cocktail food for a party of 50. This book gives lots of new recipe ideas, from the ultra-sophisticated to the casual, and some advice on how to estimate quantities and how to deal with any problems that you may encounter.

8

Each recipe in this book will make about 20 mouthfuls of food. For a drinks party you should allow 10 mouthfuls of food per head; 4 mouthfuls with pre-lunch or dinner drinks; 8 savoury plus 4 sweet mouthfuls for a wedding reception (but increase this to 15 mouthfuls if the guests are unlikely to go on for a meal afterwards).

Bear in mind how the food will be prepared and carefully select the menu so that there is not too much work to do on the day of the party. Some items freeze well; some are quick to make; some need last-minute attention. The recipes indicate how much preparation can be done in advance. Don't leave too many things to be done after the guests have arrived or you will be a slave at your own party.

As a general rule, choose food that will give a variety of texture, colour and flavour and think about its appearance too. Cold cocktail bits can be arranged as an assortment on a platter. This is best done in tightly packed rows decorated with cress and olives or slices of radish. Food accompanied by a dip can be served on a round plate with the dip in the centre. Hot bits are best served with only one kind on each plate.

Make a shopping list well in advance and be prepared to spend some time doing this thoroughly. Check the availability of anything unusual – hunting around at the last minute can be irritatingly time-consuming. Suppliers tend to be keen to let you know that most foods are available all year round, but when it comes to the crunch there can be some obscure reason why they haven't, after all, got what you require. 'Spinach only arrives from Italy on Tuesdays.' 'Crab claws are scarce in spring because the crabs are not yet large enough to harvest', and so on. Pin your supplier down and give your order well in advance. It is far better to change the menu sooner than later if there is any doubt about availability.

When it comes to preparation, the most speedy method of tackling cocktail party food is undoubtedly by a production line system. For example, Smoked Salmon Wheels (p. 45) are best made in the following stages:

1. Lay out all the bread slices in pairs.
2. Flatten them with a rolling pin.
3. Butter all the bread.
4. Cover the bread with smoked salmon.
5. Season with lemon juice and black pepper.
6. Roll up and chill in the refrigerator.
7. Slice all the rolls and trim them neatly.

The choice of menu will also depend on whether waiters or waitresses will be helping on the day of the party. If there is to be no help at all, it is best to limit the choice of food to 5 items and not to include more than 2 hot bits. (That is, if allowing 10 mouthfuls of food per guest, choose 5 different items and make 2 of each kind for each person.) If you are employing help, allow one server for every 35 guests for the food, one bartender for every 50 guests if only serving a limited bar (say sherry, wine and a soft drink), and one bartender per 30 guests if serving a mixed bar or cocktails.

Deciding on how much drink to supply can be a tricky question. It is disastrous for a cocktail party to run dry and as most off-licences supply on a sale or return basis, it is best to over-order. Remember, though, that any bottles left over must be returned completely intact, including the labels.

There are many options as to how much variety of drink to supply. It is perfectly acceptable to offer only wine or champagne. A small bar of perhaps wine, one or two kinds of spirits and sherry is another alternative, or a full bar with even a choice of two or three cocktails, if you are really ambitious. The budget will probably be the deciding factor. Whatever you decide, always include some mineral water and fruit juice for the non-drinkers, drivers and those just trying to sober up before going home.

The drink can be served either from a tended bar or wine and a small selection can be passed round on trays. One bottle of wine will fill 6 glasses. If only wine or champagne are being served, allow half a bottle per person. In the case of wine, two-thirds should be white and one-third red. For a mixed bar, in my experience, gin and whisky are the most popular spirits with vodka and bacardi coming a close second. Campari, dry and sweet martini and sherry should also be available. For a mixed bar for 50 people a reasonable order would consist of:

Gin, 3 bottles	**Red Wine**, 4 bottles
Whisky, 3 bottles	**Soda Water**, 6×500 ml
Vodka, 1 bottle	**Tonic Water**, 12×500 ml
Dry Martini, 1 bottle	**American Dry**, 6×500 ml
Sweet Martini, 1 bottle	**Tomato Juice**, 3 litres
Dry Sherry, 2 bottles	**Orange Juice**, 12 litres
Sweet Sherry, 1 bottle	**Bitter Lemon**, 6×500 ml
Brandy, ½ bottle	**Coca Cola**, 12 cans
White Wine, 9 bottles	**Mineral Water**, 12 litres

There are many books available with recipes and suggestions for cocktails. Unless you really want to go to town, a choice of three cocktails should be enough. Look closely at the list of ingredients before you start: some recipes require a dash of this and a drop of the other and suddenly the whole exercise can become quite costly. Remember, again, that unless you have 'help', you can easily become a slave at your own party.

12

If there is not sufficient refrigerator space for cooling wine, allow 5 kg (10 lb) of ice to chill each case. Place the bottles in a large plastic bowl (a baby's bath or even a clean dustbin is ideal) and pour the ice on top. If ice is only needed for drinks, make a few extra trays and store the cubes in a plastic box in the freezer. Crushed ice for cocktails can be made in a liquidizer or food processor at the last minute.

For a cocktail party to be enjoyable, it is important to keep the number of guests manageable. It is all too easy for an over-crowded room to feel like a zoo. As a rough guide, two average-sized reception rooms will be comfortable for 50 people. But remember to count helpers when totting up the numbers and don't forget to allow space for your bar. The type of party will indicate the space and facilities needed. For instance, a wedding reception is likely to involve a few grannies and to last for longer than an evening drinks party so provision should be made for a few small tables and chairs.

It is a good idea to rehearse the party in your mind to check whether you have everything you need. Where will the coats go? Have you enough plates? Can all the food be eaten with fingers only? Will you need napkins? What about ashtrays? Glasses? Coasters? Off licences will usually supply glasses free of charge if they are providing the drink. If you need more than glasses, there are many catering equipment hire companies (see the Equipment Checklist on page 15).

For a formal cocktail party, it is usual to send a written or printed invitation and this should state what time the guests are expected to leave as well as to arrive. The idea is to give them the opportunity to make arrangements for a meal afterwards, but it can also be useful to the host in preventing the party from lasting all evening. It is usually sensible, though, to assume that there will be a few hangers on and to have some more substantial food available (in your freezer, for instance) in case they would like to stay for dinner. For a more casual party, a telephone call to the guests is all that is necessary. If the time the party should finish is important, let them know then – tactfully.

A cocktail party is an ideal way to entertain. It can be anything you like – extravagant, economical, small and sophisticated, for 5 or 500 people. With careful planning and by following these guidelines, the host or hostess can prepare the food, still be free to enjoy the party themselves and be remembered for having given 'a cocktail party with a difference'.

EQUIPMENT CHECK LIST

CHINA
6-inch plates for guests to put
food on
10-inch plates for serving hot
food and food with dips
Small bowls for serving dips

GLASSWARE
(allow 1½ glasses per guest)
Port/sherry glasses
Brandy balloons
Tulip-champagne and white wine
glasses
Whisky tumblers for mixed drinks
and soft drinks
Tall tumblers for cocktails and
soft drinks
Goblets for red wine and mixed
drinks
Water jugs for serving fruit juice

TABLEWARE
Oval serving dishes
Round serving dishes
Ice bowls and spoons
Serving trays for passing drinks
Ashtrays
Tablecloths to cover bar, serving
tables and any small tables
used
Linen napkins for service
Paper napkins (small cocktail size
ones are very handy)
Tea cloths
Plastic ice bath
Trestle tables for bar and food
Card tables, if needed, round the
room
Chairs
Coat rail hangers, tickets and pins

FISH

Top: *Smoked Halibut on Rye with Salmon Roe and Lime;* right: *Smoked Trout Mousse and Smoked Salmon Parcels;* bottom: *Spinach Roulade with Smoked Salmon Mousse and Taramasalata Toasties;* centre: *New Potatoes with Sour Cream and Mock Caviar and a Choux Puff with Curried Crab and Apple.*

Fritto Misto with Green Mayonnaise

100 g (4 oz) squid, cleaned
100 g (4 oz) sole, whiting or plaice, skinned and
boned
100 g (4 oz) scampi
100 g (4 oz) whitebait
Oil for deep-frying
Seasoned flour
FOR THE BATTER
50 g (2 oz) plain flour
Pinch of salt
1 egg, separated
150 ml (¼ pt) milk and water, mixed half and half
2 tsp oil
FOR THE SAUCE
1 bunch watercress
300 ml (½ pt) mayonnaise

First make the sauce: Wash the watercress thoroughly in salted water and remove the stalks. Purée with a tbsp of boiling water. Stir into the mayonnaise and set aside in a small round dish.

Cut the squid into rings, the white fish into strips and the scampi in half. To make the batter: Sift the flour and salt into a bowl, make a well in the centre and drop the egg yolk into this. Mix, gradually adding the milk and water and incorporating the flour from the sides, until smooth and creamy. Add the oil. Beat the egg white until stiff and fold into the mixture.

Heat the oil for frying until a drop of batter will sizzle slowly. Dust the fish with seasoned flour, dip in the batter and fry, a few pieces at a time, until golden brown. Drain on absorbent paper and sprinkle with salt. Serve immediately on a round plate with the green mayonnaise in the centre.

SMOKED TROUT MOUSSE AND SMOKED SALMON PARCELS

1 large smoked trout
3 tbsp double cream, lightly whipped
Lemon juice
1 tsp horseradish sauce
Salt and ground black pepper
175 g (6 oz) smoked salmon
20 tiny sprigs of dill

Cut the head and tail off the smoked trout and remove the skin and bones. Mince the flesh or chop it in a food processor. Mix with the whipped cream and season with the lemon juice, horseradish, salt and black pepper. Cut the smoked salmon into 40 strips, roughly 2.5 cm (1 in) by 8 cm (3 in). Lay two strips of smoked salmon on the work-top, arranged in a cross. Put a spoonful of smoked trout mousse in the centre of the cross and fold the ends over the top. Decorate with dill.

TIP: The smoked trout mousse freezes well. The parcels can be made the day before and stored in the refrigerator, covered in cling film.

CHOUX PUFFS WITH CURRIED CRAB AND APPLE

20 choux puffs (see recipe, p. 146)
175 g (6 oz) white king crab meat, frozen or
tinned
½ red apple, grated with the skin on
150 ml (¼ pt) mayonnaise
Curry Paste
Milk
Paprika

Defrost the frozen crab meat slowly. Drain well and pat dry with absorbent paper. Mix with the grated apple. Flavour the mayonnaise with enough curry paste to give a mild, spicy flavour. (If the mayonnaise is very thick, thin it to a coating consistency with a little milk.) Mix the crab and apple with the mayonnaise.
Slit the choux puffs halfway through with a diagonal cut from top to bottom. Fill with the crab mixture and sprinkle with paprika.

SCALLOP MOUSSELINIS

2 large scallops
175 g (6 oz) haddock, skin removed
1 egg white
150 ml (¼ pt) double cream, chilled
Parsley, finely chopped
Salt and ground white pepper
Anchovy essence
Lemon juice
20 puff pastry croûtes (see recipe, p. 150)
1 tbsp mayonnaise
1 tbsp fresh herbs, finely chopped

Remove the corals and tough muscles (opposite the corals) from the scallops. Discard the muscles. Plunge the corals into boiling water, then immediately into cold water. Drain and cut into small pieces and set aside. Pat the scallops very dry with absorbent paper. Purée with the haddock and egg white in a liquidizer or food processor. Turn into a bowl, cover and chill for several hours. Lightly whip 2 tbsp cream, gradually beat the rest into the scallop mixture. Fold in the whipped cream. Add the chopped corals, parsley and season with salt, pepper, anchovy essence and lemon juice. Butter two sheets of tin foil. Spoon the scallop mixture in lines about 5 cm (2 in) away from the narrow edge of each sheet. Carefully roll up into a sausage and twist the ends to tighten.

Set the oven to 180°C/350°F/Gas Mark 4. Fill a roasting tin with 5 cm (2 in) of boiling water. Place the mousselines in the roasting tin and cook for about 20 minutes. Unwrap one mousseline to check that it feels quite firm. If not, continue to cook for a few minutes more. Chill overnight. Mix the mayonnaise with the fresh herbs. Unroll the scallop mousselines and cut into slices. Spread each puff pastry croûte with a little herb mayonnaise and top with a round of mousseline.

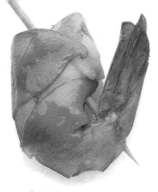

MEDITERRANEAN PRAWNS WITH MANGE-TOUTS

20 Mediterranean prawns
3 tbsp peanut oil
I tbsp lemon juice
I clove garlic, crushed
Salt and ground black pepper
1 tsp chopped mint
10 mange-touts

Peel the prawns and put them in a dish. Pour over the oil, lemon juice, garlic, salt and pepper. Leave to marinate for about 6 hours. Add the chopped mint. Top and tail the mange-touts. Plunge them into boiling salted water for 3 minutes, then immediately into cold water. Drain and pat dry on absorbent paper. Cut the mange-touts in half along the seams. Wrap in a spiral around each prawn and skewer into place with a cocktail stick.

MUSSELS WITH GARLIC BUTTER IN THEIR SHELLS

20 mussels
300 ml (½ pt) water
½ onion, sliced, a few sprigs parsley, 1 bay leaf
50 g (2 oz) butter
2 cloves garlic, crushed
1 tbsp parsley, finely chopped
Salt and ground black pepper
1 tbsp breadcrumbs
1 tbsp Gruyère, finely grated

Tap the mussels on the work-top and discard any that stay open. Scrub the rest and put them in a large pan with the water, onion, parsley sprigs and bay leaf. Cover and simmer for 2 minutes, shaking the pan occasionally until the mussels have opened. Strain and discard any mussels which remain closed. Remove the top half of each shell. Soften the butter and beat in the garlic and parsley and season with salt and black pepper. Mix the breadcrumbs and cheese together. Just before serving, heat the grill. Put a dob of garlic butter on each mussel and sprinkle with the breadcrumbs and cheese. Grill until browned.

HERB-COATED KNOTS OF PLAICE WITH SAFFRON DIP

1 medium-sized plaice, filleted
1 egg, beaten
Salt
Milk
Dry white breadcrumbs
1 heaped tbsp mixed fresh herbs, finely chopped
Seasoned flour
Oil for deep-frying
FOR THE SAFFRON DIP
150 ml (¼ pt) fish stock
4 strands saffron
150 ml (¼ pt) thick mayonnaise
Salt and ground black pepper
Pinch of turmeric
Squeeze of lemon juice.

Cut the plaice fillets into thin strips, roughly ½ cm (¼ in) wide and 10 cm (4 in) long, and tie them into knots. Mix the beaten egg with a pinch of salt and a little milk. Mix the breadcrumbs and herbs together. Dip the knots of plaice first into the seasoned flour, then into the egg and milk and lastly into the breadcrumbs. Make sure they are evenly coated.

TO MAKE THE SAFFRON DIP: Boil the fish stock until reduced to 1 tbsp. Soak the saffron strands in the hot stock. Leave to cool. Strain the stock and mix it with the mayonnaise. Season with salt, black pepper, turmeric and lemon juice. Serve in a small dish. Heat the oil until a piece of bread will sizzle vigorously in it. Fry the plaice until golden brown. Drain on absorbent paper and sprinkle with salt. Serve immediately on a round plate with the saffron dip in the centre, or leave to cool and reheat for 10 minutes in an oven set at 190°C/375°F/Gas Mark 5 just before serving.

TIP: The knots of plaice can be coated with egg and breadcrumbs the day before, covered in cling film and stored in the refrigerator overnight. Sole can be used instead of plaice, if preferred.

MINI ARNOLD BENNETT OMELETTES

3 eggs, separated
1 tbsp double cream
1 tbsp grated Parmesan cheese
Ground black pepper
100 g (4 oz) smoked haddock, cooked
2 tbsp whipped cream
1 tomato, skinned, deseeded and
    chopped
Cayenne pepper and 1 tsp of lemon juice

Set the oven to 190°C/375°F/Gas Mark 5. Line a Swiss roll tin roughly 20 cm (8 in) by 30 cm (12 in) with greased greaseproof paper. Mix the egg yolks with the cream and Parmesan cheese. Stiffly whisk the egg whites and fold into the yolks. Season with black pepper. Turn into the tin and bake for 10-12 minutes. Cool. Chop the haddock finely, stir in the whipped cream and tomato, season with lemon juice and black and Cayenne pepper. Turn the omelette onto greaseproof paper. Peel off the lining paper and cut the omelette in half. Spread with the haddock. Roll up like a tiny Swiss roll. Trim and cut into 20 smaller rolls.

SMOKED HALIBUT ON RYE WITH SALMON ROE AND LIME

10 slices of white rye bread
Butter for spreading
175 g (6 oz) smoked halibut
1 lime
Ground black pepper
50 g (2 oz) salmon roe

Cut two 5 cm (2 in) rounds from each slice of bread and spread with butter. Cut rounds of smoked halibut and lay on top of the buttered bread. With a potato peeler, remove thin strips of rind from the lime, taking care not to remove any of the pith. With a sharp knife, cut the rind into the finest shreds. Plunge into boiling water, then immediately into cold water. Squeeze the juice from the lime, grind a little black pepper into it, and brush over the smoked halibut. Put a small mound of salmon roe on top of each smoked halibut round. Decorate with shreds of lime.

TIP: Smoked halibut is bought sliced, like smoked salmon, from most good delicatessens, but check in case you need to order it in advance.

SPINACH ROULADE FILLED WITH SMOKED SALMON MOUSSE

100 g (4 oz) frozen finely chopped spinach
15 g (½ oz) butter
2 eggs, separated
Salt and ground black pepper
Ground nutmeg
225 g (8 oz) smoked salmon pieces
Milk
2 tsp mayonnaise
2 tsp whipped cream
Lemon juice

Set the oven to 190°C/375°F/Gas Mark 5. Defrost the spinach. Line a Swiss roll tin roughly 20 cm (8 in) by 30 cm (12 in) with greased greaseproof paper. Melt the butter, add the spinach and stir over a high heat until the excess moisture has evaporated. Cool a little, add the egg yolks and season with salt, black pepper and nutmeg. Whisk the egg whites until stiff and fold into the spinach mixture. Turn into the tin and bake for 10-12 minutes. Leave to cool.

Purée the smoked salmon in a liquidizer or food processor, adding a little milk to make a thick paste. Stir in the mayonnaise and cream and season with lemon juice and black pepper.

Lay a sheet of greaseproof paper on the work-top and turn the cold roulade on to it. Peel off the lining paper and cut the roulade in half widthways. Spread the smoked salmon mousse over each half and roll them up like tiny Swiss rolls. Trim the untidy edges and cut each roulade into 10 smaller rolls.

GRILLED CLAMS WITH PROVENÇALE TOP

20 littleneck clams
75 g (3 oz) butter, softened
1 shallot, finely chopped
1 tinned tomato, finely chopped
1 clove garlic, crushed
1 tbsp breadcrumbs
Chopped parsley

Make sure that the clams are still alive by tapping the shells. Discard any that remain open. Push the sharp edge of a knife blade hard between the shells, opposite the hinge. Twist the knife to open the clams and remove the top shell from each one. Heat the grill. Beat the shallot, tomato, garlic and breadcrumbs into the butter. Put a spoonful of this on each clam and grill for a few minutes, until the tops are lightly browned and the clams are cooked. Decorate with parsley.

PRAWN AIGRETTES

1 quantity savoury choux pastry (see recipe, p. 146)
100 g (4 oz) prawns, cooked and peeled
25 g (1 oz) strong Cheddar cheese, finely diced
Oil for deep-frying
2 tbsp grated Parmesan cheese

Mix the prawns and diced cheese into the choux pastry.
Heat the oil until a small piece of the paste will sizzle vigorously in it.
Use 2 teaspoons to shape the mixture into even-sized balls and drop
them into the hot oil (make sure each one has prawns inside it). Fry a
few at a time until puffed up and golden brown. Drain on absorbent
paper and then sprinkle with Parmesan cheese. Serve straightaway,
and hand cocktail sticks and napkins separately.

DILL BLINIS WITH SOUR CREAM AND GRAVLAX

100 g (4 oz) boneless salmon
1 tsp olive oil
1 tsp fresh dill, chopped
1 tsp salt
½ tsp caster sugar
½ tsp crushed green peppercorns
1 × 150 ml (5 fl oz) carton soured cream
FOR THE BLINIS
100 g (4 oz) plain and wholemeal flour,
*   mixed half and half*
Pinch of salt
½ tsp bicarbonate of soda
½ tsp cream of tartar
1 egg, beaten,
250 ml (8 fl oz) milk
1 tsp chopped dill

Lay the salmon skin-side down on a piece of tin foil. Rub with olive oil and sprinkle with dill, salt, caster sugar and peppercorns. Wrap up tightly and chill for 24 hours, turning twice.

To make the blinis: Sift the flour, salt, bicarbonate of soda and cream of tartar together into a mixing bowl. Make a well in the centre, add the egg and beat. Stir in the milk until the batter is the consistency of lightly whipped cream. (It may not be necessary to add all the milk.) Add the dill and leave to stand for 10 minutes.

Grease a heavy frying pan or griddle and heat it. When very hot, drop 2 or 3 small spoonfuls of batter on to the surface, keeping them well separated. When the underside is brown and bubbles have risen to the surface, turn the blinis to brown the other side.

To serve the blinis: Wrap them in tin foil and warm in a moderate oven. Cut the gravlax into thin strips. Put a spoonful of sour cream in the middle of each blini and arrange the strips of gravlax on top in a lattice pattern.

NOTE: True blinis are made with a yeast batter but this is very time-consuming. The recipe above cheats a little to be speedy, but is delicious nonetheless.

NEW POTATOES WITH SOUR CREAM AND MOCK CAVIAR

20 even-sized tiny new potatoes
Oily French dressing (4 parts oil to 1 of vinegar)
1 × 150 ml (5 fl oz) carton sour cream
1 × 50 g (2 oz) jar black lumpfish roe

Scrub the potatoes and cook in gently simmering salted water until tender, about 20 minutes. Drain and, while still hot, soak in the French dressing until cool. Lift the potatoes out of the dressing and pat dry with absorbent paper. Cut a small slice from the bottom of each potato so that it can sit flat. Carefully scoop a hollow out of the top with a melon-baller. Fill the hollows with a spoonful of sour cream and top with the lumpfish roe.

TIP: The potatoes can be boiled and soaked in French dressing overnight.

SMOKED MUSSELS IN CHEESE PASTRY

2 × 100 g (4 oz) tins smoked mussels
1 quantity cheese pastry (see recipe,
  p.147)
½ egg, beaten

Drain the smoked mussels and lay on absorbent paper to dry. Roll the pastry out thinly and stamp out 5 cm (2 in) rounds with a plain pastry cutter. Put a smoked mussel in the middle of each one. Brush the edges with the beaten egg and fold over like a tiny Cornish pasty. Seal together with a fork or knife, marking a pattern on the pastry at the same time. Chill. Just before serving, set the oven to 200°C/400°F/Gas Mark 6, brush the pastry with beaten egg and bake for 10-15 minutes. Or bake ahead of time and serve cold, but do not reheat.

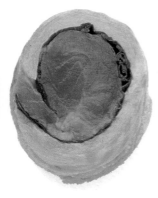

MARINATED TURBOT AND SALMON CATHERINE WHEELS

1 × 100 g (4 oz) salmon fillet, skinned
100 g (4 oz) turbot fillet, skinned
Juice of ½ lemon
2 tbsp white wine
15 g (½ oz) caster sugar
1 tbsp fresh tarragon, finely chopped, or 1 tsp dried
100 g (4 oz) fresh spinach
150 ml (¼ pt) mayonnaise
Salt and ground black pepper
20 puff pastry croûtes (see recipe, p. 150)

With a very sharp knife, slice the salmon and turbot fillets in half horizontally to give four very thin fillets. Place them between two layers of cling film and flatten them with a rolling pin. Marinate the salmon in the lemon juice, white wine, sugar and half the tarragon for about 4 hours. Add the turbot and marinate for a further 2 hours. Wash the spinach and remove the tough stalks. Plunge it first into boiling salted water and then into cold water. Lay the leaves flat on a clean tea towel.

Drain and pat the fish dry with absorbent paper. Lay the two salmon fillets on the work-top, cover with spinach leaves and put the turbot on top. Roll up like Swiss rolls, wrap tightly in tin foil and refrigerate for at least 1 hour.

To assemble the catherine wheels: Cut the rolls of fish into thin slices. Mix the remaining tarragon with the mayonnaise and season with salt and black pepper. Spread each croûte of puff pastry with some mayonnaise and top with a salmon and turbot catherine wheel.

TIP: Ask the fishmonger for long flat fillets rather than thick cutlets.

CEVICHE SKEWERED WITH COCKTAIL AVOCADO

5 large scallops
175 g (6 oz) salmon
Juice of 1 lime
1 shallot, finely chopped
2 tbsp olive oil
½ red chilli, finely chopped
2 ripe cocktail avocado pears

Wash the scallops and remove the tough muscles (opposite the coral). Cut them into quarters. Skin the salmon and remove any bones. Cut into bite-sized pieces. Put the fish in a dish and sprinkle over the lime juice, shallot and oil. Cover tightly with cling film and chill overnight. Not more than 1 hour before serving, add the red chilli to the ceviche and marinate for a further 15 minutes. Meanwhile peel the avocados, cut in half lengthways and then into chunks. Drain the ceviche and pat dry on absorbent paper. Turn the avocado in the marinade to prevent it from going brown. Thread onto cocktail sticks with the avocado sandwiched between a piece of salmon and a piece of scallop.
TIP: Any firm white fish may be substituted for the scallop.

TARAMASALATA TOASTIES

½ slice crustless white bread
1 clove garlic, crushed
100 g (4 oz) smoked cod's roe, skinned
150 ml (¼ pt) salad oil
Lemon juice
Ground black pepper
20 slivers of black olive
20 toastie cases (see recipe, p. 148)

Soak the bread in cold water and squeeze dry. Put it into a bowl with the crushed garlic and cod's roe. With a wooden spoon or electric whisk, gradually beat the oil in, drop by drop. (Alternatively, put the bread, garlic and cod's roe into a food processor and gradually add the oil.) Season with lemon juice and black pepper. Put the taramasalata into a piping bag fitted with a fluted nozzle and pipe in whirls into the toastie cases. Decorate with a sliver of black olive.

TIP: The taramasalata will keep in the refrigerator for up to a week.

MUSHROOM AND OYSTER BOUCHÉES

25 g (1 oz) butter
100 g (4 oz) flat black mushrooms, finely chopped
1 shallot, finely chopped
20 cooked bouchée cases (see recipe, p.149)
Salt and ground black pepper
2 × 100 g (4 oz) tins smoked oysters
FOR THE LEMON HOLLANDAISE
1 egg yolk
50 g (2 oz) butter
1 tbsp lemon juice
Salt and ground black pepper

Melt the butter in a frying pan, add the mushrooms and shallots and cook gently until soft. Season with salt and black pepper.
TO MAKE THE LEMON HOLLANDAISE: Place the egg yolk in a small bowl with a pinch of salt and a knob of the butter. Set over a pan of barely simmering water. Stir until slightly thickened and gradually beat in the remaining butter and lemon juice, allowing the sauce to thicken each time before adding more. Season with black pepper.

42

Put a spoonful of the mushroom mixture in the base of each bouchée case. Pop an oyster (or half an oyster if they are too large) into each bouchée case on top of the mushroom mixture. Preheat the grill. Top each bouchée with a dollop of lemon hollandaise and grill until lightly browned. Serve straightaway.

TIP: Fresh oysters can be used instead of smoked. Ask the fishmonger to open them for you but be sure to use them on the same day. Fry the oysters briskly in a little butter just before adding to the bouchée cases.

LOBSTER MOUSSE IN PASTRY CASES

1 quantity cheese pastry (see recipe, p.147)
225 g (8 oz) cooked lobster meat
2 tbsp mayonnaise
2 tbsp double cream, whipped
Salt, ground black pepper and Tabasco
Lemon juice
7 g (¼ oz) gelatine
Paprika

Roll the pastry thinly and stamp out 5 cm (2 in) rounds with a plain pastry cutter. Press into tiny patty tins and chill for 30 minutes. Fill each pastry case with a scrumpled up piece of tin foil and bake for 10-15 minutes at 200°C/400°F/Gas Mark 6. Cool.

Purée the lobster meat with the mayonnaise until smooth. Turn into a bowl and fold in the cream. Season with salt, black pepper, Tabasco and lemon juice. Put a spoonful of water into a small pan and sprinkle the gelatine over. Soak for 10 minutes, then warm gently until clear and runny. Add to the lobster and mix well. Pipe into the pastry cases. Sprinkle with paprika.

SMOKED SALMON WHEELS

*8 slices brown bread, crusts
    removed
Butter for spreading
175 g (6 oz) smoked salmon
Lemon juice
Ground black pepper
Mustard and cress, to decorate*

Lay 2 slices of bread on the work-top with the edges overlapping by 1
cm (½ in): Flatten them with a rolling pin, making sure that the edges
are well pressed together. Butter the bread and cover with smoked
salmon. Brush with lemon juice and sprinkle with black pepper. Roll up
like a Swiss roll. Repeat with the other 6 slices. Pack tightly together in
a box covered with cling film and chill for 30 minutes. Trim the untidy
edges from each smoked salmon roll and cut into 5. Decorate with
mustard and cress.

TIP: The smoked salmon rolls can be frozen before they are sliced.
Wrap each roll individually in cling film before freezing.

MEAT

Left to right: *Smoked Chicken Bites; Salami on Black Rye with Marinated Beetroot; Ham, Cream Cheese and Chive Catherine Wheels; Mini Antipasto; Steak Tartare.*

TOASTIES WITH PÂTÉ AND GREEN PEPPERCORNS

225 g (8 oz) chicken or duck livers
100 g (4 oz) butter
1 medium-sized onion, chopped
1 clove garlic, crushed
Salt and ground black pepper
2 tbsp natural yoghurt
1 × 70 g (2½ oz) jar or tin green peppercorns
20 toastie cases (see recipe, p. 148)

Discard any discoloured bits from the livers. Melt the butter in a heavy-based frying pan, add the onion and garlic and cook gently until soft and transparent. Add the livers and cook, turning occasionally until they are brown all over and cooked right through. Season well with salt and black pepper. Purée the pâté in a liquidizer or food processor with the yoghurt and a teaspoonful of green peppercorns. Put the pâté into a piping bag fitted with a fluted nozzle and pipe in whirls into the toastie cases. Decorate with a green peppercorn on top.

TIP: The pâté can be kept in the refrigerator for up to 3 days. It also freezes well.

48

CHINESE BACON ROLLS

10 rashers streaky bacon
100 g (4 oz) chicken livers
1 tsp brown sugar
1 tbsp hot water
1 tbsp soy sauce
Pinch of five spice powder
1 clove garlic, crushed
Pinch of salt
20 slices water chestnuts

Stretch the bacon with the back of a knife and cut each rasher in half. Discard any discoloured bits from the livers and cut into bite-sized pieces. Dissolve the brown sugar in the hot water and add the soy sauce, spice powder, garlic and salt. Add the chicken livers and leave to marinate for 2-4 hours. Drain the livers well. Place each piece of liver with a slice of water chestnut and wrap in a strip of bacon. Set on a baking tray with the join underneath. Heat the grill and cook the bacon rolls for 10 minutes until golden brown and crisp.

TIP: The bacon rolls can be made the day before and chilled overnight.

RADICCHIO WITH SALADE TIÈDE

20 of the smallest radicchio leaves
2-3 leaves of curly endive
100 g (4 oz) chicken livers
1 tbsp walnut oil
2 rashers streaky bacon, diced
50 g (2 oz) button mushrooms, sliced

Wash and dry the radicchio leaves. Wash and dry the curly endive and tear into smaller pieces. Discard any discoloured bits from the liver and cut into small thin slices. Just before serving, heat the oil in a heavy frying pan. Add the sliced liver and bacon and cook briskly until well browned. Add the mushrooms and cook for another minute. Add this mixture, including any liquid, to the endive. Season with salt and black pepper and toss well. Tuck a little of the mixture inside the radicchio leaves and secure with a cocktail stick.

TIP: This recipe must be made and served at the last minute. The livers will be dry and tough if reheated and the radicchio leaves soon wilt once the warm salad is inside them. It is therefore not suitable for parties of more than 20 people.

PORK AND PRAWN TOASTS

175 g (6 oz) minced pork
50 g (2 oz) cooked, peeled prawns, finely chopped
1 tbsp fresh coriander, finely chopped
1 clove garlic, crushed
1 tsp anchovy essence
½ small egg, beaten
Salt and ground black pepper
3 slices stale bread, crusts removed
Oil for deep-frying
Extra sprigs of coriander, to decorate

Put the pork, prawns, coriander, garlic, anchovy essence and beaten egg together in a bowl and season well with salt and black pepper. Knead and squeeze the mixture together until it has a paste-like consistency. Spread the pork and prawn mixture thickly on the bread. Cut each slice into eight triangles. Heat the oil until a piece of bread will sizzle vigorously in it. Fry a few triangles at a time, meat-side down, until crisp and brown. Drain on absorbent paper and keep warm while the remaining toasts are cooking. It is important to let the oil regain heat each time or the toasts will be greasy and soggy. Serve straight away, decorated with sprigs of coriander.

VENISON SAUSAGES WITH CRANBERRY SAUCE

175 g (6 oz) minced belly pork
75 g (3 oz) minced veal
75 g (3 oz) minced venison
4 tbsp fresh white breadcrumbs
1 tsp mixed ground spice
½ tsp dried sage
Salt and ground black pepper
A little flour
Dripping
Cranberry sauce

Mix the minced meats together and add the breadcrumbs, spice and sage and season with salt and black pepper. With floured hands, shape the mixture into little sausages about 5 cm (2 in) long. Dust with flour. Turn the heat down and continue to fry, turning occasionally.

Put the dripping in a roasting tin and melt over a moderate heat on top of the stove. When hot add the sausages and brown on all sides until cooked all the way through. Serve on cocktail sticks on a plate with cranberry sauce in the middle.

52

MINI BARBECUE RIBLETS

500 g (1 lb) pork spare ribs
1 tbsp clear honey
1 tbsp soy sauce
2 tbsp orange juice
150 ml (¼ pt) tomato ketchup
1 clove garlic, crushed
Salt and ground black pepper

With a sharp knife, scrape away ½ cm (¼ in) of meat from one end of each riblet to expose a little bone (so that they can be held easily with the fingers). Mix all the rest of the ingredients together. Put the riblets into a shallow container, pour the marinade over, cover and chill overnight. The following day, heat the oven to 190°C/375°F/Gas Mark 5. Put the ribs with the marinade into a roasting tin and bake for about 1 hour until the ribs are very tender and the marinade has reduced to a dark sticky glaze. Alternatively drain the ribs and cook them over a not too fierce barbecue.

TIP: Ask the butcher to cut the ribs apart and then into 5 cm (2 in) lengths. If he cannot be persuaded to do this, the job can be accomplished with a sharp knife and a cleaver. But do take care.

SALAMI WITH MARINATED BEETROOT ON RYE

100 g (4 oz) raw beetroot
2 tbsp French dressing
1 tsp seed mustard
Pinch cumin
10 slices black rye bread
Butter for spreading
225 g (8 oz) salami, about 3.5 cm (1½ in) in
  diameter

Cut the beetroot into thin slices. Stamp out small fluted rounds with a decorative pastry cutter. Mix the French dressing with the mustard and cumin. Put the beetroot rounds into a dish, pour the dressing over and leave to marinate for several hours.

Cut the rye bread into 3.5 cm (1½ in) rounds with a plain cutter and spread with butter. Slice the salami quite thickly and set a slice on top of each bread round. Drain the beetroot well, pat dry with absorbent paper and use to decorate the salami.

STEAK TARTARE

100 g (4 oz) fillet or rump steak
1 tbsp oil
1 raw egg yolk
½ small onion, finely chopped
1 tsp parsley, finely chopped
Salt and freshly ground black pepper
Worcestershire sauce
20 dried white bread croûtes (see p. 150)
1 hard-boiled egg or 20 capers

Trim the steak and chop or mince it two or three times until it is very smooth. Beat in the oil, egg yolk, chopped onion and parsley and season with salt, black pepper and Worcestershire sauce. Put a spoonful of steak tartare on top of each bread croûte and decorate with sieved hard-boiled egg yolk and chopped white, or with a caper.

TANDOORI CHICKEN WITH CUCUMBER AND YOGHURT DIP

225 g (8 oz) boneless chicken meat
1× 150 ml (5 fl oz) carton natural yoghurt
Pinch of chilli, cumin and coriander powder
1 tsp garam masala
1 tsp tomato purée
Juice and grated rind of half a lemon
1 clove garlic, crushed
1 tsp fresh ginger, peeled and chopped
Salt and ground black pepper
FOR THE CUCUMBER AND YOGHURT DIP
¼ cucumber
1× 150 ml (5 fl oz) carton natural yoghurt
1 tbsp double cream
1 tbsp mint, finely chopped
Salt and ground black pepper

Cut the chicken into bite-sized chunks. Place all the remaining ingredients together in a liquidizer or food processor and blend until smooth. Lay the pieces of chicken in a shallow dish, pour over the marinade, cover and chill overnight.

The following day, just before serving, lift the chicken out of the marinade and place in a roasting tin. Preheat the grill or oven to the highest temperature. Cook the chicken for about 10 minutes until reddish brown and tender. Spear with cocktail sticks and serve on a round dish surrounding the cucumber and yoghurt dip.

CUCUMBER AND YOGHURT DIP: Chop the cucumber finely and pat dry with absorbent paper to get rid of any excess moisture. Mix all the ingredients together and season with salt and ground black pepper.

KOFTA KEBABS

225 g (8 oz) lamb
½ tsp ground coriander
½ tsp ground cumin
2 tsp mint, chopped
2 tsp coriander leaves, chopped or parsley, chopped
Mint leaves, to decorate

Finely chop or mince the lamb and mix it
thoroughly with all the seasonings. Shape
into tiny oval nuggets and thread two onto a
cocktail stick. Grill or cook over a barbecue for
10 minutes. Serve hot, decorated with the
mint leaves.

MINI ANTIPASTO

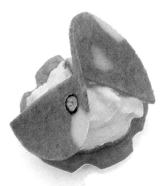

3 large carrots
175 g (6 oz) Boursin
Milk
¼ green pepper, deseeded and finely
  chopped
¼ red pepper, deseeded and finely chopped
Salt and ground black pepper
10 slices Mortadella, cut into thin slices

Peel the carrots. With the tip of a potato peeler, cut grooves the length of the carrot and all the way around. Soften the Boursin with a little milk and mix with the chopped peppers. Season with salt and black pepper. Cut the Mortadella into small rounds, about 2.5 cm (1 in) in diameter, with a plain pastry cutter.

Put a spoonful of the Boursin mixture on top of each piece of carrot. Make a cut in each round of Mortadella from the outside to the centre and arrange on top of the Boursin in a twist.

TIP: Most cooked sausages or salamis can be substituted for the Mortadella.

WAFER-THIN SLICES OF RAW BEEF WITH MUSTARD MAYONNAISE

225 g (8 oz) fillet of beef
5 slices granary bread, crusts removed
Butter for spreading
150 ml (¼ pt) thick mayonnaise flavoured with
Dijon mustard

Place the fillet of beef in the freezer until almost frozen. With a very sharp knife, cut the nearly frozen meat into wafer-thin slices. Place the slices of meat between two layers of cling film and flatten with a rolling pin.

Butter the bread and spread with a little mustard mayonnaise. Cover each slice with raw beef and cut into four triangles. Place the remaining mayonnaise in a piping bag fitted with a small fluted nozzle and pipe a curl in the corner of each triangle.

TIP: Any lean, tender cut of beef can be used in this recipe but a neat result is most easily achieved with fillet steak.

PORK AND MANGO WITH SATÉ SAUCE

225 g (8 oz) lean pork
1 mango
FOR THE SATÉ SAUCE
2 tbsp crunchy peanut butter
½ small onion, very finely chopped
1 clove garlic, crushed
1 tsp fresh ginger, peeled and chopped
2 tsps brown sugar
Pinch chilli powder and lemon grass
25 g (1 oz) coconut cream
150 ml (¼ pt) boiling water

Cut the pork into bite-sized chunks. Peel the mango and cut the flesh into chunks about the same size as the pork. Make into little kebabs with a piece of pork and a piece of mango threaded on to a cocktail stick. Grill for about 10 minutes, turning halfway through cooking. Serve on a dish around the warm saté sauce.

TO MAKE THE SATÉ SAUCE: Combine all the ingredients in a pan and bring to the boil. Add a little extra water if the sauce is too thick.

SMOKED CHICKEN BITES

225 g (8 oz) smoked chicken meat, minced
100 g (4 oz) butter, softened
1 tbsp chives, finely chopped
1 tsp seed mustard
Salt and ground black pepper
5 tbsp toasted granary breadcrumbs, crushed

Beat the chicken and butter together until smooth (or combine in a food processor). Add the chopped chives and mustard and season with salt and black pepper. Shape into small balls and roll in the breadcrumbs. **TIP:** The smoked chicken mixture freezes well. The Bites are also delicious served on cocktail sticks and dipped in mustard-flavoured mayonnaise or chilli dip.

MINI CHEESE AND HAM CROISSANTS

225 g (8 oz) puff pastry
100 g (4 oz) thinly sliced ham
100 g (4 oz) Gruyère or Emmenthal
cheese, thinly sliced
1 egg, beaten

Roll the puff pastry out thinly and cut it into ten 5 cm (2 in) squares. Cut each square in half and pull one point to make an elongated triangle. Put a little ham and cheese in each one. Roll up from the longest edge towards the point and twist to form a croissant shape. Place on a wet baking sheet and chill for 30 minutes. Set the oven to 200°C/400°F/Gas Mark 6. Brush with beaten egg and bake for 15-20 minutes, until well risen, crisp and golden brown.

TIP: The croissants can be filled and shaped the day before, tightly covered with cling film and chilled overnight.

NUGGETS OF MARINATED LAMB

225 g (8 oz) boneless lamb
150 ml (¼ pt) peanut oil
1 tsp coriander seed, crushed
1 tsp fennel seed, crushed
2 cardamom pods and 2 allspice, crushed
1 tsp garam masala
Salt and ground black pepper
½ lemon
Handful fresh rosemary

Trim the lamb and cut into 1 cm (1 in) cubes. Mix all the marinade ingredients together except the lemon. Squeeze the juice from the lemon, then finely slice the skin and add both to the marinade. Mix the cubes of meat with the marinade, cover and chill overnight.

The following day, drain the cubes of lamb and thread onto cocktail sticks with two pieces of meat on each stick. Scatter over the fresh rosemary and grill or barbecue for 10 minutes, turning halfway through cooking and brushing with marinade. Serve hot.

TIP: This is also delicious served with saté sauce, p. 61.

HAM, CREAM CHEESE AND CHIVE CATHERINE WHEELS

8 slices brown bread, crusts removed
Butter for spreading
175 g (6 oz) cream cheese
Milk
50 g (2 oz) ham, finely chopped
1 tbsp chives, finely chopped
Ground black pepper
1 punnet mustard and cress

Lay two slices of bread on the work-top with the edges overlapping by 1 cm (½ in). Flatten them with a rolling pin, making sure the edges are well pressed together. Butter the bread. Repeat with the other slices. Soften the cream cheese with a little milk and mix with the ham and chives and season with black pepper. Spread a thick layer over the slices of bread. Roll up like Swiss rolls. Pack tightly together in a box, cover with cling film and chill for 30 minutes. Unwrap, trim the untidy edges and slice each roll into five. Serve decorated with the mustard and cress.

MOROCCAN LAMB PIES

125 g (5 oz) butter
½ small onion, finely chopped
½ tsp ground cumin
25 g (1 oz) flaked almonds
2 tsp honey
A handful of sultanas
225 g (8 oz) cooked minced lamb
Salt and ground black pepper
8 sheets filo pastry

Melt 25 g (1 oz) of the butter. Add the onion and cook gently until soft and transparent. Stir in the cumin powder and flaked almonds and continue to cook until the almonds are a little browned. Add the honey and sultanas. Drain the mixture on absorbent paper and leave to cool. Mix with the minced lamb. Season with salt and black pepper. Brush half the sheets of filo pastry with melted butter, cover with the remaining sheets and brush again with butter. Cut each pair of pastry sheets into five long strips. Place a spoonful of the lamb filling at one end of each strip of pastry. Form a triangle by folding the right hand corner to the opposite side, then fold over and then across from left to right. Continue folding until the strip of pastry is used up.

Heat the oven to 200°C/400°F/Gas Mark 6. Place the lamb pies on a greased baking tray. Brush the tops with melted butter and bake for about 10 minutes until golden brown. Serve warm.

TIP: Prepared triangles keep in the refrigerator for up to two days or freeze them open on a tray, then wrap in plastic until needed. They can be brushed with butter and baked from frozen.

CHICKEN AND LOBSTER BOUCHÉES

225 g (8 oz) cooked chicken meat
100 g (4 oz) cooked lobster meat
150 ml (¼ pt) mayonnaise
Milk or single cream
Salt and ground black pepper
Lemon juice
Tabasco
25 g (1 oz) red lumpfish roe
20 cooked bouchée cases (see recipe,
p.149)

Chop the chicken and lobster meat. Thin the mayonnaise with a little milk or cream to a coating consistency. Mix the mayonnaise with the chicken and lobster meat and season with salt, black pepper, lemon juice and Tabasco. Spoon into the bouchée cases and decorate with red lumpfish roe.

MINI HAMBURGERS

350 g (12 oz) lean minced beef
1 tsp parsley, finely chopped
Salt and ground black pepper
20 dried bread croûtes (see recipe, p.150)
Mayonnaise flavoured with French mustard
2 dill pickles, finely sliced
Tomato and chilli relish
3 small tomatoes, finely sliced
2 spring onions, cut into strips

Mix the minced beef with the parsley and season with salt and black pepper. Shape into tiny hamburger-shaped patties about 3.5 cm (1½ in) in diameter. Grill for 3 minutes a side, until dark brown on the outside and still a little juicy in the middle. (This can be done on a barbecue.) Spread the bread croûtes with mustard mayonnaise and a little relish, place a slice of pickle on top. Finally, add a slice of tomato and the hot mini hamburger. Decorate with strips of spring onion.

MOSTLY VEGETABLE

Left to right: *Seasoned Soft Cheese with Paprika; Tabouli Bites; Ratatouille Bouchées; Watercress Roulade with Tomato and Cream Cheese; Cherry Tomatoes with Avocado.*

WATERCRESS, CREAM CHEESE AND TOMATO ROULADE

1 bunch watercress, washed
1 tbsp parsley, chopped
1 tbsp grated Parmesan cheese
2 eggs, separated
100 g (4 oz) cream cheese, softened with milk
2 tomatoes, skinned and deseeded and chopped
Salt and ground black pepper

Set the oven to 190°C/375°F/Gas Mark 5. Line a Swiss roll tin, roughly 20 cm (8 in) by 30 cm (12 in), with greased greaseproof paper. Remove the stalks from the watercress and dry thoroughly. Chop and mix with the parsley, Parmesan cheese and egg yolks. Beat well and season. Whisk the egg whites until stiff and fold into the watercress mixture. Turn into the tin and bake for 10-12 minutes. Cool. Mix the cream cheese with the tomato and season with salt and black pepper. Lay the cold roulade onto a sheet of greaseproof paper. Peel off the lining paper and spread with the cream cheese mixture. Roll up like a tiny Swiss roll. Trim the untidy edges and cut into about 20 smaller rolls.

GARLIC MUSHROOMS IN BREADCRUMBS

20 even-sized mushrooms
2 cloves garlic, crushed
2 tsp parsley, finely chopped
100 g (4 oz) butter, softened
Salt and ground black pepper
1 tsp lemon juice
Flour
1 egg, beaten with a little milk
Dry white breadcrumbs
Oil for deep-frying

Wipe the mushrooms and remove the stalks. Add the garlic and parsley to the butter and season with salt, black pepper and lemon juice. Put a dob of butter on each mushroom in the cavity left by the stalk. Mix the egg with a pinch of salt and a little milk. Dip the mushrooms first into the flour, then into the egg and milk, and lastly into the breadcrumbs. Chill for 1 hour. Heat the oil until a piece of bread will sizzle vigorously in it. Fry the mushrooms until golden brown, drain on absorbent paper and sprinkle with salt. Serve straightaway.

SPINACH AND RICOTTA FILO TRIANGLES

225 g (8 oz) frozen chopped spinach
175 g (6 oz) butter
100 g (4 oz) Ricotta
Salt, black pepper and ground nutmeg
8 sheets filo pastry

Defrost the spinach. Melt 25 g (1 oz) butter in a heavy pan, add the spinach and heat, stirring constantly, until any liquid has boiled away. Stir in the Ricotta. Season. Melt the remaining butter. Lay half the sheets of filo pastry on the work-top and brush with butter, cover with the remaining sheets of pastry and more melted butter. Cut each pair of pastry sheets lengthways into five strips. Place a spoonful of filling at one end of each strip. Form a triangle by folding the right-hand corner to the opposite side, then fold over and then across from the left-hand corner to the right edge. Continue folding until the strip of pastry is used up. Heat the oven to 200°C/400°F/Gas Mark 6. Place the filo triangles on a greased baking tray. Brush with melted butter and bake for about 10 minutes until golden brown. Serve warm.
TIP: See p. 67 for details on storing and freezing.

Choux Puffs with Stilton Salad

20 choux puffs (see recipe, p. 146)
100 g (4 oz) Stilton, grated
1 stick celery, finely chopped
2 tsp chives, chopped
6 walnuts, chopped
1 tsp walnut oil
Squeeze of lemon juice
Salt and ground black pepper

Mix the grated Stilton, chopped celery, chives and walnuts together. Moisten with the oil and lemon juice and season with salt and black pepper. Make a diagonal slit through each choux puff from the top down towards the bottom. Pile in the Stilton salad and serve straight-away.

TIP: Choux puffs freeze perfectly wrapped tightly in a plastic bag. Pop them frozen into a moderate oven (180°C/375°F/Gas Mark 5) for 10 minutes to defrost and crisp them.

SEASONED SOFT CHEESES

500 g (1 lb) cream cheese
25 g (1 oz) Cheddar cheese, finely grated
½ tsp Dijon mustard
Pinch of Cayenne
Salt and ground black pepper
50 g (2 oz) Roquefort cheese
1 tbsp mixed chopped parsley, chervil and
* chives*
1 small clove garlic, crushed
FOR DECORATION
1 tbsp paprika
1 tbsp toasted sesame seeds
1 tbsp parsley, finely chopped
1 tbsp ground black pepper

Divide the cream cheese into 4 separate batches – 100 g (4 oz) in each one. Mix the Cheddar cheese, Dijon mustard and Cayenne with one batch and season with salt and black pepper. Mix the Roquefort into the second batch, the chopped herbs and garlic into the third and leave the last one plain. Roll all the different cheeses into about 40 balls, keeping them in their separate batches. Lightly dust the Cheddar-flavoured ones with paprika, the Roquefort with sesame seeds, the herb and garlic cheese with parsley and the plain ones with black pepper. Serve them mixed together in a basket lined with a napkin or, better still, with vine leaves.

TIP: The cheeses can be flavoured and shaped the day before but not finished until the day.

MUSHROOM AND ROQUEFORT STRUDELS

20 even-sized mushrooms
100 g (4 oz) Roquefort, softened (or other soft blue cheese)
8 sheets filo pastry
100 g (4 oz) butter, melted
Salt and ground black pepper
1 egg, beaten

Set the oven to 200°C/400°F/Gas Mark 6. Grease a baking tray. Wipe the mushrooms and carefully remove the stalks. Fill the cavities where the stalks were with Roquefort. Brush half the sheets of filo pastry with melted butter, cover with the other 4 sheets. Brush again with butter. Cut the sheets into small squares. Put a filled mushroom in the centre of each square and season with salt and ground black pepper. Draw the edges of the pastry up together to look like a small sack. Pinch the 'neck' together firmly with the fingers. Set on the baking tray and brush with more melted butter. Bake for 15-20 minutes until the pastry is golden brown. Serve straightaway.

TIP: The strudels can be prepared, but not baked, the day before.

TABOULI BITES

50 g (2 oz) cracked wheat
1 cucumber
2 tomatoes, peeled, deseeded and chopped
½ green pepper, deseeded and chopped
1 shallot, finely chopped
1 tbsp mint, finely chopped
1 tbsp parsley or coriander leaf, finely
*   chopped*
2 tbsp olive oil
Salt, ground black pepper and lemon juice

Soak the cracked wheat in cold water for 1 hour. Drain well, wrap in a clean tea towel and squeeze out all the excess moisture. Spread the wheat on a tray to dry. Cut the cucumber in half lengthways and scoop out the seeds with a teaspoon. Put all the prepared vegetables into a mixing bowl with the soaked wheat, add the mint, parsley and oil. Season well with salt, black pepper and lemon juice. Spoon the tabouli into the hollowed-out cucumber and cut each half into about 10 pieces.

TORTELLONI WITH HOT PROVENÇALE PEPPER DIP

5 tbsp olive oil
1 small onion, finely chopped
2 cloves garlic, crushed
1 green pepper, deseeded and finely chopped
1 red pepper, deseeded and finely chopped
1 × 230 g (8 oz) tin of tomatoes
½ tsp marjoram and 1 tsp dried basil
Salt and ground black pepper
40 fresh tortelloni (any type will do)

Heat 3 tbsp oil in a heavy pan. Add the onion and garlic and fry gently until soft and transparent. Stir in the peppers, tomatoes and marjoram and basil and season with salt and black pepper. Simmer gently until the dip is well reduced, dark and oily. Bring a large pan of salted water to the boil and add 1 tbsp oil. Cook the tortelloni in the water until tender (about 12 minutes). Drain and rinse with boiling water. Return to the pan and toss in 1 tbsp oil. Thread onto cocktail sticks and serve on a plate with the hot Provençale pepper dip in a small dish in the centre.

CAMEMBERT PASTRY PARCELS

½ Camembert, well chilled
1 quantity cheese pastry recipe (p. 147)
2 tbsp good quality gooseberry preserve
1 egg, beaten

Cut the Camembert into 2.5 cm (1 in) cubes. Roll the pastry out thinly and cut into 7 cm (3 in) squares. Put a little gooseberry preserve in the centre of each square and top it with a cube of Camembert. Brush the edges of the pastry with beaten egg and draw them up to the top to make a parcel rather like a sack. Pinch the 'neck' tightly together and snip off the excess pastry (it is vital to seal the parcel or the Camembert will leak out). Heat the oven to 200°C/400°F/Gas Mark 6. Grease a baking tray. Brush the Camembert parcels with beaten egg, place on the baking tray and bake for 10-15 minutes, until the pastry is golden brown. Serve straightaway.
TIP: The pastry parcel can be made the day before and chilled overnight.

QUAIL-EGG FLOWERS

10 small fat pickling cucumbers
150 ml (¼ pt) wine vinegar
150 ml (¼ pt) water
175 g (6 oz) sugar
2 tbsp salt
2 tbsp oil
2 cloves garlic, crushed
1 tsp crushed black peppercorns
Good pinch ground coriander
150 ml (¼ pt) soy sauce
2 tbsp brown sugar
20 quails' eggs, hard-boiled and peeled

Cut 2.5 cm (1 in) from the end of each cucumber (the middles can be used to make Tabouli Bites, p. 79). With a melon-baller, scoop most of the flesh out of the cucumber ends to make little cups. With a sharp knife, cut deep zig-zags from the rim of the cucumber to look like petals. Mix the vinegar, water, sugar and half the salt together and soak the cucumber flowers in this for 30 minutes.

Heat the oil in a frying pan and add the remaining salt, garlic, peppercorns, coriander, soy sauce and brown sugar. Turn the quails' eggs in the hot soy sauce mixture until evenly brown. Allow the eggs to cool in the sauce, turning them occasionally. Drain the cucumber flowers well and put a quail's egg into each one. Spear with a cocktail stick through the base of the cucumber into the quail's egg, to look like a stalk. Or alternatively slice a little off the base of the cucumber flowers so that they will sit flat and arrange them on a plate.

TIP: To hard-boil quails' eggs, boil them gently for 3 minutes.

CHÈVRE TARTS

1 quantity cheese pastry (see recipe, p. 147)
225 g (8 oz) Chèvre (goat's cheese)
1 red apple
6 walnuts, chopped
Walnut oil
Squeeze of lemon juice
Salt and ground black pepper

Roll the pastry thinly and stamp out 5 cm (2 in) rounds. Press into tiny patty tins and chill for 30 minutes. Fill each pastry case with a scrumpled piece of tin foil and bake for 10-15 minutes at 200°C/400°F/ Gas Mark 6. Cool. Cut the Chèvre into ½ cm (¼ in) dice. Cut the apple, with the skin on, into pea-sized balls with a melon-baller. Put the Chèvre, apple and walnuts together in a bowl and moisten with the oil and lemon juice. Season with salt and black pepper. Spoon into the pastry cases and serve straightaway.

TIP: If cooking several batches of pastry cases in one go, pile the tins on top of each other instead of filling with tin foil. The filling will soon discolour so this recipe is not very suitable for large parties.

CHICORY WITH COTTAGE CHEESE, ORANGE AND WALNUTS

2 heads of chicory
2 small oranges
1 × 125 g (5 oz) carton cottage cheese
6 walnuts, finely chopped
1 tsp parsley, chopped
Salt and ground black pepper

Separate the chicory leaves and wash and dry them. Use only the smaller leaves. Grate the rind from the oranges and add it to the cottage cheese together with the walnuts and chopped parsley. Season with salt and black pepper. Peel the oranges with a sharp knife and cut into segments, discarding all the pith and pips. Drain the segments on absorbent paper. Spoon a little of the cottage cheese mixture into the chicory leaves and set a segment of orange on top.

MINI FRIED GRUYÈRE SANDWICHES

6 slices soft white bread
Butter for spreading
Dijon mustard
100 g (4 oz) Gruyère, finely sliced

Butter the bread and lay half the slices butter-side down on the work-top. Spread the unbuttered side with a little mustard and cover with the cheese. Top with the remaining bread so that you have a sandwich with the butter on the outside. Heat a heavy frying pan or griddle and fry the sandwiches slowly until they are golden brown on both sides and the cheese inside has melted. Trim the crusts and cut each sandwich into 8 triangles. Serve straight away.

TIP: If making this for more than 20 people, heat the oven to 220°C/425°F/Gas Mark 7, put the sandwiches on a baking tray and bake for 10 minutes on the first side and 5 minutes on the second.

FALAFEL

454 g (15 oz) tinned chick peas
1 egg, lightly beaten
½ tsp turmeric
2 tbsp coriander leaves, chopped
¼ tsp ground cumin
¼ tsp Cayenne pepper
1 clove garlic, crushed
1 tbsp tahina
25 g (1 oz) cracked wheat, soaked and
*   squeezed dry*
Salt and ground black pepper
50 g (2 oz) flour
Oil for deep frying

Put the chick peas into a food processor or liquidizer with the egg, turmeric, coriander leaves, cumin, Cayenne pepper, garlic, tahina and soaked cracked wheat. Season with salt and black pepper. Blend until smooth. Shape the mixture into small patties and dust heavily with seasoned flour. Heat the oil until a piece of bread will sizzle vigorously in it. Fry the patties until lightly browned. Drain well on absorbent paper and serve hot.

TEX MEX MUFFINS WITH CHILLI DIP

75 g (3 oz) butter, softened
75 g (3 oz) cream cheese
1 small egg, beaten
50 g (2 oz) self-raising flour
50 g (2 oz) cornmeal
Pinch salt
½ small green pepper, finely chopped
½ small red pepper, finely chopped
FOR THE DIP
1 tbsp olive oil
½ medium onion, finely chopped
1 clove garlic, crushed
Pinch of chilli powder
1 × 230 g (8 oz) tin tomatoes

Grease about 20 tiny patty tins. Heat the oven to 180°C/350°F/Gas Mark 4. Beat the butter and cream cheese together until light and fluffy. Beat in the egg. Mix the flour, cornmeal and salt together and gradually add to the butter and cream cheese mixture, stirring until well mixed. Add the peppers. Spoon the mixture into the tins. Bake for 20 minutes or until golden brown.

TO MAKE THE DIP: Heat the oil in a frying pan and in it gently brown the onion and garlic. Add the chilli powder and continue to cook for another minute. Stir in the tinned tomatoes and simmer for 30 minutes. Liquidize the dip and serve hot in a small bowl surrounded by the warm muffins skewered with a cocktail stick.

TIP: The muffins can be frozen, then defrosted and reheated in a moderate oven for a few minutes before serving.

MINI PITTAS WITH NIÇOISE FILLING

5 round 'mini' pittas
1× 198 g (7 oz) tin tuna fish
¼ cucumber, finely chopped
3 tomatoes, peeled, deseeded and chopped
½ small onion, finely chopped
½ green pepper, finely chopped
50 g (2 oz) French beans, cooked
1 hard-boiled egg, finely chopped
Salt and ground black pepper

Drain a little but not all of the oil from the tuna fish and mash the tuna well with the cucumber, tomatoes, onion, green pepper, beans and hard-boiled egg. Season with salt and black pepper. Cut the pitta bread into quarters. Spoon a little of the filling into the pockets.

TIP: The filling can be prepared the day before. Cover it tightly with cling film and chill overnight. But do not fill the pittas until the very last minutes as they quickly curl at the edges.

CHERRY TOMATOES WITH AVOCADO

10 cherry tomatoes
1 very ripe avocado pear
50 g (2 oz) cream cheese
Salt and ground black pepper
Worcestershire sauce
Tabasco
Lemon juice

Cut the tomatoes in half and scoop out the flesh and seeds. Leave to drain, turned upside down on a sheet of absorbent paper. Purée the flesh of the avocado pear in a liquidizer or food processor. Add the cream cheese and continue to process until very smooth. Season to taste with salt, pepper, Worcestershire sauce, Tabasco and plenty of lemon juice (as this prevents the avocado from turning brown). Place the avocado mixture in a piping bag fitted with a fluted nozzle and pipe whirls into the tomato halves.

TIP: To save time, the tomatoes can be prepared the day before.

WALNUT AND CHÈVRE SABLÉS

75 g (3 oz) plain flour
Pinch of salt, dry mustard and Cayenne pepper
75 g (3 oz) butter
75 g (3 oz) Cheddar cheese, finely grated
25 g (1 oz) crumbled Chèvre (goat's cheese)
25 g (1 oz) walnuts, chopped

Sift the flour and seasonings into a mixing bowl. Cut the butter into pieces and then rub it into the flour. When lumps of dough start to form, add the cheese and carefully draw the dough together, using the fingertips only. Knead gently and roll out on a lightly floured surface to approximately ¼ cm (⅛ in) thick. Stamp out 2.5 cm (1 in) rounds, place on a baking tray and chill for 1 hour. Heat the oven to 200°C/400°F/Gas Mark 6. Mix the Chèvre and walnuts together and sprinkle a little on top of each sablé. Bake for about 10 minutes, until golden brown. Serve warm or cold.

TIP: This dough is very rich. Keep it cool and handle it as little as possible to prevent it becoming greasy. The mixture can easily be made by combining all the ingredients in a food processor. The sablés can be stored overnight in an airtight container.

RATATOUILLE BOUCHÉES

1 small onion
1 clove garlic, crushed
½ small aubergine
½ courgette
1 small green pepper
1 × 230 g (8 oz) tin tomatoes
1 tbsp olive oil
Salt and ground black pepper
Dried basil
20 cooked bouchée cases (see recipe,
p.149)

Chop all the vegetables very finely. Heat the oil in a heavy pan, add the onion and garlic and fry gently until soft and transparent. Add the aubergine, courgette and green pepper, cover the pan and continue to cook gently for 10 minutes. Add the tomatoes, season with salt, black pepper and basil, bring to the boil and simmer until the vegetables are cooked and the ratatouille is well reduced and shiny. If serving cold, allow the ratatouille to cool completely before using. To serve hot, warm the bouchée cases and fill with spoonfuls of hot ratatouille.
TIP: Ratatouille freezes well.

93

AUBERGINE SAMOSAS

225 g (8 oz) plain flour
½ tsp salt
4 tbsp vegetable oil
4 tbsp water
FOR THE FILLING
1 tbsp oil
1 medium-sized aubergine, peeled and finely
chopped
1 clove garlic, crushed
¼ tsp ground allspice
¼ tsp marjoram
Salt and ground black pepper
1 tsp tomato purée
Oil for deep-frying

Sift the flour and salt into a bowl and add the oil. Rub it in until the mixture resembles coarse breadcrumbs. Slowly add the water while mixing the dough to a stiff ball with the fingertips. Knead for about 10 minutes. Rub a little extra oil over the dough, wrap it in cling film and leave to rest for at least 30 minutes. Meanwhile, make the filling: heat the oil, add the aubergine, garlic, allspice and marjoram and season with salt and black pepper. Fry the mixture gently until soft and well cooked. Stir in the tomato purée. Leave to cool.

Knead the dough again and divide into 10 balls. Roll them out thinly to about 10 cm (4 in) in diameter and cut in half. Spoon a little filling on to one side of each piece of pastry, damp the edges and fold over to form triangles. Press the edges well together, marking a pattern with a knife and fork. Heat the oil until a piece of bread will sizzle vigorously in it. Fry the samosas until golden brown. Drain on absorbent paper and serve immediately, or leave to cool and serve cold.

TIP: Samosas can also be made with the Spinach and Ricotta filling (see p. 74) or the Lamb filling (see p. 66).

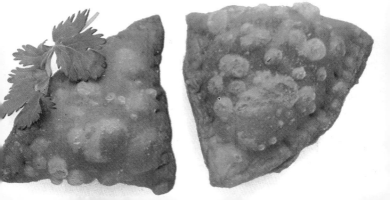

QUICK AND EASY

Centre: *Carrots with Curried Cream Cheese;* top: *Rare Roast Beef with Pickle;* bottom: *Tomato, Mozzarella and Black Olive.*

PARMA HAM BUNDLES

Wedge of ripe melon
½ a papaya
2 figs
175 g (6 oz) Parma ham, very thinly sliced

Remove the skin and seeds from the melon and papaya and scoop into balls with a melon-baller. Cut the figs into bite-sized chunks. Slice the Parma ham into strips about 2.5 cm (1 in) wide. Wrap each piece of fruit neatly in a strip of Parma ham and secure with a cocktail stick.

STUFFED MANGE-TOUTS

20 small mange-touts
100 g (4 oz) Boursin
Milk

Top and tail the mange-touts and plunge them into boiling salted water for 2 minutes, then immediately into cold water. Drain and pat dry with absorbent paper. With a very sharp vegetable knife, split them on the curved side. Soften the Boursin with a little milk and place in a large piping bag fitted with a medium plain nozzle. Pipe a squiggle of cheese into each mange-tout.

TIP: To save time, the mange-touts can be prepared the day before, but do not stuff them until the day of the party.

99

SARDINE CRESCENTS

100 g (4 oz) puff pastry
75 g (3 oz) tinned sardines
Salt, ground black pepper and lemon juice
1 egg, beaten

Roll the pastry out thinly. Drain and mash the sardines and season with salt, pepper and lemon juice. Spread the mixture over the pastry and fold in half. Roll into an oblong, fold into three, turn so that the folded edge is to the left and roll again. Cut out crescent shapes stamping a semi-circle out of one end of the pastry with a 5 cm (2 in) plain pastry cutter. Then place the cutter partially over the cut round edge of the pastry strip so that the next cut will give a crescent shape. Continue to cut until all the pastry is used. Place on a wet baking tray and chill for 30 minutes. Set the oven to 200°C/400°F/Gas Mark 6. Brush with beaten egg and bake for 15-20 minutes until golden brown. Serve hot.

TIP: The sardine crescents can be baked the day before and warmed just before serving.

FRESH DATES STUFFED WITH CREAM CHEESE AND ALMONDS

20 fresh dates
225 g (8 oz) cream cheese
Milk
25 g (1 oz) ground almonds
100 g (4 oz) browned, nibbed almonds

With a sharp vegetable knife, split the dates lengthways along the top and remove the stone. Soften the cream cheese with a little milk and stir in the ground almonds. Place this mixture in a piping bag fitted with a fluted nozzle and pipe lines of it into the dates. As each date is filled, dip the top of the cream cheese into the nibbed almonds so that it becomes coated in nuts.

PRAWNS AND SCALLOPS IN GARLIC BUTTER

(About 40 mouthfuls)
20 Queen scallops
3 spring onions, cleaned and trimmed
2 tbsp olive oil
25 g (1 oz) butter
3 cloves garlic, crushed
3 tbsp dry vermouth
350 g (12 oz) prawns, cooked and peeled

Remove the tough muscle opposite the coral from the scallops. Cut the spring onions into thin strips. Heat the oil and butter in a heavy-based frying pan and gently fry the garlic. Pour in the vermouth and simmer until the liquid is reduced and buttery – about 2 tablespoonsful. Add the scallops and toss over the heat for a few minutes until cooked. Stir in the prawns and spring onions and cook for a further few minutes until heated through. Pass the prawns and scallops round in the pan, handing cocktail sticks for the guests to help themselves with.
TIP: Queen scallops are usually only available frozen.

TUNA TOASTS

1 packet melba toasts (bought from a delicatessen)
1 × 200g (7 oz) tin tuna fish
½ small onion, finely chopped
2 tbsp mayonnaise
Lemon juice
Salt and ground black pepper
Cayenne pepper

Cut the melba toast into small rectangles. Drain the tuna fish well and mash with the onion. Stir in the mayonnaise and season with lemon juice, salt and black pepper. Place a spoonful on top of each melba toast and decorate with a tiny sprinkle of Cayenne pepper.

CARROTS WITH CURRIED CREAM CHEESE

3 medium-sized carrots
225 g (8 oz) cream cheese
Milk
Curry paste
Salt and ground black pepper
Coriander leaves

Peel the carrots. With the tip of a potato peeler, cut grooves the length of the carrot and all the way around. Cut into slices about ½ cm (¼ in) thick. Soften the cream cheese with milk and flavour with curry paste. Place in a piping bag fitted with a large fluted nozzle and pipe whirls on to the carrot rounds. Decorate each one with a whole coriander leaf.

MINI PIZZAS

20 dried bread croûtes (see recipe, p.150)
50 g (2 oz) strong Cheddar cheese,
*   finely sliced*
1 tsp oregano
4 tomatoes, skinned and sliced
10 black olives, stoned and halved

Put a slice of tomato on each of the dried bread croûtes. Cut the cheese into small squares and lay on top of the tomato. Sprinkle with oregano and decorate with half a black olive. Cook the mini pizzas under a hot grill until the cheese has melted. Serve straightaway.

TIP: The mini pizzas can be grilled before the party and left to cool. Reheat them in a moderate oven just before serving.

TOMATO, MOZZARELLA AND BLACK OLIVE

100 g (4 oz) Mozzarella cheese
2 tomatoes, peeled
10 black olives, stoned and halved

Cut the Mozzarella into 1 cm (½ in) cubes. Cut the tomatoes in half. Remove the seeds and cut the flesh of each tomato into 10. Thread a cube of Mozzarella on to each cocktail stick, followed by a strip of tomato and lastly half a black olive.

TIP: Try to buy Mozzarella that is fairly firm or it may break when threaded on to the cocktail sticks.

MELON AND HONEY-ROAST HAM

½ honeydew melon
225 g (8 oz) piece of honey-roast ham

Scrape the seeds from inside the melon and scoop the flesh into balls with a melon-baller. Cut the ham into 1 cm (½ in) cubes. Thread the balls of melon and the cubes of ham alternately on to cocktail sticks. **TIP:** Don't push the cocktail stick right through the food as it will be awkward to eat. The old way of serving cocktail stick kebabs is hedgehog-fashion in an upturned melon, cabbage or pineapple. Or serve them with other items arranged in rows on a serving dish.

ASSORTED MINI SANDWICHES

(Each filling is enough for 5 rounds of sandwiches or 20 mini sandwiches)

CELERIAC

225 g (8 oz) Celeriac, thickly peeled and grated
2 tbsp thick mayonnaise
½ tsp Dijon mustard
1 tsp capers
1 tsp gherkin, finely chopped
Salt and ground black pepper

CREAM CHEESE, TOMATO AND CHIVE

175 g (3 oz) cream cheese
Milk
2 tomatoes, skinned, deseeded and chopped
1 heaped tbsp chives, chopped
Salt and ground black pepper

SARDINE AND EGG

1 × 125 g (5 oz) tin sardines in oil, drained and mashed
2 hard-boiled eggs, chopped
Salt and ground black pepper

SALMON AND WATERCRESS

1 × 225 g (8 oz) tin salmon or fresh salmon, cooked and flaked
½ bunch watercress, destalked, washed and chopped
Salt, ground black pepper and lemon juice
TO DECORATE
Watercress, mustard and cress, slices of radish, olives

Two slices of bread, filled, will cut into four mini sandwiches. Any thinly sliced bread will do, all sorts of granary, rye and other types are now available ready cut. Choose a colour to compliment the filling. For instance, the celeriac filling is pale brownish and therefore will look more attractive between white bread than brown. Spread the bread with softened butter. Don't skimp on the butter – after all it is an ingredient of any sandwich and will also prevent moisture from the fillings soaking into the bread.

The fillings are made by mixing all the ingredients together and seasoning to taste. Use them generously. When the sandwiches are made, trim the crusts so that you have a completely square sandwich. Cut each one into four triangles. Set them upright on a platter so that the filling can be seen. The effect of this is best with alternate rows of brown and white sandwiches. Decorate with water cress, mustard and cress, slices of radish or whole olives.

TIP: An electric carving knife makes it much easier to cut perfectly neat sandwiches. Once made, cover the sandwiches with a damp towel to keep them fresh.

Other recipes that could be used as sandwich fillings are Smoked Trout Mousse (p.20), Ham, Cream Cheese and Chives (p.65), Smoked Chicken (p.62), Chicken and Lobster (p.68), Pâté (p.48) Avocado (p.91), Niçoise (p.90), Cottage Cheese, Orange and Walnut (p.85), and Tuna Fish (p.103).

FRENCH BREAD OPEN SANDWICHES

A party can be quickly put together by serving French bread with almost anything that can be bought from the local shop. The trick is to buy a very fresh and narrow French stick, about 5 cm (2 in) in diameter and slice it about ½ cm (¼ in) thick. For a casual party the bread can be buttered and spread with pâté and decorated with an olive, topped with a thin slice of Brie and a twist of cucumber, or herring in sour cream with rings of raw onion. For a more sophisticated effect, the top should be completely covered. Use thin slices of smoked salmon, smoked halibut, Parma ham, German salami or raw beef (p. 60) stamped out with a sharp cutter to fit the slice of French bread exactly. Decorate the fish fillings with dill or a spoonful of real or mock caviar. Meat fillings can be decorated with mustard or herb mayonnaise.

ASPARAGUS AND PARMA HAM

20 spears of fresh asparagus, cooked
175 g (6 oz) Parma ham, thinly sliced
Ground black pepper

Trim the tough stalks from the asparagus so that the spears measure about 7 cm (3 in). Sprinkle with black pepper. Cut the Parma ham into strips about 5 cm (2 in) wide. Wrap the strips around the asparagus spears so that a little asparagus is showing at each end.

BEETROOT WITH HORSERADISH CREAM CHEESE

10 slices of rye bread
175 g (6 oz) cream cheese
Milk
Horseradish relish
225 g (8 oz) cooked beetroot, peeled

Stamp two 5 cm (2 in) rounds out of each slice of rye bread. Soften the cream cheese with the milk and flavour with horseradish relish. Spread this mixture over the rounds of black rye bread. Slice the beetroot and cut into squares. Use to decorate the bread rounds just before serving.
TIP: It is possible to buy cream cheese that is already flavoured with horseradish.

SPICED NIBBLES

225 g (8 oz) chick peas
1 rasher streaky bacon, chopped
6 tbsp peanut oil
Good pinch of chilli powder
1 tsp paprika pepper
1 tsp tomato purée
Salt and ground black pepper
225 g (8 oz) whole blanched almonds
75 g (3 oz) sugar
1 tsp ground cumin
Oil for deep-frying
225 g (8 oz) cashew nuts

Soak the chick peas overnight. Drain and cook in boiling water with the bacon until they are tender. Drain the chick peas well and pat dry with absorbent paper. Heat 3 tbsp of the peanut oil in a frying pan and add a pinch of chilli powder, the paprika pepper and tomato purée. Gently fry the chick peas in the spicy mixture until they are well covered and soaked in oil. Drain, sprinkle with salt and ground black pepper and leave to cool.

Heat the remaining peanut oil, add the almonds and sprinkle the sugar over. Fry them gently until the almonds become golden brown and the sugar caramelizes. Put the almonds in a bowl and toss with the cumin and 1 tsp of salt. They can be served warm or cold.

Heat the oil for deep-frying until a piece of bread will sizzle vigorously in it. Add the cashew nuts and fry until deep golden brown. Remove from the oil immediately, drain well and spread on absorbent paper. Sprinkle with plenty of salt, black pepper and a pinch of chilli. Serve warm or cold.

TIP: The almonds and cashew nuts can be stored for up to two weeks in airtight containers.

BACON AND SCALLOP ROLLS

(Makes 20)
10 rashers streaky bacon
20 queen scallops
Salt, freshly ground black pepper
Lemon juice

Remove the rind from the bacon, stretch each rasher with the back of a knife and cut in half. Remove the tough muscle opposite the coral. Season the scallops with salt, black pepper and lemon juice. Wrap a piece of bacon loosely around each scallop and pack tightly together in a roasting tin with the join underneath, to stop them from unravelling. Heat the grill to the fiercest temperature and cook the bacon rolls for 5-10 minutes, turning halfway through the cooking, until crisp and brown. Serve straightaway, skewered with a cocktail stick.

TIP: Bacon and scallop rolls can be made the day before but should be cooked on the day. If using seafood, always be sure that it is very fresh.

BACON AND BANANA ROLLS

(Makes 20)
10 rashers streaky bacon
2 bananas

Remove the rind from the bacon, stretch each rasher with the back of a knife and cut in half. Cut the bananas into chunks. Wrap a piece of bacon loosely around each banana chunk and pack tightly together in a roasting tin with the join underneath, to stop them from unravelling. Heat the grill to the fiercest temperature and cook the bacon rolls for 5-10 minutes, turning halfway through cooking, until crisp and brown. Serve straightaway, skewered with a cocktail stick, or leave in a cool place and reheat for 5 minutes in a hot oven just before serving.
TIP: These rolls can also be made with lychees or chunks of mango instead of the bananas.

PUFF PASTRY ANCHOVIES

100 g (4 oz) puff pastry
Anchovy paste
Caster sugar
Beaten egg

Roll the pastry out thinly and spread with a thin layer of anchovy paste. Sprinkle with caster sugar. Fold in half and roll into an oblong. Fold the strip into three, turn so that the folded edge is to the left and roll again. Stamp out fish shapes with a shaped pastry cutter and place on a wet baking tray. Chill for 30 minutes. Set the oven to 200°C/400°F/Gas Mark 6. Brush with beaten egg and bake for 15 minutes until golden brown. Serve hot.

TIP: Any shaped cutter can be used to make the anchovies or the pastry can be cut into fingers. The pastries can be made the day before, stored in an airtight container overnight, and reheated before serving.

QUAIL AND GULL EGGS WITH CHILLI DIP

20 quails' eggs
20 gulls' eggs
Celery salt, sea salt or
*   chilli dip (see recipe, p. 88)*

Gently boil the quails' eggs for 3 minutes. Drain them, cover with cold water and leave to cool. Gulls' eggs are bought ready boiled. If the shells look pretty, leave the eggs unpeeled. Serve the quails' and gulls' eggs in their shells (with a separate dish for the débris) with the celery salt, sea salt or chilli dip in a small dish on the side.

MEDITERRANEAN PRAWNS WITH AÏOLI DIP

20 Mediterranean prawns
FOR THE AÏOLI DIP
3 cloves garlic, crushed
2 egg yolks
Pinch of salt
1 tsp Dijon mustard
150 ml (¼ pt) olive oil and 150 ml (¼ pt) salad oil
Squeeze of lemon juice
2 tbsp wine vinegar
Ground black pepper

Carefully peel the prawns, leaving the heads intact. Put the garlic, egg yolk, salt and mustard into a mixing bowl or in the bowl of a food processor. Gradually add the oil, drip by drip, beating all the time. The mixture should become very thick by the time half the oil is added. Stir in the lemon juice and vinegar. Add the remaining oil rather more confidently. Season with salt and black pepper. Spoon the aïoli into a small dish and place in the centre of a round serving plate. Arrange the peeled prawns around the edge of the dip.

RARE ROAST BEEF AND PICKLE

225 g (8 oz) sliced rare roast beef
4 dill pickles

With a very sharp knife, cut the beef into 2.5 cm (1 in) strips. Cut the dill pickles into 20 chunks. Pleat the strips of meat on to cocktail sticks and thread a chunk of pickle on to each one.
TIP: Pastrami or salami makes a delicious substitute for the roast beef in this recipe.

CRUDITÉS

A selection of:
½ cucumber, cut into sticks
2 carrots, peeled and cut into sticks
½ green pepper, deseeded and cut into sticks
½ red pepper, deseeded and cut into sticks
1 bunch spring onions, cleaned and trimmed
12 cherry tomatoes
100 g (4 oz) button mushrooms
1 bunch radishes, with a little stalk left on
¼ cauliflower, cut into florets

Prepare the vegetables and arrange them in clusters on a round plate, leaving room for a bowl of dip in the centre. If preparing them in advance, put vegetables cut into sticks into bundles and secure at each end with an elastic band. Keep in a bowl of iced water.

The vegetables listed above are the most commonly used for crudités, but more unusual ones can be offered too, such as sticks of aubergine, turnip, baby beets, French beans, mange-touts. One attractive idea is to choose vegetables on a particular colour scheme: green, purple (aubergine, red cabbage, beetroot, purple beans) or red and white.

HOT BRIE OR CAMEMBERT DIP

1 whole Camembert or baby Brie

Lift the cheese out of its straw case, remove the wrapping and rewrap in tin foil. Replace in the straw case without the lid. Heat the oven to 180°C/375°F/Gas Mark 5 and heat the cheese for about 20 minutes, until it is warm and runny. With a sharp knife, remove the crust from the top of the cheese and set in the centre of the crudités. If the cheese starts to cool and harden, warm it again in the oven.

SPINACH AND BOURSIN DIP

100 g (4 oz) frozen chopped spinach
50 g (2 oz) cream cheese
50 g (2 oz) Boursin
Milk
Salt, ground black pepper, nutmeg

Defrost the spinach, squeeze very dry and drain on absorbent paper. Mix together the Boursin and cream cheese and soften with a little milk. Beat in the spinach and season with salt, pepper and nutmeg.

Carrot and Cardamom Dip

225 g (8 oz) carrots
15 g (½ oz) butter
300 ml (½ pt) water
1 bay leaf and 2 cardamom pods
2 tbsp Greek yoghurt
2 tsp chervil, finely chopped
Salt and ground black pepper

Pare and slice the carrots. Melt the butter in a pan, add the carrots, cover and fry gently for 10 minutes. Add the water, bay leaf and cardamom pods and simmer until the carrots are tender. Strain, remove the bay leaf and cardamom and leave to cool. Purée with the yoghurt, stir in the chervil and season to taste with salt and black pepper.

SMOKED SAUSAGE, BACON AND PEPPER KEBABS

225 g (8 oz) spicy smoked sausage
4 rashers rindless streaky bacon
½ red pepper
½ green pepper

Cut the smoked sausage into 20 chunks. Grill the streaky bacon until golden brown and cut it into 1 cm (½ in) pieces. Deseed the peppers and cut into pieces about the same size as the bacon. Arrange on cocktail sticks. Heat the oven to 180°C/375°F/Gas Mark 5 and just before serving cook the smoked sausage kebabs for 10 minutes.

TIP: Almost any type of smoked sausage is suitable for this recipe. Kabanos, Polish pork sausages, are highly spiced and particularly good.

ASPARAGUS CROUSTADE

5 slices brown bread, crusts removed
Butter for spreading
10 spears tinned asparagus
Ground black pepper

Flatten the bread with a rolling pin. Butter each slice, cut in half and lay the slices, butter-side down, on the work-top. Drain the asparagus well and pat dry with absorbent paper. Put a spear of asparagus along the edge of each piece of bread, season with black pepper and roll up tightly. Cut each roll in half and set on a baking tray. Chill for 30 minutes. Heat the oven to 220°C/425°F/Gas Mark 7 and bake the croustades until crisp and golden brown. Serve hot or cold.

CRAB CLAWS DIPPED IN SMOKED COD'S ROE SAUCE

20 crab claws, shells removed but with the
*   tips of the claws intact*
Juice of half a lemon
Ground black pepper
FOR THE SAUCE
50g (2 oz) smoked cod's roe, skinned
Ground black pepper
I shallot, finely chopped
I clove garlic, crushed
Juice of half a lemon
I tsp tomato purée
Dash of Worcestershire sauce
Dash of Tabasco
3 tbsp double cream, lightly whipped
1 tsp mayonnaise

If using frozen crab claws, defrost them slowly overnight, sprinkled with lemon juice and black pepper. Put the cod's roe, shallot, garlic, lemon juice and tomato purée into a liquidizer or food processor and blend until smooth. Pour the mixture into a bowl and season with

128

Worcestershire sauce, Tabasco and black pepper. Fold in the whipped cream and mayonnaise. Serve the sauce in a small bowl set in the centre of a serving dish surrounded by the crab claws.

TIP: Crab claws are sold frozen and ready prepared for cocktail parties with the tip of the claw attached to the shelled white meat. It is a good idea to order them in advance. Have a dish handy for the guests to put the shells in.

MEXICAN TOASTADAS

2 cocktail avocados
1 tbsp mayonnaise
20 dried bread croûtes (see recipe,
* p. 150)*
20 slices of garlic sausages, approx 3 cm
* (1½ in) in diameter*
100 g (4 oz) Cheddar cheese, finely grated

Peel the cocktail avocados and cut each one into 10 slices. Heat the grill. Spread a little mayonnaise on each of the dried bread croûtes, then cover with a slice of garlic sausage, followed by a slice of avocado. Sprinkle with grated cheese and place under the grill until the cheese has melted. Serve straightaway.

BRIE AND BLACK GRAPES

¼ medium-ripe Brie
20 black grapes, halved and pipped

Cut the Brie into 20 pieces, each about 1 cm (½ in) square. Thread half a black grape on to a cocktail stick, followed by a piece of Brie and then another half black grape. Make sure that the rounded ends of the grapes are outermost.

TIP: The grapes can be prepared in advance but the Brie must be cut on the day of the party.

SWEET

From the outside: *Caramel Choux Puffs; Strawberry Tartlets; Walnut and Lemon Curd Mini Meringues.*

FRUIT FONDUE

*A selection of fruit: Cantaloupe melon, apples,
    bananas, oranges, black grapes, strawberries,
    cherries*
Lemon juice
FOR THE DIPS
100 g (4 oz) plain chocolate
1 tbsp golden syrup
2 tsp brandy
2 tbsp milk
425 ml (¾ pt) double cream, whipped
1 × 125 g (5 oz) carton cottage cheese, sieved
Icing sugar to taste
Grated rind and juice of 2 small oranges

Chill the fruit for a few hours. Prepare it for eating with the fingers: peel and deseed the melon and cut the flesh into slices. Quarter, core and thickly slice the apples. Peel the bananas and cut into chunks. Break the oranges into segments, picking off any pith. Wash the grapes, strawberries and cherries, leaving the stalks on. Brush the apple and banana with lemon juice and arrange the fruits on a well chilled dish. The dips are handed separately to dunk the fruit in.

TO PREPARE THE DIPS: Put the chocolate, syrup, brandy and milk together in a small pan and melt over a low heat, stirring occasionally until completely smooth. Serve warm. Fold 150 ml (¼ pt) of whipped cream into the sieved cottage cheese and sweeten to taste. Serve in a small bowl. Mix the remaining 300 ml (½ pt) of whipped cream with the orange rind and juice and sweeten with icing sugar.

MINI MERINGUES

Makes about 10 of each sort
3 egg whites
125 g (5 oz) caster sugar
25 g (1 oz) soft brown sugar
25 g (1 oz) walnuts, finely ground
50 g (2 oz) soft fruit (strawberries,
*   raspberries, apricots, etc.)*
2 tsp lemon curd
150 ml (¼ pt) double cream, whipped
25 g (1 oz) unsalted butter
50 g (2 oz) icing sugar, sifted
1 tsp coffee essence
½ egg yolk

Set the oven to 100°C/200°F/Gas Mark ½. Cover a baking tray with a sheet of oiled greaseproof paper. Beat the egg whites until stiff. Add 75 g (3 oz) of the caster sugar and continue to beat until very stiff and shiny. Divide the mixture into three. Add 25 g (1 oz) sugar to one-third of the mixture; the brown sugar to the next third; and the remaining caster sugar and ground walnuts to the last batch. Place the walnut meringues in small spoonfuls on the prepared baking tray and pipe the other sorts with a fluted nozzle in little whirls. Cook them for about 1 hour. They are ready when light and dry and when the paper can be pulled off easily.

Wash and coarsely chop the soft fruit and mix with half the whipped cream. Use this to sandwich the plain meringues together. Mix the lemon curd with the remaining cream and use as a filling for the walnut meringues. Soften the butter and beat in the remaining ingredients until light and fluffy. Sandwich the brown sugar meringues together with the coffee filling.

TIP: The plain and brown sugar meringues can be made in advance and stored for several weeks in an airtight container.

SWEET PANCAKES

20 thin pancakes about 10 cm (4 in) in
*   diameter*
50 g (2 oz) Petit Suisse
2 tbsp whipped cream
Caster sugar
225 g (8 oz) berries (strawberries,
*   blueberries, etc.)*
Jam the same flavour as the berries

As soon as the pancakes are cooked, put them on a heated plate, cover and keep warm in a low oven. Sweeten the Petit Suisse with caster sugar and mix with the cream. To serve: put a dollop of the Petit Suisse mixture to one side of each pancake and top it with a smaller dollop of jam. Arrange a few berries on top of this and fold up neatly.
TIP: Pancakes freeze well.

GOLDEN GRAPES

20 white grapes
225 g (8 oz) granulated sugar
A little water

Place the sugar with a little water in a heavy-based pan, set over a very low heat and melt to a golden caramel. Dip the base of the pan in cold water to stop the cooking, then stand it in hot water to keep the caramel liquid. Dip the fruit into the caramel (taking great care not to touch the caramel with the fingertips) and leave to set on an oiled baking tray.

TIP: Caramel is scorching hot and can cause serious burns so take great care when using it.

CARAMEL CHOUX PUFFS

1 quantity choux pastry (see recipe, p.146),
without seasonings or Parmesan
150 ml (¼ pt) double cream, whipped
1 tbsp Grand Marnier
Grated rind of 1 orange
100 g (4 oz) granulated sugar

Set the oven to 200°C/400°F/Gas Mark 6. Wet two baking trays. Put the choux pastry in a piping bag fitted with a fluted nozzle and pipe in rounds on to the baking trays. Bake for 20-30 minutes, until puffed up and golden brown. Remove from the oven and make a small hole in the side of each bun. Return to the oven to dry out. Cool on a wire rack. Mix the whipped cream with the Grand Marnier and orange rind. Place in a piping bag fitted with a medium-sized plain nozzle and fill the choux buns through the small hole in the side. Set the wire rack with the choux buns on over an oiled baking tray. Put the granulated sugar in a heavy-based pan and set over a low heat and melt to a golden caramel. Dribble the caramel over the top of the choux buns.
TIP: Caramel is scorching hot and can cause serious burns so take great care when using it.

EASY CHOCOLATE TRUFFLES

100 g (4 oz) cream cheese
275 g (10 oz) icing sugar, sifted
225 g (8 oz) plain chocolate
Vanilla essence
Cocoa powder, sifted, or chocolate strands

Soften the cream cheese and gradually mix in the icing sugar. Break the chocolate into small pieces and melt in a bowl set over a pan of simmering water. Stir the melted chocolate into the cream cheese mixture and add the vanilla essence. Roll into small balls and coat the truffles in cocoa or chocolate strands. Chill for 2 hours before serving.

ALMOND TARTLETS

50g (2oz) unsalted butter
50g (2oz) caster sugar
1 egg and squeeze of lemon juice
15g (½oz) plain flour, sifted
50g (2oz) ground almonds
20 unbaked pastry cases (see recipe p. 151)
25g (1oz) flaked almonds
2tbsp apricot jam, sieved

Set the oven to 190°C/375°F/Gas Mark 5. Cream the butter and sugar together until light and fluffy. Gradually beat in the egg. Add the lemon juice and fold in the flour and ground almonds. Pipe into the pastry cases, filling each one to just below the top. Scatter with the flaked almonds and bake for 10-15 minutes until golden brown. Remove from the oven and brush the tops with hot apricot jam.

STRAWBERRY TARTLETS

20 pastry cases (see recipe p. 151)
100 g (4 oz) Petit Suisse
Caster sugar to taste
Vanilla essence
20 medium-sized strawberries
Redcurrant jelly
Squeeze of lemon juice

Sweeten the Petit Suisse with caster sugar and vanilla and spread a little in the bottom of each pastry case. Wash the strawberries if necessary, and remove the hulls. Set a whole berry on top of each tartlet. Warm the redcurrant jelly with the squeeze of lemon juice and brush over the tartlets.

TIP: If making these in quantity, it is quicker to pipe the Petit Suisse mixture into the tartlet cases using a large plain nozzle.

CURD MERINGUE TARTLETS

20 pastry cases (see recipe p. 151)
100g (4oz) satsumas
150g (6oz) caster sugar
25g (1oz) butter
1tbsp lemon juice
2 eggs, separated

Wash and quarter the satsumas and 'finely mince' them in a liquidizer or food processor. Put in a bowl with 50g (2oz) caster sugar, butter, lemon juice and egg yolks. Set the bowl over a pan of simmering water and stir gently until the mixture thickens slightly. Cool and spoon into the tartlet cases. Set the oven to 180°C/350°F/Gas Mark 4. Beat the egg whites stiffly and gently fold in the remaining caster sugar. Place in a piping bag fitted with a fluted nozzle and pipe in whirls on top of the tartlets. Bake in the oven for 15-20 minutes, until the meringue is brown on top.

BASES

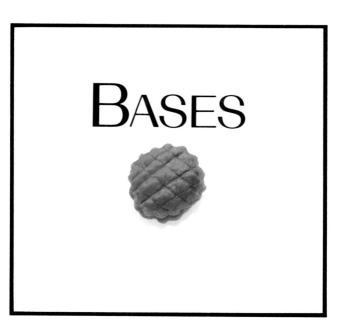

SAVOURY CHOUX PASTRY

70 g (2½ oz) plain flour, sifted
Salt, ground black pepper and a pinch of dry
   mustard
Cayenne pepper and 1 tsp Parmesan cheese
50 g (2 oz) butter
150 ml (¼ pt) water
2 eggs, beaten

Sift the flour with the seasonings and add the Parmesan cheese. Put the butter and water together in a pan and bring slowly to the boil. Immediately the liquid boils, tip in all the flour at once, remove from the heat and beat the mixture until it becomes thick and leaves the sides of the pan. Leave to cool. Beat in the eggs a little at a time until the mixture is smooth and shiny. It may not be necessary to add all the eggs, the mixture should fall easily from a lifted spoon.
TO MAKE INTO CHOUX PUFFS: Set the oven to 200°C/400°F/Gas Mark 6. Pipe the pastry into small blobs on to a damp baking tray. Brush with beaten egg and sprinkle with Parmesan cheese. Bake for 20-30 minutes until puffed up and golden brown. Remove from the oven and make a hole in the side of each puff. Return to the oven to dry out.

CHEESE PASTRY

100 g (4 oz) plain flour
50 g (2 oz) butter
15 g (½ oz) Parmesan cheese, grated
Pinch of Cayenne pepper
Pinch of dry mustard
½ egg, beaten
Cold water

Put the flour into a mixing bowl and rub in the butter. Add the Parmesan, Cayenne and mustard. Bind to a firm dough with the beaten egg and a little water. Knead gently.

TIP: The pastry can be frozen or made the day before.

TOASTIE CASES

10 slices bread
Butter for spreading

Set the oven to 220°C/425°F/Gas Mark 7. Cut the bread into 5 cm (2 in) rounds with a plain pastry cutter. Spread the rounds with butter. Press them firmly into tiny patty tins, moulding the bread to the shape of the tin and making the edges very thin. Bake in the hot oven until golden brown and crisp. Remove from the tins and cool on a wire rack.

BOUCHÉE CASES

20 frozen bouchée cases
1 egg, beaten

Heat the oven to 220°C/425°F/Gas Mark 7. Place the bouchée cases on wet baking trays and carefully brush the rims with beaten egg. Bake for 10 -15 minutes, until well risen and golden brown. Remove from the oven and use the handle of a wooden spoon to push down the pastry in the centre of each bouchée case. Cool on a wire rack.

TIP: Bouchée cases can be made from puff pastry but ready-made frozen ones are both neat and quick to make. They can be bought in a variety of sizes – the smaller the better for cocktail recipes.

Puff Pastry Croûtes

225 g (8 oz) puff pastry

Set the oven to 220°C/425°F/Gas Mark 7. Roll the pastry out very thinly and stamp out rounds with a 5 cm (2 in) pastry cutter. Lay them on a wet baking tray and prick them all over. Chill for one to two hours. Set the oven to 220°C/425°F/Gas Mark 7. Bake for 15 minutes until well browned and crisp. Flatten any croûtes that are very puffed up. Cool them on a wire rack and store in an airtight tin.

Dried Bread Croûtes

Cut any sort of sliced bread into 5 cm (2 in) rounds. Place them on a baking tray and bake in an oven set at 170°C/325°F/Gas Mark 3 until crisp and dry. They can be stored for up to 2 weeks in an airtight container.

SWEET PASTRY CASES

100 g (4 oz) plain flour
50 g (2 oz) butter
Pinch of caster sugar
1 egg yolk
1 tbsp chilled water

Sift the flour into a mixing bowl and rub in the butter. Add the egg yolk and enough water to bind to a firm dough. Roll out thinly and stamp out 5 cm (2 in) rounds with a fluted pastry cutter. Press into tiny patty tins and chill for 30 minutes. Fill each pastry case with a scrumpled piece of tin foil and bake for 10-15 minutes at 200°C/400°F/Gas Mark 6. Remove the tin foil halfway through cooking to allow the pastry cases to dry out and become crisp and golden brown.

Menu Suggestions

DRINKS PARTY

Smoked Trout Mousse and
  Smoked Salmon Parcels
New Potatoes with Sour Cream
  and Mock Caviar
Cherry Tomatoes with Avocado
Parma Ham Bundles
Mini Antipasto
Choux Puffs with Stilton Salad
Radicchio with Salade Tiède
Herb-coated Knots of Plaice with
  Saffron Dip
Pork and Prawn Toasts
Mushroom and Roquefort
  Strudels

BARBECUE PARTY

Pork and Mango with Saté Sauce
Mini Hamburgers
Kofta Kebabs
Tandoori Chicken with Cucumber
  and Yoghurt Dip
Mini Barbecued Riblets
Nuggets of Marinated Lamb
Crudités and Dips
Spiced 'Nibbles'
Mini Pittas with Niçoise Filling
Tex Mex Muffins with Chilli Dip
Curd Meringue Tartlets
Fruit Fondue

ITALIAN DRINKS PARTY
Mini Pizzas
Tuna Toasts
Tomato, Mozzarella and Black
  Olives
Asparagus with Parma Ham
Mini Antipasto
Salami with Marinated Beetroot
  on Rye
Tortelloni with Hot Provençale
  Dip
Garlic Mushrooms
Fritto Misto with Green
  Mayonnaise

WEDDING RECEPTION
Smoked Salmon Wheels
Toasties with Pâté and Green
  Peppercorns
Carrots with Curried Cream
  Cheese
Mushroom and Oyster Bouchées
Bacon Rolls
Mediterranean Prawns with Aïoli
  Dip
Assorted Mini Sandwiches
French Bread Open Sandwiches
Strawberry Tartlets
Caramel Choux Puffs
Mini Meringues

FURTHER READING

Brennan, Jennifer, *Thai Cooking* (1981)
Haroutunian, Arto der, *Vegetarian Dishes from the Middle East* (1982)
Jaffrey, Madhur, *Indian Cookery* (1982)
Leith, Prue and Polly Tyrer, *Entertaining with Style* (1986)
Leith, Prue and Caroline Waldegrave, *Leith's Cookery Course* (1979)
Stewart, Martha, *Hors d'Oeuvres* (1985)
Worrall-Thompson, Antony, *The Small and Beautiful Cookbook* (1984)

RECIPE INDEX

Garlic mushrooms in breadcrumbs, 73
Golden grapes, 139
Grilled clams with Provençale top, 32

Ham, cream cheese and chive catherine wheels, 65
Herb-coated knots of plaice with saffron dip, 26-7
Hot Brie or Camembert dip, 123

Kofta kebabs, 58

Lobster mousse in pastry cases, 44

Marinated turbot and salmon catherine wheels, 38-9
Mediterranean prawns with aïoli dip, 120
Mediterranean prawns with mange-touts, 24
Melon and honey-roast ham, 107
Mexican toastados, 130
Mini antipasto, 59
Mini Arnold Bennett omelettes, 28
Mini barbecue riblets, 53
Mini cheese and ham croissants, 63

Quail-egg flowers, 82-3
Quail and gull eggs, 119

Radicchio with salade tiède, 50
Rare roast beef and pickle, 121
Ratatouille bouchées, 93

Salami with marinated beetroot on rye, 54
Sardine crescents, 100
Savoury choux paste, 146
Scallop mousselinis, 22-3
Seasoned soft cheeses, 76-7
Smoked chicken bites, 62
Smoked halibut on rye with salmon roe and lime, 29
Smoked mussels in cheese pastry, 37
Smoked salmon wheels, 45
Smoked sausage, bacon and pepper kebabs,
Smoked trout mousse and smoked salmon parcels, 20
Spiced nibbles, 114-15
Spinach and Boursin dip, 124
Spinach and Ricotta filo triangles, 74
Spinach Roulade filled with smoked salmon mousse, 30-1

Steak tartare, 55
Strawberry tartlets, 151
Stuffed mange-touts, 99
Sweet pancakes, 138
Sweet pastry cases, 151

Tabouli bites, 79
Tandoori chicken with cucumber and yoghurt dip, 56-7
Taramasalata toasties, 41
Tex Mex muffins with chilli dip, 88-9
Toastie cases, 148
Toasties with pâté and green peppercorns, 148
Tomato, Mozzarella and black olive, 106
Tuna toasts, 103
Tortelloni with hot Provençale dip, 80

Venison sausages with cranberry sauce, 52

Wafer-thin slices of raw beef with mustard mayonnaise, 60
Walnut and chèvre sablés, 92
Watercress, cream cheese and tomato roulade, 72

Burmese phrasebook
  2nd edition

Published by
  Lonely Planet Publications
  Head Office: PO Box 617, Hawthorn, Vic 3122, Australia
  Branches: 155 Filbert St, Suite 251, Oakland, CA 94607, USA
               10 Barley Mow Passage, Chiswick, W4 4PH, UK
               71 bis rue du Cardinal Lemoine, 75005 Paris, France

Printed by
  Colorcraft Ltd, Hong Kong

Cover Photograph
  Temple Art, Bagan, Myanmar (Tony Wheeler)

Published
  January 1997

National Library of Australia Cataloguing in Publication Data

Bradley, David, 1947-
  Burmese phrasebook.

  2nd ed.
  Includes index.
  ISBN 0 86442 341 1.

  1. Burmese language - Conversation and phrase books - English. I. Title.
  (Series: Lonely Planet language survival kit).

495.883421

© Copyright Lonely Planet Publications 1997

All rights reserved. No part of this publication may be reproduced, stored in a
retrieval system or transmitted in any form by any means, electronic, mechanical, photocopying, recording or otherwise, except brief extracts for the purpose
of review, without the written permission of the publisher and copyright owner.

Contents

From the Publisher
This edition was edited by Sally Steward. Penelope Richardson designed and illustrated the book, and Simon Bracken designed the cover. Thanks to Joe Cummings, author of the Lonely Planet guide to *Myanmar (Burma)*, for his comments. Burmese script used is Avalaser for Macintosh.

About the Author
David Bradley has written various sociolinguistic and historical linguistic studies of Burmese and related languages, including Lonely Planet's *Thai Hill Tribes* phrasebook, and has worked extensively in Southeast Asia and China for over 25 years. He teaches Linguistics and Burmese at La Trobe University in Melbourne.

This Edition
This edition was updated and expanded by David Bradley. Vicky Bowman and San San Hnin Tun assisted with the updating. Vicky Bowman studied Burmese at the School of Oriental and African Studies, University of London, and lived in Myanmar for three years, from 1990 to 1993. In her spare time, she translates modern Burmese writing. San San Hnin Tun is a native speaker of Burmese who lectures in Burmese and French at Cornell University, USA. Thanks to Kyaw Zan Tha for assisting in checking proofs.

Introduction

Burmese is in the Tibeto-Burman language family, as are most of the languages of Myanmar (Burma) and many in neighbouring China, India, Thailand and Nepal. As the national language, it has over 40 million speakers, more than 30 million of whom use it as their first language. Thus it has more speakers than any other Tibeto-Burman language, including Tibetan.

After Tibetan, Burmese was one of the earliest Tibeto-Burman languages to develop a writing system. The earliest surviving inscription is at the Myazedi in Bagan (Pagan); it is known as the Rajakumar after the person who had it prepared. Dated 1112 AD, it is in four languages: Pali, Mon, Pyu and Burmese.

Burmese has some minor dialect differences; the standard dialect is that of Mandalay and Yangon, which is spoken throughout the central area of Myanmar, and taught in schools everywhere. Rakhine (Arakanese) in the west and Tavoyan in the south are slightly different, while Intha (spoken by the people of Inle Lake), Yaw, Danu and Taungyo are more divergent. There are many other languages spoken in Myanmar, some of them in the same language family and others quite unrelated. Nevertheless Burmese is spoken by nearly everyone in the country; and widespread literacy has been achieved through schools and adult literacy programmes.

Like many other languages, Burmese has two varieties: one is used in writing and associated formal activities, the other is used in speaking and other informal situations. The main differences are in vocabulary, especially the most frequent words and particles; for example 'this' is *di* in spoken Burmese, but *i* in the written language. Everything in this phrasebook is the spoken informal variety, which is appropriate for all situations a traveller is likely to encounter.

Since 1989, the government prefers the literary form Myanmar to refer to the country, its language and its people as a whole. The former English name 'Burma' is derived from the spoken form. The English form of many other places and groups was also changed at the same time. In this phrasebook, we use Myanmar to refer to the country, and Burmese for the language (as it is more commonly referred to outside the country), while for other placenames, the current name is given first, then the former name in parentheses; for example, the capital, Yangon (Rangoon); the western state of Rakhine (Arakan); and so on.

There are 33 consonants in the writing system, and there are traditionally held to be 12 vowel sounds. As in other languages spoken in the region there are various combinations of consonants; and the vowel of each syllable is written using another symbol above, below, before, or after the consonant that it follows. There are additional markings to represent the tones. Given the written form, it is almost always possible to know how to pronounce a word; but because of changes in pronunciation over the centuries the reverse is not true.

The spelling used here is the revised spelling introduced in 1980, as formulated by the Myanmar (Burma) Language Commission. The best available bilingual dictionary is their *Myanmar-English Dictionary* published in 1993. Various English-Myanmar dictionaries are available; the *Guide* dictionary of 1992 is fairly up to date, but reprinted editions of the *U Tun Nyein* and other older dictionaries can also be found; most of these use pre-1980 spelling, which is slightly different. None of these is convenient to carry around; but the available pocket dictionaries like the *Thalun* have many gaps. Also, note that nearly all these dictionaries use primarily or exclusively written language. If you are serious about learning Burmese, you may also want to get one of the better monolingual dictionaries, such as the one-volume 1991 or five-volume 1980 dictionaries of the Myanmar Language Commission.

Many Burmese nouns are borrowed from English, though the meaning and sound may be somewhat different. If you are totally stumped, you can try the English noun in the middle of a Burmese sentence, and this may sometimes work. There are also some loanwords from Hindi. Much of the more formal vocabulary comes from Pali, the language of Theravada Buddhism; but this is pronounced in a Burmese way, and so sounds different from Thai, Sri Lankan or other Pali pronunciation.

Outside the country, you can study the language at various places. These include: in Australia, at La Trobe University in Melbourne; in England, at the School of Oriental and African Studies, University of London; in the USA, at Northern Illinois University, Cornell University and sometimes elsewhere; in Germany, at Heidelberg and Humboldt Universities; in Thailand at Mahidol University; in China at Beijing University and various places in Yunnan Province; in Japan at Osaka University of Foreign Studies and Tokyo University of Foreign Studies; in France at the Ecole des Langues Orientales in Paris; and a few others.

Apart from the spoken/written difference, Burmese is not a difficult language. The three tones are largely a matter of relative stress and are less difficult to keep apart than the five tones of Thai or the six tones of Vietnamese, and some effort to produce them will be rewarded by the delight of Burmese people. Other aspects of pronunciation can best be learned by listening and imitation. Enjoy your time in Myanmar, and good luck in speaking the language!

Getting Started

There are always a few key essentials you should memorise before you begin your travels. A standard greeting is one of the most useful: *min-gǎla-ba* is good for any formal situation and in cities; while 'Are you well?' *ne-kaùn-yéh-là* is fine for any informal encounter. You can reply *ne-kaùn-ba-deh*, 'I am well'. For more on greetings, see page 36. To understand the little tone marks you've just read — the *ǎ* and *aù* — turn to pages 11-12.

Saying 'thank you' can be done with a smile (refer to page 40). 'I understand' is *nà-leh-ba-deh*; 'I don't understand' is *nà-mǎleh-ba-bù*. 'How much?' is *beh-lauq-lèh?*; 'Where?' is *beh-hma-lèh?* For quick reference to other key words, go to the Vocabulary chapter.

If you have time, other useful words to memorise are the numbers (pages 124-126) and some key verbs (page 22-23). At this stage, don't worry about your pronunciation or getting the grammar right — just take the plunge and start speaking. And if native speakers laugh, don't panic. They are laughing because they are surprised and delighted that you are taking the trouble to learn their language.

Pronunciation

In this book, Burmese pronunciation is the same as that used in the textbooks by Okell, the most up-to-date Burmese course available. The tones and some of the consonants may seem difficult at first. The best way to overcome this problem is to listen to the way the speakers differentiate between the tones.

Tones

Burmese tones are largely a matter of relative stress between adjoining syllables. They exist in English too — think about the different stresses, and hence meaning, between 'He's thought less' and 'He's thoughtless'.

There are three tones, plus two other possibilities, for any syllable. Every syllable has one of these five alternatives.

Creaky High Tone

This is made with the voice tense, producing a high-pitched and relatively short creaky sound, such as occurs with the English words 'heart' and 'squeak'. It is indicated by an acute accent above the vowel, for example *ká,* 'dance'.

Plain High Tone

The pitch of the voice starts quite high, then falls for a fairly long time, similar to the pronunciation of words like 'squeal', 'car' and 'way'. It is indicated by a grave accent above the vowel, for example *kà* which, conveniently, is also the Burmese word for 'car'.

11

Low Tone

The voice is relaxed, stays at a low pitch for a fairly long time, and does not rise or fall in pitch. It is indicated by no accent above the vowel, for example *ka*, 'shield'.

Stopped Syllable

This is a very short syllable, on a high pitch, cut off at the end by a sharp catch in the voice (a glottal stop); this is like the sound in the middle of the exclamation used in a dangerous situation, 'oh-oh', or the Cockney pronunciation of 't' in a word like 'bottle'. If you have trouble with this sound, try replacing it with a 't'; but keep the syllable short. It is indicated in this book by a 'q' after the vowel, for example *kaq*, 'join'. However, the 'q' is not pronounced.

Reduced (Weak) Syllable

This is a shortened syllable, usually the first syllable of a two-syllable word, which is said without stress, like the first syllable of 'again' in English. Only the vowel 'a', sometimes preceded by a consonant, occurs in a reduced syllable; this is indicated by a˘ above the vowel. For example *ălouq*, 'work'. Any syllable but the last in a word can be reduced.

Vowels

Burmese vowel sounds should be easy for speakers of English and other European languages. They occur in open, nasalised and stopped forms.

Nasalisation of vowels is like that found in French; speakers of English or other languages can approximate this by putting a weak 'n' at the end of such a syllable. This nasalisation is indicated by *n* after the vowel, as in *ein*, 'house'.

non-nasalised

i	sounds like 'be';
e	like the 'a' in 'bay'
eh	like the first 'e' in 'elephant'
a	like the 'a' in 'father'
aw	as the British pronounce 'law'
o	like the 'o' in 'go', the French 'au' and German long 'o'
u	like the 'oo' in 'too'

nasalised	stopped	
in	*iq*	like 'sin' and 'sit'
ein	*eiq*	like 'lane' and 'late''
	eq	as in 'bet'
an	*aq*	like 'man' and 'mat'
oun	*ouq*	like 'bone' and 'boat'
un	*uq*	like the German *Bund* and 'foot'
ain	*aiq*	as in the English 'might' and the German *mein*
aun	*auq*	as in 'brown' and 'out'

PRONUNCIATION

Consonants

Consonants only occur at the beginning of a syllable; there are no consonants that occur after the vowel. Many of these are similar to consonants in English or other European languages.

b, d, j, g, m, n, ng,	as in English. The *w* sound can occur
s, sh, h, z, w, l, y	on its own, or in combination with other consonants
th	as in 'thin'
dh	as in 'the', 'their'
ny	similar to the consonants at the beginning of British 'new'
hm, hn, hny, hng, hl	made with a puff of air just before the nasal or *l* sound
p', t', s', c', k'	aspirated
p, t, c, k	unaspirated

Aspirated Consonants

The aspirated sounds are made with a puff of air after the sound; this is the way the letters 'p', 't', 'k' are pronounced in English at the beginning of a word. The unaspirated sounds are without this puff of air, as the letters 'p', 't', 'k' sound after an 's' as in 'spin' 'stir' 'skin', or as in French 'p', 't', 'k'.

The unaspirated *c* and aspirated *c'* are similar to the 'ch' in 'church'. Remember that *sh* as in 'ship', *s* as in 'sip', and the aspirated *s'* are three different sounds. Another difficulty is in saying the *ng* at the beginning of a syllable; try saying 'hang on', then leave off the 'ha' to get an idea of the sound.

Like most languages, Burmese changes when spoken rapidly.

One change which happens even in slow speech is that the aspirated and unaspirated sounds *p'*, *p*; *t'*, *t*; *s'*, *s*; *c'*, *c* and *k'*, *k* within a word change into the voiced sounds *b*, *d*, *z*, *j* and *g*, and the *th* sound changes into the voiced sound *dh*. This happens automatically to the consonant at the beginning of the second, third or later syllable in a word, unless the syllable before it is a stopped syllable. For example:

yauq-cà	'man'	the *c* does not become *j* because of the stopped syllable
băzaq	'mouth'	the original *s* becomes *z*

Transliteration

In Burmese writing, *c*, *c'*, *j* are written using the letters for *k*, *k'*, *g* plus *y* or *r*, so anglicised forms of Burmese often represent them as *ky*, *gy* and so on. One example is the unit of currency, *caq*, which is usually written 'kyat' in the Roman alphabet. Aspirated consonants (*k'*, *s'*, *t'* and *p'*) may be spelt with an 'h' before or after the consonant.

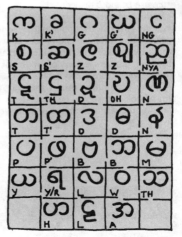

A creaky tone may be indicated by a final **t** eg Hpakant (in Kachin State).

Various combinations of letters may be used to represent the same vowel sound: **e** and **eh** are both often transliterated as 'ay'; **ain** may be represented as 'aing', **auq** as 'auk', and so on. For these reasons and because the official English forms of many placenames changed in 1989, the Burmese versions of common placenames and tourist sites are given on pages 70 to 72.

There is no 'r' in Burmese but the sound appears in some foreign words such as *re-di-yo,* 'radio' or *da-reiq-s'an,* 'animal' (Pali). Sometimes it is substituted with a **y** . Similarly there is no 'f' or 'v' in Burmese; loan words containing these consonants often use **p'** and **b** respectively.

In the transliteration system used in this book, transliterated syllables (with the exception of the reduced syllable **ă**) have been separated by hyphens and breaks between words, or groups of words, by spaces. This is intended to make it easier for the learner. However, native speakers often do not speak with a clear division between words or syllables.

If you pronounce things the way they are written in the phrasebook you should be understood. If this doesn't work, try showing the written version of what you want, and people will say it for you.

Grammar

The following outline of Burmese grammar is not a complete description, but it gives the basic structure, and shows you how to put together correct phrases and sentences not included in the phrasebook. Once you are familiar with this grammar it will be easy to learn sentence patterns for specific situations, allowing you to plug in new vocabulary as the need arises.

Word Order

Burmese places the verb at the end of the sentence. One or more nouns may precede the verb; usually but not always the subject noun comes before the object noun.

I'd like to eat something.	*cănaw/cămá tăk'ú-gú sà-jin-badeh* ('I [m/f] something eat-want')
I don't want to eat chicken.	*cănaw/cămá ceq-thà măsà-jin-bù* ('I [m/f] chicken not-eat-want')

Unlike English which has prepositions, and modal verbs such as 'will' before the verb, Burmese has particles after the word that they belong with.

He will be able to go to Yangon (Rangoon).	*thu yan-goun-go thwà-nain-meh* ('He Yangon-to go-can-will')

17

Nouns

Each noun has one form. You can show that something is plural with the particle *t(w)e* or *d(w)e* (the 'w' can be omitted) after the noun, although it isn't always necessary. There is no article corresponding to 'the' or 'a/an'.

> with the children   *k'ălè-dwe-néh* or *k'ălè-de-néh*
>   ('child-*d(w)e*-with')

One of the main differences between Burmese and English grammar is that a noun may simply be left out, without being replaced by a pronoun, if it is clear what is being said. For a foreigner, it is probably easier and less likely to lead to misunderstanding to leave the nouns and pronouns in.

The main noun particles, which come last of all in the noun phrase, are as follows:

to	*ko (go)*
from (places)	*ká (gá)*
from (people)	*s'i-ká (s'i-gá)*
with	*néh*
at/in/on	*hma*

If you want to distinguish between the subject and object of the verb, add the particle *ká (gá)* to the end of the subject and *ko (go)* to the end of the object.

> Father gives a book to his daughter at home.
> *sa-ouq pè-deh ăp'e-gá thămì-go ein-hma*
> ('father-*gá* daughter-*go* home-at book gives')

GRAMMAR

Possessives

In Burmese the possessor precedes the noun possessed; the particle *yéh*, or a creaky high tone on the last syllable of the possessor, comes between.

my house	*cǎnáw-yéh/cǎmá-yéh ein*
	('my [m]-*yéh*/my [f]-*yéh* house')
daughter's car	*thǎmì-yéh-kà*
	('daughter car')

Counting Phrase

In Burmese the number always follows the noun, and is followed by a 'counter', one of a small set of words used in counting. More details are given in the Numbers chapter, page 123.

Pronouns

Instead of a noun, you may use a pronoun; in Burmese there are many different pronouns. You can get by with only a few; these are the polite forms for use with non-intimates. One unusual feature is that the sex of the speaker (you) determines which pronoun is used for both 'I/we' and 'you'.

	I	you	he/she/it
male speaker	*cǎnaw*	*k'ǎmyà*	*thu*
	ကျွန်တော်	ခင်ဗျား	သူ
female speaker	*cǎmá*	*shin*	*thu*
	ကျွန်မ	ရှင်	သူ

GRAMMAR

Thus a man uses *cănaw* for himself and *k'ămyà* for 'you', but a woman uses *cămá* for herself and *shin* for 'you'. Very often a person's title, occupation or kinship can be used to signify 'you' or 'I'. Examples include:

older man ('uncle')	*ù-lè*	ဦးလေး
older woman ('aunty')	*daw-daw*	ဒေါ်ဒေါ်
man (same age) ('big brother')	*ko-ko*	ကိုကို
woman (same age) ('big sister')	*má-má*	မမ
professional person (m)	*s'ăya*	ဆရာ
professional person (f)	*s'ăya-má*	ဆရာမ

The term *s'ăya/s'ăya-má* literally means 'teacher' but as it is a term of respect, visitors of all occupations may find that this is the way they are addressed. As noted earlier, pronouns can be left out altogether if the meaning is clear.

> (I) want to go   *thwà-jin-deh*

If you want to emphasise that a pronoun is plural, you can add *dó* after it eg *cămá-dó*, 'we (females)'. To show what case or function in the sentence a pronoun has, the same particles as for nouns (see page 18) are attached to them.

> with you (female speaking)   *shin-néh*
> from him/her/them   *thú-s'i-gá*

To summarise: the noun phrase can be completely omitted, it can have only a single noun or pronoun, or it can be rather long, as the next examples show:

to these adults	*di lu-jì-dwe-go* ('these adults to')
at father's house	*ăp'e-yéh ein-hma* ('father's house at')
with the soldiers	*siq-thà-dwe-néh* ('soldiers with')

You may notice that certain particles sometimes have one form and sometimes another; as the plural *twe/dwe* and case particles such as *ko/go*. The preceding syllable determines which form (voiced or non-voiced) to use. Unless the preceding syllable is stopped (eg *taq*), the following syllable is 'voiced' and begins with *g*, *d*, *b* etc. Voicing happens naturally: it is easier to say *kà-go* than *kà-ko*, for example.

GRAMMAR

Verbs

Verbs come at the end of the sentence. Like nouns, they usually include particles and other grammatical markers; these particles show things such as tense. In fact every verb except for an abrupt or impolite command has at least one particle after it.

Tense & Negation

A verb particle indicating the tense occurs in almost every sentence. It is *teh/deh* for the present and past tenses and *meh* for the future tense. A further particle is *pi/bi*, which shows a completed action. See also Negation, page 24.

I go/I went	*thwà-deh*
I have gone	*thwà-bi*
I will go	*thwà-meh*
I eat/I ate	*sà-deh*
I have eaten	*sà-bi*
I will eat	*sà-meh*

Useful Verbs

agree	*thăbàw tu-deh*
bring	*yu-deh*
come	*la-deh*
cost	*koun cá-deh/cá-deh*
depart (leave)	*t'weq-teh*
do	*louq-teh*
eat	*t'ămin sà-deh*
go	*thwà-deh*
have	*shí-deh*
help	*ku-nyi-deh*
know (someone/something)	*thí-deh*
know (how to)	*taq-teh*
like	*caiq-teh*
make	*louq-teh*
meet	*twéh-deh*
need	*lo-deh*
prefer	*po caiq-teh*
return	*pyan-deh*
say	*pyàw-deh/s'o-deh*

GRAMMAR

see	*myin-deh*
stay	*ne-deh*
take	*yu-deh*
understand	*nà-leh-deh*
want	*lo-jin-deh*

Adjectives

In Burmese adjectives work exactly like verbs: they come after the noun, and are followed by various verb particles. For this reason there is no equivalent of the verb 'to be' in a sentence with an adjective in Burmese; the adjective *is* the verb.

This person is big. *di lu cì-deh*
   ('this person big-*deh*')
This car is blue. *di kà pya-deh*
   ('this car blue-*deh*')

To put an adjective-verb with a noun in Burmese there are two possibilities: a few colour and size adjectives can be stuck on after the noun. Any adjective can be put in a relative clause before the noun, the clause being marked by *téh/déh* between the verb and the following noun.

house *ein*
   a big house *ein-jì*
   a house that is big *cì-déh ein*

GRAMMAR

Comparisons

Comparisons are made with specific modal verbs preceding the adjective verb, eg *po* for 'more'. The word equivalent to 'than' is *t'eq*. It is placed after the relevant noun.

> This room is better than that room.
> *di ăk'àn-gá ho ăk'àn-t'eq po-kaùn-deh*
> ('this room that room-*t'eq* more good [better]')

> My car is faster than his/her car
> *cănaw/cămá-yéh kà thú-kà-t'eq po-myan-deh*
> ('my car his car-*t'eq* more fast [faster]')

Equivalence is expressed by putting the noun(s), linked by *néh* (meaning 'and/with') before *ătu-du,* or, more emphatically, *ătu-du-ba-bèh,* 'the very same', for example:

> This car is the same as that car.
> *di-kà(néh) ho-kà-néh ătu-du-ba-bèh*
> ('this car-*néh* that car-*néh* the very same')

> It is the same as this one.
> *di-ha-néh ătu-du-ba-bèh*
> ('this thing-*néh*-the very same')

Negation

Any sentence can be negated by putting *mă-* before the verb, and *p'ù/bù* at the end of the sentence. The particle *teh/deh* is dropped in the negative.

> That room is good. *ho ăk'àn kaùn-deh*
> ('that room good-*deh* ')

That room is not good. *ho ăk'àn măkaùn-bù*
('that room *mă*-good-*bù*')

This is like negation in written French, with one part before the verb and the second part after.

Modal Verbs

There are a number of modal verbs in Burmese. The following is a list of the most useful. Most of the modals come after the verb and before the tense particle. For example:

must, have to *yá*
    I go.   *thwà-deh*
    I had to go.   *thwà-yá-deh*
    I must go.   *thwà-yá-meh*
    I must go to Yangon   *cănaw/cămá yan-goun-go*
    (Rangoon).   *thwà-yá-meh*

can (be skilled at) *taq/daq*
    The teacher can speak   *s'ăya băma-zăgà pyàw-*
    Burmese.   *daq-teh*
    I can speak Burmese.   *băma-zăgà lo pyàw-daq-teh*

can (be physically able) *nain*
    I can see the house.   *cănaw ein-ko myin-nain-deh*

GRAMMAR

want to	*c'in/jin*
I leave	*t'weq-deh*
I want to leave	*t'weq-c'in-deh*
I eat	*sà-deh*
I want to eat	*sà-jin-deh*
Mother wants to go	*ăme yan-goun-go*
to Yangon (Rangoon).	*thwà-jin-deh*

continue	*ne*
(equivalent to '-ing')	
The soldier is riding on	*siq-thà mì-yăt'à sì-ne-deh*
the train.	

try to	*cí/jí*
Please try to eat some	*myăma-t'ămìn-hìn sà-jí-ba*
Burmese food.	

have ever	*p'ù/bù*
(I) have never been to	*băgan mă-yauq-p'ù-bù*
Bagan (Pagan).	

Note that the modal *p'ù/bù*, 'have ever' and the second part of the negation, *p'ù/bù*, are the same, and can be together in one sentence, as above, creating the negative sense, 'have never'.

Politeness

The language has a very frequent and important small particle that makes the whole sentence more polite. It comes after the verb and after the modal if there is one (see page 25 for an explanation of modals), but before any other particles such as those indicating tense. The form is *pa/ba*, ပါ. You don't need to put it into every sentence, but do put it into any requests or commands that you make, and try to put it in a few sentences at the start and end of every conversation. A request or command does not have a tense particle, but without the politeness particle it is abrupt.

Please go.	*k'ămyà/shin thwà-ba*
Go!	*thwà*
Please give (me) a book/ one book.	*sa-ouq tăouq pè-ba*

To Be

There are several equivalents for the English verb 'to be'. Firstly, with adjectives, there is no word for 'to be' (see page 23). It is also quite possible to have no word for 'to be' when two nouns are together, for example:

He/She is a teacher.	*thu s'ăya* ('he/she teacher')
They are at school.	*thu-dó caùn-hma* ('they school-at')

However, such a sentence is commonly finished off with the 'politeness' particle, *ba* (see page 26):

He/She is a teacher.	*thu s'ăya-ba*

Sometimes this kind of sentence uses the verb *p'yiq* 'to become', but this suggests that something has changed.

He/She is (now) a teacher.	*thu s'ăya p'yiq-teh*
He/She has become a teacher.	*thu s'ăya p'yiq-pi*

Another related verb is *shí* 'to have' or 'to exist' (there is/are):

There is a monastery here.   *di-hma caùn shí-deh*
                             ('here monastery exists')
I have a car.   *cǎnaw/cǎmá kà shí-deh*
                             ('I car have')

A further possibility is *ne,* 'to be at', 'to live' or 'to stay'.

They are at school.   *thu-dó caùn-hma ne-deh*
                      ('they school-at are')

As with *p'yiq,* the addition of *ne* suggests a different meaning: they live there, or stay there for some time, rather than just happening to be there now.

Questions

There are two types of questions in Burmese: those with a 'yes' or 'no' answer, and those asking for specific information about a noun or adverb.

'Yes/No' Questions

A yes/no question ends in *là*, while an information question ends in *lèh*. Before verbs, the tense particles *teh/deh* and *meh* get shortened before *là* and *lèh* to *dhǎ* and *mǎ:*

Do you want to buy a   *(k'ǎmyà/shin) leq-hmaq*
ticket?   *weh-jin-dhǎlà?*
                       ('you ticket buy-want-*dhǎlà*)
Is he a teacher?   *thu s'ǎya-là?*
                       ('he/she teacher-*là*')

To make a yes/no question where you are seeking to confirm a piece of information, add the particle *'naw'* to the end of a statement. This particle is equivalent to phrases like 'isn't it?', 'don't they?', and 'n'est-ce pas?' in French.

> You've got a car, haven't you?   *kà shí-deh naw?*

You can use *naw* to ask if it's alright to do something:

> Can I take your picture?   *daq-poun yaiq-meh naw?*
> (lit: I will take a photo, OK?)

One of the most useful questions is *yá-dhǎlà* (or, more informally *yá-là*). This very versatile phrase can mean amongst other things 'Is it possible?', 'Is it feasible?', 'Is it permissible?' 'Can I....' and 'Do you mind?' For example:

> Is it OK to take pictures?   *daq-poun yaiq-ló yá-dhǎlà?*
> Can one go by car?   *kà-néh thwà-ló yá-là?*
> Can I take a look at the room.?   *ǎk'àn thwà-cí-ló yá-dhǎlà?*

An affirmative answer is *yá-deh* or *yá-ba-deh (*when spoken fast, *yá-deh* sometimes sounds more like *yá-reh).* If it's not OK, the reply will be *mǎyá-bù* or *mǎyá-ba-bù.*

GRAMMAR

Information Questions

In English, information questions begin with a 'wh' question word, and all questions have other grammatical complications such as word order changes. In Burmese a statement and a question have exactly the same word order; the question words all begin with b.

what	*ba*	What do (you) want?
		ba lo-jin-dhălèh?
		What is that?
		da ba-lèh?
who	*bădhu*	Who will you go with?
		(k'ămyà/shin) bădhu-néh thwà-mălèh?
		Who is this monk?
		di p'oùn-jì bădhu-lèh?
where (at)	*beh-hma*	Where do you live?
		(k'ămyà/shin) beh-hma ne-dhălèh?
		Where is ... ?
		... beh-hma-lèh?
where (from)	*beh-gá*	Where did (you) get this food from?
		di ăsa beh-gá yá-dhălèh?
		Where have you come from?
		(k'ămyà/shin) beh-gá la-dhălèh?
where (to)	*beh-go*	Where will (you) go tomorrow?
		maneq-p'yan beh-go thwà-mălèh?
		Where are you going?
		k'ămyà/shin beh-go thwà-mălèh?

GRAMMAR

which (noun) *beh* + noun   Which fruit will (you) buy?
                              beh ăthì weh-mălèh?

Some question words are more adverbial:

when (past)   *beh-dòun-gá*

When did you attend school?
(k'ămyà/shin) càun beh-dòun-gá teq-thălèh?

when (future) *beh-dáw*

When will it open?
beh-dáw p'wín-mălèh?
When will he become a teacher?
thu s'ăya beh-dáw p'yiq-mălèh?

why   *ba-p'yiq-ló*

Why is the bus late?
baskà ba-p'yiq-ló nauq-cá-dhălèh?

how much   *beh-lauq*

How much is it to go to ...?
... thwà-yin beh-lauq-lèh?
How much is the room?
ăk'àn-gá beh-lauq-lèh?

how many   *beh-hnă* + counter   (see pages 19 & 123)
How many people came?
lu beh-hnăyauq la-dhălèh?

(see pages 19 & 123)

Remember, don't change the word order in a question, and there is no need for the pitch of the voice to rise; *là* or *lèh* at the end with a plain high tone is all you need.

GRAMMAR

Answers

To reply to a question, you can produce a full sentence by repeating everything in the question and providing the necessary new information, but shorter answers are more common and easier.

Answering 'Yes/No' Questions

For a 'yes/no' question, you can simply repeat the verb, with or without negation and modal as required.

Do you want to go to Yangon (Rangoon) by car?
k'ǎmyà/shin yan-goun-go kà-néh thwà-jin-dhǎlà?

> (Yes, I) want to go (to Yangon by car).
> *thwà-jin-ba-deh*

> (No, I) don't want to go (to Yangon by car).
> *mǎthwà-jin-ba-bù*

Will grandmother eat something?
ǎp'wà t'ǎmìn sà-mǎlà?

> Yes she will (eat).
> *sà-meh*

> No, she won't (eat).
> *mǎsà-bù*

Instead of repeating the verb and modal, you can simply say:

> Yes. *houq-kéh*
> > or more politely *houq-pa-deh*
> > or, to a monk, *hman-ba*

> No. *mǎhouq-p'ù*
> > or more politely *mǎhouq-pa-bù*
> > or, to a monk, *mǎhouq-pa-bù p'a-yà*

GRAMMAR

In a sentence without a verb, you can say 'yes' or 'no', or repeat the whole sentence with or without negation.

Is he a student?	*thu caùn-thà-là*
Yes.	*houq-kéh*
No.	*mǎhouq-p'ù*

Answering Information Questions

To answer an information question, you can simply provide the noun or adverb information necessary, or you can give the full sentence.

What do (you) want?	*ba lo-jin-dhǎlèh*
(I want) a ticket.	*leq-hmaq (lo-jin-deh)*
(I) don't want anything.	*ba-hmá mǎlo-jin-bù*

Who will come?	*bǎdhu la-mǎlèh*
Nobody will come.	*bǎdhu-hmá mǎla-bù*
Mother will come.	*ǎme la-meh*

If the question is answered in the negative, 'nothing' is *ba-hmá*, and 'nobody' is *bǎdhu-hmá*. With these, you usually need at least a negated verb (and modals if there are any in the question).

Adverbs

The third type of word in Burmese is the adverb or adverb phrase. These can be before or after any noun phrase in the sen-

GRAMMAR

tence, but not normally at the end. Adverbs describing the manner of the verb's action tend to be just before the verb, while sentence adverbs such as those of time tend to be closer to the beginning of the sentence.

> Yesterday I [m/f] arrived at Yangon (Rangoon).
> *mǎné-gá cǎnaw/cǎmá yan-goun yauq-teh*

> This evening (I) will see a show.
> *nyá-ne pwèh thwà-cí-meh*

> Can you come back next year?
> *nauq-hniq pyan-la-nain-mǎlà*

> This horse runs quickly.
> *di myìn myan-myan pyè-deh*

As the last example shows, some adverbs are doubled versions of adjective-verbs: *myan* 'fast', *myan-myan* 'quickly'; *kaùn* 'good', *kaùn-gaùn* 'well'.

Some Useful Words

in front	*shé*	ရှေ့
behind/after (in time)	*nauq*	နောက်
inside	*ăt'èh*	အထဲ
outside	*ăpyin*	အပြင်
between	*ăcà/jà*	အကြား:/ကြား:
above/on top of	*ăt'eq-/ăpaw*	အထက်/အပေါ်
below/under	*auq*	အောက်
because	*ba p'yiq-ló-lèh-s'o-dáw*	ဘာဖြစ်လို့လဲဆိုတော

because (after a verb)	*ló*	လို့
but	*da-be-méh*	ဒါပေမဲ့
and (after a noun)	*lèh*	လည်း
and (after a noun)/with	*néh*	နဲ့
and then...	*pì-dáw*	ပြီးတော့
for (after a noun)	*ătweq*	အတွက်
every (after a noun)	*tàin/dàin*	တိုင်း
only (after a noun)	*bèh*	ပဲ
very	*theiq*	သိပ်

The grammar in this chapter may seem difficult, but if you remember that the verb comes after the nouns, and that the grammatical particles are put on the end of the word they belong with, that is actually the major part of the battle. No one will mind if you make a few mistakes, so go for it!

GRAMMAR

Greetings & Civilities

In formal situations and in cities, the first thing you say when meeting a stranger is *min-găla-ba*, literally 'It's a blessing'. When you already know someone, a greeting can start by asking about their health. This is no more of a genuine request for a medical report than the English 'how are you?', and is usually answered positively.

Greetings

Are you well?
(k'ămyà/shin)   (ခင်ဗျား:/ရှင်) နေကောင်း:ရဲ့လား။
ne-kaùn-yéh-là?

(I) am well.
ne-kaùn-ba-deh   နေကောင်း:ပါတယ်။

What about you?
k'ămyà-yò/shin-yò   ခင်ဗျား:ရော/ရှင်ရော
ne-kaùn-yéh-là?   နေကောင်း:ရဲ့လား။

Instead of this, especially outside the cities, greetings may be in the form of asking whether you have eaten (the usual answer, even if you're hungry, is yes, unless you are, for example, arriving at someone's house for dinner!); where you are going, or where you have come from. The answers to these questions can be quite vague; the questions are not meant to be intrusive.

36

Have you eaten?
  t'ămìn sà-pì-bi-là?   ထမင်းစားပြီးပြီလား။
(I) have eaten.
  sà-pì-ba-bi   စားပြီးပါပြီ။

A common greeting, which you may hear people calling out from
the roadside, is:

Where are you going?
  beh thwà-măló-lèh?   ဘယ်သွားမလို့လဲ။

To this, a general, non-specific reply is *di-nà-lè-bèh,* ဒီနားလေးပဲ
(literally 'Just around here') will suffice. If you want to be more
specific, common replies are:

I am going to the market.
  zè thwà-măló   ဈေး သွားမလို့။
I am travelling.
  k'ăyì thwà-măló   ခရီး သွားမလို့။
I am going to town.
  myó-dèh thwà-măló   မြို့ ထဲသွားမလို့။

Alternatively, you may be asked if you are going home, or where
you have come from:

Are you going home?
  pyan-táw-mălà?   ပြန်တော့မလား။
I am going home.
  pyan-táw-meh   ပြန်တော့မယ်။
I am going back to my hotel.
  ho-teh-go pyan-táw-meh   ဟိုတယ်ကို ပြန်တော့မယ်။

Where have you been?
beh-gá la-dhǎlèh?   ဘယ်က လာသလဲ။

The answer may be more or less general:

I have come from Yangon
(Rangoon).
   yan-goun-gá la-ba-deh   ရန်ကုန်က လာပါတယ်။
I have come from the school/
temple
   caùn-gá la-ba-deh   ကျောင်းက လာပါတယ်။
I've come from America.
   ǎme-rí-kan-gá la-ba-deh   အမေရိကန်က လာပါတယ်။

Names

Each Burmese person has a two-syllable
name (or sometimes more;
infrequently only one). There
is no family name, no change
of name on marriage, and no
abbreviation, except among
intimates. Before this
name, one of a vari-
ety of titles may be
put, like our 'Mr';
but these titles are
used according to
age, prestige and
closeness — not
marital status.

	for men		**for women**	
to someone older/respected:	*ù*	ဦး	*daw*	ဒေါ်
to someone the same age:	*ko*	ကို	*mámá*	မမ/
			daw	ဒေါ်
to someone younger/intimate:	*maun*	မောင်	*má*	မ

Use of a name without one of these titles is also possible among close friends; so a man called Soe Win could be called U Soe Win, Ko Soe Win, Maun(g) Soe Win or just Soe Win, or even Ko Soe; a lady named Khin Than could be called Daw Khin Than or Ma Khin Than; (using just Khin Than, Khin or Than alone would imply quite close friendship).

What is your name?
  k'ǎmyá/shín na-meh   ခင်ဗျား/ရှင် နာမည်
  beh-lo k'aw-dhǎlèh?   ဘယ်လို ခေါ်သလဲ။
My name is ...
  (cǎnáw/cǎmá) ... ló   ကျွန်တော်/ကျွန်မ ... လို့
  k'aw-ba-deh   ခေါ်ပါတယ်။

The day of the week a person is born determines what letter the name begins with.

			Wednesday	
			morning	*l, w*
			afternoon	*y*
Sunday	*vowels*		Thursday	*p, p', b,m*
Monday	*k, k', g, ng*		Friday	*th, h*
Tuesday	*s, s', z, ny*		Saturday	*t, t', d, n*

If you are given a name, make sure it begins with the right letter. Sometimes an occupational title is used instead of, or before, another title.

General Aung San (born on Sunday)
bo-jouq aun s'àn — ဗိုလ်ချုပ်အောင်ဆန်း

U Nu (born on Saturday)
ù nú — ဦးနု

Daw Aung San Suu Kyi (born on Tuesday; father's name used first)
daw aun s'àn sú ci — ဒေါ်အောင်ဆန်းစုကြည်

Teacher Hla Han (m)
s'ăya ù hlá han — ဆရာ ဦးလှဟန်

Teacher Daw Khin Khin Myint (f)
s'ăya-madaw k'in k'in myín — ဆရာမဒေါ်ခင်ခင်မြင့်

Doctor Ba U
dauq-ta bá ù — ဒေါက်တာ ဘဦး

Thanking & Being Thanked

In Myanmar a smile is often enough, in situations where someone is doing their job or a small favour. Thanking is reserved for larger favours. If you think something you want is a favour, you could use *cè-zù pyú-pi*, literally 'having thanked you', before the request. This makes it even more polite than just *pa/ba* at the end.

Please help.
cè-zù pyú-pì ku-nyi-pè-ba — ကျေးဇူးပြီ ကူညီပေးပါ။

However, as more people in Myanmar meet foreigners, saying 'thank you' is becoming more common:

Thanks.
cè-zù-bèh　　　　　　　ကျေးဇူးပဲ။

Thank you.
cè-zù tin-ba-deh　　　　　ကျေးဇူးတင်ပါတယ်။

The response may be:

It's nothing (you're welcome).
keiq-sá măshí-ba-bù　　　ကိစ္စမရှိပါဘူး။

USEFUL TIP

Women should use *shin* ('you') when addressing someone, and *căma* ('I') for the first person.

Men should use *k'ămyà* for 'you' and *căno* for 'I'.

These words are appropriate for most situations, but should not be used in addressing monks.

Apologies & Sympathy

Unlike in English, expressing sorrow or sympathy frequently with unknown strangers is not widespread. Don't say 'Sorry' every time you brush someone in the street or to attract someone's attention.

GREETINGS & CIVILITIES

(I) am sorry.
wùn-nèh-ba-deh   ဝမ်းနဲ့ပါတယ်။

To express pleasure or congratulate someone you can say:

(I) am glad.
wùn-tha-ba-deh   ဝမ်းသာပါတယ်။

You can put these phrases after another sentence:

Pleased to meet you.
twé-yá-da wùn-tha-ba-deh   တွေ့ရတာ ဝမ်းသာပါတယ်။
(I) am very sorry that (your)
father died.
ăp'e s'oùn-thwà-da   အဖေဆုံးသွားတာ
theiq wùn-nèh-ba-deh   သိပ်ဝမ်းနဲ့ပါတယ်။

One very frequent phrase is:

Don't feel bad about it/Don't
be embarrassed.
à-măna-ba-néh   အားမနာပါနဲ့ ။

People say this when they want to give you something or do something for you, and don't want you to refuse because it's a favour;
but sometimes they will say this even if they hope you will refuse.
If someone says this to you and you accept, you should probably
thank them. If you want to decline the offer, or to be polite, you
might reply:

I do feel bad about it.
à-na-ba-deh   အားနာပါတယ်။

Attracting Someone's Attention

The polite way to attract someone's attention is to say the pronoun form 'you': *k'ămyà,* ခင်ဗျား; if you are a man and *shin,* ရှင်, if you are a woman. If the person you wish to talk with has an obvious title, you should use that instead: 'teacher', *s'ăya,* ဆရာ (m), *s'ăya-má,* ဆရာမ (f); 'military officer (lieutenant)', *siq-bo,* စစ်ဗိုလ်; 'general' *bo-jouq,* ဗိုလ်ချုပ် and so on. For monks there is a special honorific vocabulary. Women should avoid touching monks or their clothes, or even approaching too close.

You may also tack these words ('you' or any kind of title) onto the end of anything you say, to make a request or statement even more polite.

Please come, sir.
   la-ba, k'ămyà/shin   လာပါ ခင်ဗျား/ရှင်။
Good, teacher.
   kaùn-ba-deh, s'ăya   ကောင်းပါတယ် ဆရာ။
 Yes (to a monk; literally
 'correct, Buddha')
   hman-ba, p'ăyà   မှန်ပါ ဘုရား။

Goodbyes

There is no single phrase for 'goodbye'; rather, one leads up to departure with thanks if someone has helped you. Then you normally say that you were glad to meet them, and say that you are going. You may finally say that you will see them later. As in English, this does not necessarily imply a commitment to see them again. The phrases used also depend on whether you are leaving or being left behind.

Thank you very much!
ămyà-jì cè-zù-tin-ba-deh   အများကြီး ကျေးဇူးတင်ပါတယ်။

I'm glad to meet you.
k'ămyà/shin-néh twé-ya-da   ခင်ဗျား/ရှင်နဲ့
wùn-tha-ba-deh   တွေ့ ရတာ ဝမ်းသာပါတယ်။

I enjoyed talking to you
săga-pyàw-ló kaùn-ba-deh   စကားပြောလို့ ကောင်းပါတယ်။

Are you going home?
pyan-dáw-mălà   ပြန်တော့မလား။

Are you leaving now?
thwà-dáw-mălà   သွားတော့မလား။

I'm leaving now.
thwà-ba-oùn-meh   သွားပါအုံးမယ်။

I'm leaving, OK?
thwà-meh naw   သွားမယ်နော်။

I'm going home, OK?
pyan-meh naw   ပြန်မယ်နော်။

Please don't go!
măthwà-ba-néh-oùn   မသွားပါနဲ့ အုံး။

OK, go (goodbye).
kaùn-ba-bi   ကောင်းပါပြီ။

See you again/later
twé-meh, naw   တွေ့ မယ်နော်။

or *nauq-twé-dhè-da-páw*   နောက်တွေ့ သေးတာပေါ့။

Small Talk

After you have said hello, there are various things that a local person is likely to talk about. Some of these, such as one's salary and age, may surprise foreigners. Other topics Westerners often discuss, such as the weather, are less frequently discussed in Myanmar.

Nationalities

Where do you live?
k'ămyà/shin   ခင်ဗျား/ရှင်
beh-hma ne-dhălèh?   ဘယ်မှာနေသလဲ။
What is your nationality?
k'ămyà/shin ba-lu-myò lèh?   ခင်ဗျား/ရှင် ဘာလူမျိုးလဲ။

You can ask this question to find out about ethnicity (Shan, Chin etc), whose names are listed on page 73.

I live in ...	*cănaw/cămá ...*	ကျွန်တော်/ကျွန်မ ...
	pye-hma ne-ba-deh	ပြည်မှာနေပါတယ်။
I am ...	*cănaw/cămá ...*	ကျွန်တော်/ကျွန်မ ...
	lu-myò-ba	လူမျိုးပါ။
Chinese/China	*tăyouq*	တရုတ်
French/France	*pyin-thiq*	ပြင်သစ်
Thai/Thailand	*yò-dăyà*	ယိုးဒယား

For all other nationalities, the words are just like English.

45

Age

How old are you?

(k'ămyà/shin) ătheq beh-lauq shí-bi-lèh? — ခင်ဗျား/ရှင် အသက် ဘယ်လောက်ရှိပြီလဲ။

I am ... years old.

(cănaw/cămá ătheq) ... hniq shí-bi — ကျွန်တော်/ကျွန်မ အသက် ... နှစ် ရှိပြီ။

See the Numbers & Amounts chapter, pages 124-126, for the numbers.

Occupations

What is your occupation?

(k'ămyà/shin) ba ălouq louq-dhălèh? — (ခင်ဗျား/ရှင်) ဘာအလုပ်လုပ်သလဲ။

I am a/ an ...	*cănaw/cămá ... ba*	ကျွန်တော်/ကျွန်မ ... ပါ။
accountant	*săyìn-kain*	စာရင်းကိုင်
artist	*păgyi-s'ăya*	ပန်းချီဆရာ
businessperson	*sì-bwà-yè-dhămà*	စီးပွားရေးသမား
clerk	*săyè*	စာရေး
dentist	*thwà-beq-s'ăya-wun*	သွားဘက်ဆရာဝန်
diplomat	*than-tăman*	သံတမန်
doctor	*s'ăya-wun*	ဆရာဝန်
engineer	*seq-hmú-pyin-nya-s'ăya*	စက်မှုပညာဆရာ
	in-jin-ni-ya	ယိုးဒယား
farmer	*leh-dhămà*	လယ်သမား
government worker	*ăhmú-dàn/ ăya-shí/ ăsò-yá wun-dàn*	အမှုထမ်း အရာရှိ အစိုးရ ဝန်ထမ်း
journalist	*dhădìn-za-s'ăya*	သတင်းစာဆရာ

nurse	*thu-na-byú*	သူနာပြု
photographer	*daq-poun-s'ăya*	ဓါတ်ပုံဆရာ
researcher	*thú-te-thi*	သုတေသီ
scientist	*theiq-pan-pyin-nya-shin*	သိပ္ပံပညာရှင်
soldier	*siq-thà*	စစ်သား
student	*caùn-dhà*	ကျောင်းသား
teacher	*caùn-s'ăya*	ကျောင်းဆရာ
tourist	*k'ăyì-dhe/tò-riq*	ခရီးသည်/တိုးရစ်
university lecturer	*tek-kădho kăt'í-ká*	တက္ကသိုလ်ကထိက
waiter	*săbwè-dò*	စားပွဲထိုး
worker	*ălouq-thămà*	အလုပ်သမား
writer	*sa-yè-s'ăya*	စာရေးဆရာ

Some typically Burmese occupations are:

actor	*thăyouq-s'aun*	သရုပ်ဆောင်
agent/broker	*pwèh-sà*	ပွဲစား
driver	*kà-maùn-thămà*	ကားမောင်းသမား
fortune-teller	*be-din-s'ăya*	ဗေဒင်ဆရာ
guide	*làn-hnyun*	လမ်းညွှန်
bazaar seller	*zè-theh*	ဈေးသည်
monk	*p'oùn-gyì*	ဘုန်းကြီး
nat medium (male)	*naq-s'ăya*	နတ်ဆရာ
nat medium (female)	*naq-gădaw*	နတ်ကတော်
rickshaw-driver	*s'aiq-kà-dhămà*	ဆိုက်ကားသမား
sailor	*thìn-bàw-dhà*	သင်္ဘောသား
shop-owner	*s'ain-pain-shin*	ဆိုင်ပိုင်ရှင်
singer	*ăs'o-daw*	အဆိုတော်

| I don't have a job. | *ălouq măshí-bù* | အလုပ်မရှိဘူး |

Religion

What is your religion?

(k'ămyà/shìn) beh-ba-dha   ခင်ဗျား/ရှင်
kò-gweh-dhălèh?   ဘယ်ဘာသာ ကိုးကွယ်သလဲ။

I am ...	*cănaw/cămá ... ba*	ကျွန်တော်/ကျွန်မ ၊ ပါ။
Buddhist	*bouq-da ba-dha*	ဗုဒ္ဓ ဘာသာ
Christian	*k'ăriq-yan ba-dha*	ခရစ်ယာန် ဘာသာ
Hindu	*hein-du ba-dha*	ဟိန္ဒူ ဘာသာ
Jewish	*gyù ba-dha*	ဂျူး ဘာသာ
Muslim	*is-lan ba-dha*	အစ္စလမ် ဘာသာ

I am not religious.
> *p'ăyà-tăyà mă-youn-kyi-bù* ဘုရားတရား မယုံကြည်ဘူး။

I am interested in Buddhism.
> *bouq-da ba-dha-ko* ဗုဒ္ဓ ဘာသာကို စိတ်ဝင်စားပါတယ်။
> *seiq-win-sà-ba-deh*

For words relating to Buddhism and for religious festivals, see page 121.

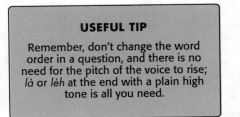

USEFUL TIP

Remember, don't change the word order in a question, and there is no need for the pitch of the voice to rise; *là* or *lèh* at the end with a plain high tone is all you need.

Family

Are you married?
> *(k'ămyà/shin) ein-daun* ခင်ဗျား/ ရှင် အိမ်ထောင်ရှိသလား။
> *shí-dhălà?*

(I, you, someone) am/is married.
> *ein-daun shí-ba-deh* အိမ်ထောင်ရှိပါတယ်။

I am not married.
> *cănaw/cămá ein-daun* ကျွန်တော်/ ကျွန်မ
> *măshí-ba-bù* အိမ်ထောင်မရှိပါဘူး။

SMALL TALK

Do you have ...?	... shí-dhǎlà?	... ရှိသလား॥
I have ...	(cǎnaw/cǎmá)	(ကျွန်တော်/ကျွန်မ)
	... shí-ba-deh	... ရှိပါတယ်॥
I have no ...	(cǎnaw/cǎmá)	(ကျွန်တော်/ကျွန်မ)
	... mǎshí-ba-bù	... မရှိပါဘူး॥

children	thà-dhǎmì	သားသမီး
father	ǎp'e	အဖေ
mother	ǎme	အမေ
older brother	ǎko	အစ်ကို
younger brother	nyi/maun	ညီ/မောင်
(of male/of female)		
older sister	ǎmá	အစ်မ
younger sister	hnǎmá/nyi-má	နှမ/ညီမ
(of male/of female)		
husband/man	yauq-cà	ယောက်ျား
wife	mèin-má	မိန်းမ
wife (more polite)	zǎnì	ဇနီး

How many brothers and sisters
do you have?
    maun-hnǎmá beh-hnǎyauq   မောင်နှမ ဘယ်နှယောက် ရှိသလဲ॥
    shí-dhǎlèh?

Language Difficulties

I'm looking for ...
    ... sha-ne-ba-deh   ... ရှာနေပါတယ်॥
Do you understand?
    nà-leh-dhǎlà?   နားလည်သလား॥

I understand.
  nà-leh-ba-deh   နားလည်ပါတယ်။

(I) don't understand.
  nà-măleh-ba-bù   နားမလည်ပါဘူး။

Please say it again.
  pyan-pyàw-ba-oùn   ပြန်ပြောပါအုံး။

I only speak a little.
  nèh-nèh pyàw-daq-ba-deh   နဲနဲ ပြောတတ်ပါတယ်။

What do you call this in
Burmese?
  da băma-lo beh-lo   ဒါ ဗမာလို ဘယ်လိုခေါ်သလဲ။
  k'aw-dhălèh?

Can you speak ...?	(k'ămyà/shin) ... lo pyàw-daq-thălà?	ခင်ဗျား/ရှင် ... လို ပြောတတ်သလား။
I speak ...	... lo pyàw-daq-teh	... လို ပြောတတ်တယ်။
I can't speak ...	... lo măpyàw-daq-bù	... လို မပြောတတ်ဘူး။
Burmese	băma-zăgà	ဗမာစကား
English	ìn-găleiq-zăgà	အင်္ဂလိပ်စကား
French	pyin-thiq-zăgà	ပြင်သစ်စကား
Japanese	jăpan-zăgà	ဂျပန်စကား

USEFUL TIP

The unaspirated **c** and aspirated **c′** are
pronounced like the 'ch' in 'chip'.

When there's a **′** after a letter, (**s′**, **t′**, etc.), say it
with a puff of air *after* the sound.

SMALL TALK

Politics

This is a sensitive topic. You should tread very carefully; many people work for M I (Military Intelligence), and others can get in trouble if they are overheard being critical of the current regime. You will see large billboards with current slogans in front of many government offices; most of these are fairly general and unexceptionable: 'Love and cherish the motherland' or similar.

politics	*nain-ngan-yè*	နိုင်ငံရေး
SLORC	*ná-wá-tá*	နဝတ
(the military regime since late 1988)		
democracy	*di-mo-kăre-si*	ဒီမိုကရေစီ
prison	*ăcìn-daun*	အကျဉ်းထောင်
political party	*pa-ti*	ပါတီ
BSPP	*làn-zin pa-ti*	လမ်းစဉ်ပါတီ
(the only party under the now-obsolete 1974 constitution)	or *má-s'á-lá*	မဆလ
election	*ywè-kauq-pwèh*	ရွေးကောက်ပွဲ
government	*ăsò-yá*	အစိုးရ
military intelligence	*t'auq-hlàn-yè/M.I.*	ထောက်လှမ်းရေး/ အမ်အိုင်း

Making Conversation

close/childhood friend
   thăngeh-jìn   သူငယ်ချင်း
friend
   meiq-s'we   မိတ်ဆွေ
We're friends.
   dó thăngeh-jìn-dwe-ba ဒို့သူငယ်ချင်းတွေပါ။

I'm here on holiday.
  ăleh la-ba-deh   အလည်လာပါတယ်။

It's very hot, isn't it!
  theiq pu-deh-naw   သိပ်ပူတယ်နော်။

Do you live near here?
  di-nà-hma ne-dhălà?   ဒီနားမှာနေသလား။

What a cute (baby,
kitten, doll etc)!
  k'yiq-săya-lè   ချစ်စရာလေး။

We like it here.
  di-hma pyaw-ne-deh   ဒီမှာပျော်နေတယ်။

We'll send you one.
  tăk'ú pó-pè-meh   တစ်ခု ပို့ပေးမယ်။

Just a minute.
  k'ănă-lè naw   ခဏလေး နော်။

address
  leiq-sa   လိပ်စာ

This is my address.
  da cănáw/   ဒါ ကျွန်တော်/
  cămá leiq-sa-ba   ကျွန်မ လိပ်စာပါ။

Really!
  houq-là   ဟုတ်လား

You're right.
  hman-ba-deh   မှန်ပါတယ်။

I don't think so.
  măt'in-bù   မထင်ဘူး။

Getting Around

Plane, train, bus and car travel within Myanmar can be arranged by a travel company, your hotel, or direct. Most 'taxis' are old jeeps, pick-ups or cars; increasingly there are new saloon cars functioning as taxis, particularly in Yangon (Rangoon). As there are no meters you should bargain for the price before you get in. Buses can be extremely crowded, although there are more and more new express, air-con buses. Shared jeeps or pickups are probably best for trips that can't be made by plane or train.

Finding Your Way

Where is the ... ?   ... beh-hma-lèh?   ... ဘယ်မှာလဲ။
  airport   le-zeiq   လေဆိပ်
  railway station   bu-da-youn   ဘူတာရုံ
  railway carriage   mì-yǎt'à-dwèh   မီးရထားတွဲ
  bus station   baq-sǎkà-geiq   ဘတ်စကားဂိတ်
  riverboat jetty   thìn-bàw-zeiq   သင်္ဘောဆိပ်

What ... is this?   da ba ... lèh?   ဒါ ဘာ ... လဲ။
  town   myó   မြို့
  street   làn   လမ်း
  bus   baq-sǎkà   ဘတ်စကား

54

When will the ... leave?	... beh-ăc'ein t'weq-mălèh?	... ဘယ်အချိန်ထွက်မလဲ။
plane	le-yin-byan	လေယာဉ်ပျံ
train	mì-yăt'à	မီးရထား
bus	baq-săkà	ဘတ်စ်ကား
riverboat	thìn-bàw	သင်္ဘော
jeep	jiq-kà	ဂျစ်ကား
taxi	ăhngà-kà	အငှားကား

I would like ...	cănaw/cămá ... lo-jin-ba-deh	ကျွန်တော်/ကျွန်မ ... လိုချင်ပါတယ်။
one ticket	leq-hmaq-dăzaun	လက်မှတ်တစ်စောင်
two tickets	leq-hmaq hnăsaun	လက်မှတ်နှစ်စောင်
a sleeper (a bed)	eiq-ya	အိပ်ရာ
a room (or cabin on a boat)	ăk'àn	အခန်း

Directions

How do I get to ...?
... ko beh-lo thwà-yá-   ... ကို ဘယ်လိုသွားရသလဲ။
dhălèh?

Can I get there by ...?	... néh thwà-ló yá-mălà?	... နဲ့ သွားလို့ရမလား။
taxi	ăhngà-kà	အငှားကား
bus	baq-săkà	ဘတ်စ်ကား
bicycle	seq-bèin	စက်ဘီး

Can I walk there?
làn-shauq-yin yá-mălà?   လမ်းလျှောက်ရင် ရမလား။

Is this the way to ...?
   di-làn ... thwà-déh-làn-là?   ဒီလမ်း ... သွားတဲ့လမ်းလား။
Is it nearby?
   di-nà-hma-là?   ဒီနားမှာလား။
Is it far?
   wè-dhǎlà?   ဝေးသလား။
How far away is it?
   beh-lauq wè-dhǎlèh?   �’ဘယ်လောက်ဝေးသလဲ။

left	*beh-beq*	ဘယ်ဘက်
right	*nya-beq*	ညာဘက်
straight [ahead]	*téh-déh*	တည့်တည့်

very far away	*theiq wè-deh*	သိပ်ဝေးတယ်။
not so far away	*theiq mǎwè-bù*	သိပ်မဝေးဘူး။

north	*myauq-p'eq*	မြောက်ဘက်
south	*taun-beq*	တောင်ဘက်
east	*ǎshé-beq*	အရှေ့ဘက်
west	*ǎnauq-p'eq*	အနောက်ဘက်

Some Useful Phrases

Where does this bus go?
   di baq-sǎkà beh-go   ဒီဘတ်စကား ဘယ်ကိုသွားသလဲ။
   thwà-dhǎlèh?
Where should I get off?
   beh-hma s'ìn'yá-mǎlèh?   ဘယ်မှာဆင်းရမလဲ။
Bus No 8 goes there.
   baq-sǎkà nan-baq-shiq   ဘတ်စကား နံပါတ်ရှစ်
   ho-beq thwà-deh   ဟိုဘက် သွားတယ်။

Can I sit here?
di-hma t'ain-ló yá-dhălà? ဒီမှာထိုင်လို့ ရသလား။

Can I put my things here?
cănáw/cămá pyiq-sì di-hma t'à-ló yá-dhălà? ကျွန်တော့်/ကျွန်မ ပစ္စည်း ဒီမှာ ထားလို့ ရသလား။

What time does the boat leave?
thìn-bàw beh-ăc'ein t'weq-mălèh? သင်္ဘော ဘယ်အချိန်ထွက်မလဲ။

How much is it to go to Maymyo?
me-myó thwà-yin beh-lauq-lèh? မေမြို့သွားရင် ဘယ်လောက်လဲ။

I'd like to sit in the front.
ăshé-gàn-hma t'ain-jin-deh အရှေ့ခန်းမှာထိုင်ချင်တယ်။

Please go slowly.
pyè-pyè thwà-ba ဖြည်းဖြည်းသွားပါ။

Please wait for me.
cănaw/cămá-go saún-ne-ba ကျွန်တော်/ကျွန်မကိုစောင့်နေပါ။
Stop here.
di-hma yaq-pa ဒီမှာ ရပ်ပါ။
Go to the corner of Fifth St.
ngà-làn-dáun-go thwà-ba ငါးလမ်းထောင့်ကို သွားပါ။
Please load my bag.
tiq-ta tin-pè-ba သေတ္တာတင်ပေးပါ။
Can I get on board now?
(buses, boats etc)
ăk'ú teq-ló yá-dhălà? အခု တက်လို့ရသလား။
What time will we reach
Bagan (Pagan)?
băgan beh-ăc'ein yauq-mălèh? ပုဂံ ဘယ်အချိန် ရောက်မလဲ။
How many hours is it by train
to Mandalay?
mì-yăt'à-néh màn-dălè-go behnă-na-yi-lèh? မီးရထားနဲ့ မန္တလေးကို ဘယ်နှစ်နာရီလဲ။

Some Useful Words

address	*leiq-sa*	လိပ်စာ
house number	*ein-nan-baq*	အိမ်နံပါတ်
bicycle	*seq-beìn*	စက်ဘီး
corner	*dáun*	ထောင့်
express train	*ămyan-yăt'à*	အမြန်ရထား
local train	*law-keh-yăt'à*	လော်ကယ်ရထား
motorcycle	*mo-ta s'ain-keh*	မော်တော်ဆိုင်ကယ်
rickshaw/side-car	*s'aiq-kà*	ဆိုက်ကား
boat deck	*kòun-baq*	ကုန်းပတ်
cabin/compartment	*ăk'àn*	အခန်း

hire	*hngà-deh*	ငှားတယ်
buy	*weh-deh*	ဝယ်တယ်
sit	*t'ain-deh*	ထိုင်တယ်
near	*nì-deh*	နီးတယ်
far	*wè-deh*	ဝေးတယ်
late	*nauq-cá-deh*	နောက်ကျတယ်
slow	*hnè-deh*	နှေးတယ်
(in a negative sense)		
fast	*myan-deh*	မြန်တယ်
early (adv)	*sàw-zàw*	စောစော
early (vb/adj)	*sàw-deh*	စောတယ်

Accommodation

Nowadays there's a range of small private guesthouses and travel agencies, who send someone to meet most flights and trains. Many new, private hotels have sprung up in recent years, and as some of these are joint ventures they can be booked directly from overseas.

Is there a ... near here?	... di-nà-hma shí-dhǎlà?	... ဒီနားမှာရှိသလား။
hotel	ho-teh	ဟော်တယ်
guesthouse	tèh-k'o-gàn	တည်းခိုခန်း
food stall	sà-thauq-s'ain	စားသောက်ဆိုင်
restaurant	sà-daw-s'eq	စားတော်ဆက်

At the Hotel

Can foreigners stay here?
nain-ngan-gyà-thà di-hma tèh-ló yá-dhǎlà? နိုင်ငံခြားသား ဒီမှာတည်းလို့ရသလား။

May I see the room?
ǎk'àn cí-bayá-ze? အခန်း ကြည့်ပါရစေ

How much is the room for one night?
ǎk'àn tǎyeq-ko beh-lauq-lèh? အခန်း တစ်ရက်ကို ဘယ်လောက်လဲ။

60

Is breakfast included in the
price?

   ăk'àn-k'á-dèh-hma   အခန်းခထဲမှာ မနက်စာ ပါသလား။
   măneq-sa pa-dhălà?

Can I pay in kyats?

   caq-néh pè-ló yá-là?   ကျပ်နဲ့ ပေးလို့ရလား။

I will stay for two nights

   hnăyeq t'èh-meh   နှစ်ရက်တည်းမယ်။

How much is ...?	... *beh-lauq-lèh?*	... ဘယ်လောက်လဲ။
one night	*tăyeq*	တစ်ရက်
two nights	*hnăyeq*	နှစ်ရက်
a single room	*tăyauq-k'an*	တစ်ယောက်ခန်း
a double room	*hnăyauq-k'an*	နှစ်ယောက်ခန်း
a cheaper room	*zè-po-nèh-déh-ăk'an*	ဈေးပိုနဲ့တဲ့အခန်း
breakfast	*măneq-sa*	မနက်စာ
lunch	*né-leh-sa*	နေ့လယ်စာ
dinner	*nyá-sa*	ညစာ

This room is good.

   di ăk'àn kaùn-deh   ဒီအခန်း ကောင်းတယ်။

(I/We'll) stay here.

   di-hma t'èh-meh   ဒီမှာ တည်းမယ်။

(We'll) stay together.

   ătu-du t'èh-meh   အတူတူ တည်းမယ်။

We'll stay in separate rooms.

   thì-gyà t'èh-meh   သီးခြား တည်းမယ်။

Requests

Do you have ...?	*... shí-dhălà?*	... ရှိသလား။
an air-conditioned room	*le-è-gàn*	လေအေးခန်း
a bathroom	*ye-c'ò-gàn*	ရေချိုးခန်း
a bed	*eiq-ya*	အိပ်ရာ
a better room	*po-kaùn-déh-ăk'àn*	ပိုကောင်းတဲ့အခန်း
hot water	*ye-nwè*	ရေနွေး
a mosquito net	*c'in-daun*	ခြင်ထောင်
a restaurant	*sà-thauq-s'ain*	စားသောက်ဆိုင်
a telephone	*p'oùn*	ဖုန်း
a toilet	*ein-dha*	အိမ်သာ

Where can I get my clothes washed?
ăwuq-beh-hma-shaw-ló yá-dhălèh? အဝတ် ဘယ်မှာလျှော်လို့ရသလဲ။

Do you serve breakfast?
măneq-sa cwè-dhălà? မနက်စာကျွေးသလား။

The room is expensive.
ăk'àn zè-jì-deh အခန်း ဈေးကြီးတယ်။
There are four of us.
cănaw-dó/cămá-dó lè-yauq shí-deh ကျွန်တော်တို့/ကျွန်မတို့ လေးယောက်ရှိတယ်။
Where is the bathroom?
ye-c'ò-gàn beh-hma-lèh? ရေချိုးခန်း ဘယ်မှာလဲ။
Will you fix the light?
daq-mì pyin-mălà? ဓါတ်မီးပြင်မလား။
Can (I/we) leave my bag for three days?
tiq-ta di-hma thoùn-yeq t'a-ló yá-dhălà? သေတ္တာ ဒီမှာ သုံးရက်ထားလို့ရသလား။
I will come back in one week.
tăpaq-ădwìn pyan-la-oùn-meh တစ်ပတ်အတွင်း ပြန်လာအုံးမယ်။

USEFUL TIP

th is pronounced as in 'thin'

Some Useful Words

blanket	*saun*	စောင်
candle	*p'ăyaùn-dain*	ဖယောင်းတိုင်
clean	*thán-deh*	သန့်တယ်
dirty	*nyiq-paq-deh*	ညစ်ပတ်တယ်
door	*dăga*	တံခါး
fan (electric)	*pan-ka*	ပန်ကာ
fan (manual)	*yaq-taun*	ယပ်တောင်

key	*tháw*	သော့
noisy	*s'u-nyan-deh*	ဆူညံတယ်
padlock	*tháw-gǎlauq*	သော့ခလောက်
pillow	*gaùn-oùn*	ခေါင်းအုံး
plug (for sink)	*ǎs'ó*	အဆို့
quiet (peaceful)	*s'eiq-nyein-deh*	ဆိတ်ငြိမ်တယ်
roof	*ǎmò*	အမိုး
sheet	*eiq-ya-k'in*	အိပ်ရာခင်း
shower	*ye-bàn*	ရေပန်း
sleep	*eiq-teh*	အိပ်တယ်
soap	*s'aq-pya*	ဆပ်ပြာ
suitcase/box	*tiq-t'a*	သေတ္တာ
tap (water faucet)	*ye-boun-bain*	ရေဘုံပိုင်
towel	*myeq-hna-thouq-pǎwa*	မျက်နှာသုတ်ပဝါ
wash (body)	*ye-c'ò-deh*	ရေချိုးတယ်
wash (clothes)	*ǎwuq-shaw-deh*	အဝတ်လျှော်တယ်
wash (hair)	*gaùn-shaw-deh*	ခေါင်းလျှော်တယ်

Around Town

It's not hard to find your way round the towns in Myanmar. You'll find many street signs are in English. Tourist maps are available in Yangon, Mandalay and Pagan. The word for street is *làn*. In downtown Yangon you can orient yourself by the central landmark, the Sule Pagoda.

Where is the ... ?	... *beh-hma-lèh?*	... ဘယ်မှာလဲ။
bank	*ban-daiq*	ဘဏ်တိုက်
market	*zè*	ဈေး
museum	*pyá-daiq*	ပြတိုက်
post office	*sa-daiq*	စာတိုက်

How far is the ...?	... *beh-lauq-wè-dhălèh?*	... ဘယ်လောက်ဝေးသလဲ။
bookshop	*sa-ouq-s'ain*	စာအုပ်ဆိုင်
botanical garden	*youq-k'á-be-dá-ú-yin*	ရုက္ခဗေဒဥယျာဉ်
church	*p'ăyà-shí-k'ò-caùn*	ဘုရားရှိခိုးကျောင်း
cinema	*youq-shin-youn*	ရုပ်ရှင်ရုံ
monastery	*p'oùn-jì-caùn*	ဘုန်းကြီးကျောင်း
park	*pàn-jàn*	ပန်းခြံ
university	*teq-kătho*	တက္ကသိုလ်

I'd like to buy a map.
mye-boun-dăboun   မြေပုံတစ်ပုံဝယ်ချင်ပါတယ်။
weh-jin-ba-deh

At the Bank
Official exchange rates are fixed and some things (including most hotel accommodation and travel) must be paid for in hard currency or foreign exchange certificates (FECs). You will be required on arrival to change some foreign currency into FECs (in Burmese 'FEC' or *bă-ma daw-la*).

I want to change ...	... *lèh-jin-ba-deh*	... လဲချင်ပါတယ်။
money	*paiq-s'an*	ပိုက်ဆံ
banknotes	*ngwe sek-ku*	ငွေစက္ကူ
travellers' cheques	*k'ăyì-c'eq-leq-hmaq*	ခရီးချက်လက်မှတ်
dollars	*daw-la*	ဒေါ်လာ
pounds	*paun*	ပေါင်
foreign currency	*nain-ngan-gyà ngwe*	နိုင်ငံခြားငွေ

Some Useful Phrases
Can I cash a cheque?
c'eq-ko ngwe-lèh-pè-ló   ချက်ကိုငွေလဲပေးလို့ရသလား။
yá-dhălà?
Please write it here.
di-hma yè-ba   ဒီမှာ ရေးပါ။
Please give me smaller change.
ăkywe-ănouq lèh-pè-ba   အကြွေအနုပ်လဲပေးပါ။
Where can I change money?
paiq-s'an beh-hma lèh-ló   ပိုက်ဆံ ဘယ်မှာလဲလို့ရမလဲ။
yá-mălèh?

AROUND TOWN

How much will you give me for 100 dollars?		
	daw-la tăya-go beh-lauq pyan-pè-mălèh?	ဒေါ်လာတစ်ရာကို ဘယ်လောက် ပြန်ပေးမလဲ။
How many kyat to a dollar?		
	tădawla beh-hnăcaq-lèh?	တစ်ဒေါ်လာ ဘယ်နှစ်ကျပ်လဲ။

At the Post Office

I'd like to send ...	... *pó-jin-ba-deh*	... ပို့ချင်ပါတယ်။
a (one) letter	*sa-dăzaun*	စာတစ်စောင်
a (one) parcel	*pa-seh-tăt'ouq*	ပါဆယ်တစ်ထုပ်
two postcards	*pó-săkaq hnăzaun*	ပို့စကတ်နှစ်စောင်
a telegram/cable	*cè-nàn tăk'u*	ကြေးနန်းတစ်ခု

How much to send ...?	... *pó-yin beh-lauq-lèh?*	... ပို့ရင် ဘယ်လောက်လဲ။
printed matter	*sa-ouq-twe*	စာအုပ်တွေ
airmail letter	*le-jaùn-sa*	လေကြောင်းစာ
registered	*re-siq-sări/sa-yìn*	ရေစစ္စရီ/စာရင်း
express	*ămyan*	အမြန်
surface	*yò-yò*	ရိုးရိုး
a fax	*'fax'*	ဖက်စ်

Please give me ...	... *pè-ba*	... ပေးပါ။
an air-letter	*èh-ya-leq-ta*	အဲယားလက်တာ
a stamp	*dăzeiq-gaùn-tăloùn*	တံဆိပ်ခေါင်းတစ်လုံး
an envelope	*sa-eiq*	စာအိတ်
a receipt	*pye-za*	ပြေစာ
a telephone directory	*teh-li-p'oùn làn-hnyun*	တယ်လီဖုန်းလမ်းညွှန်

Some Useful Phrases

I'd like to make a call.
p'oùn-s'eq-c'in-deh　　　ဖုံးဆက်ချင်တယ်။

Please call this number for me.
di teh-li-p'oùn nan-baq　　ဒီတယ်လီဖုံးနံပါတ်ခေါ်ပေးပါ။
kaw-pè-ba

Can I send a fax?
fax pó-ló yá-dhălà?　　　ဖက်စ်ပို့လို့ ရသလား။

If I send a cable (telegram)
how much per word?
cè-nàn-yaiq-yin sa-tăloùn　　ကြေးနန်းရိုက်ရင် စာတစ်လုံး
beh-lauq-lèh?　　　　　　ဘယ်လောက်လဲ။

Please give me two 5-kyat
stamps.
ngà-caq-tan dăzeiq-gàun　　ငါးကျပ်တန်တံဆိပ်ခေါင်း
hnà-loùn pè-ba　　　　　　နှစ်လုံးပေးပါ။

Please give me two
aerograms.
èh-ya leq-ta hnăyweq pè-ba　　အဲယားလက်တာ နှစ်ရွက် ပေးပါ။

I want to send this letter to
America.
di-sa ăme-rì-kà-go　　　ဒီစာ အမေရိကန်ကို ပို့ချင်တယ်။
pó-jin-deh

I want to send this letter by
airmail to France.
di-sa le-jaùn-néh　　　ဒီစာ လေကြောင်းနဲ့ ပြင်သစ်ပြည်ကို
pyin-thiq-pye-ko pó-jin-deh　　ပို့ချင်တယ်။

How much is it altogether?
à-loùn beh-lauq-lèh? အားလုံး ဘယ်လောက်လဲ။

Sights

Place and other names in Myanmar have conventional English versions, which may appear on signs and in guide-books. In some cases these can be different from the actual pronunciation of these places, and from their official anglicised names.

Main Sights in Yangon (Rangoon)

Martyrs' Tomb	*a-za-ni-goùn*	အာဇာနည်ကုန်း
Shwedagon Pagoda	*shwe-dăgoun-p'ăyà*	ရွှေတိဂုံဘုရား
Sule Pagoda	*sù-lè-p'ăyà*	ဆူလေးဘုရား
Inya Lake	*ìn-yà-kan*	အင်းလျားကန်
Royal Lake	*kan-daw-jì*	ကန်တော်ကြီး
Scott Market	*bo-jouq-zè*	ဗိုလ်ချုပ်ဈေး

Main Sights in Mandalay

Mandalay Palace	*nàn-daw*	နန်းတော်
Mahamuni Pagoda	*măha-mú-ní-p'ăyà*	မဟာမုနိဘုရား
Amarapura	*á-má-rá-pu-rá*	အမရပုရ
Mingun Bell	*mìn-gùn-k'aùn-laùn*	မင်းကွန်းခေါင်းလောင်း
Ava Bridge	*ìn-wá-tădà*	အင်းဝတံတား
Watchtower	*hmyaw-zin*	မျှော်စင်
Mandalay Hill	*màn-dălè-taun*	မန္တလေးတောင်
Central Market	*zè-jo*	ဈေးချို

USEFUL TIP

The currency, kyat, is written in this book as *caq* — pronounce it as you would the second syllable of 'cha-cha', stopping the *a* short with a catch in your voice. It's this sound that has caused it to be anglicised with a 't' on the end.

Sightseeing

How much is the entrance fee?

win-jè beh-lauq-lèh?   ဝင်ကြေး ဘယ်လောက်လဲ။

Is there an English-speaking guide?

ingăleiq săgà-pyàw-daq-téh
làn-hnyun shí-dhălà?   အင်္ဂလိပ်စကားပြောတတ်တဲ့
လမ်းညွှန် ရှိသလား။

Can I take photographs?
daq-poun yaiq-ló-yá-dhălà? ဓါတ်ပုံ ရိုက်လို့ရသလား။

When will it open?
beh-dáw p'wín-mălèh? ဘယ်တော့ဖွင့်မလဲ။

What time will it close?
beh-dáw peiq-mălèh? ဘယ်တော့ပိတ်မလဲ။

When was it built?
beh-dòun-gá s'auq-thălèh? ဘယ်တုန်းကဆောက်သလဲ။

Who built it?
bădhu s'auq-thălèh? ဘယ်သူ ဆောက်သလဲ။

It's lovely.
hlá-laiq-ta လှလိုက်တာ။

Beautiful (pagodas, Buddhas)!
ci-nyo-zăya kaùn-deh ကြည်ညိုစရာ ကောင်းတယ်။

It's wonderful/very good.
theiq kaùn-laiq-ta သိပ် ကောင်းလိုက်တာ။

It's amazing.
án-áw-zăya-bè အံ့သြစရာပဲ။

It's strange.
t'ù-zàn-laiq-ta ထူးဆန်းလိုက်တာ။

Bureaucracy

government official	*wun-dàn*	ဝန်ထမ်း
police	*yèh/păleiq*	ရဲ/ပုလိပ်
embassy	*than-yoùn*	သံရုံး
form	*poun-zan*	ပုံစံ
immigration office	*lu-win-hmú cì-jaq-yè-yoùn*	လူဝင်မှု ကြီးကြပ်ရေးရုံး

I've lost my ...	... pyauq-thwà-deh	... ပျောက်သွားတယ်။
passport	paq-săpó	ပတ်စပို့
customs form	pyiq-sì thwìn-poun-zan	ပစ္စည်းသွင်းပုံစံ
wallet	paiq-s'an-eiq	ပိုက်ဆံအိတ်

In the Country

While it is quite safe to walk in all towns, walking in the country-side may be unwise, especially in the former grey (rebel-contested) or black (rebel-controlled) areas. Nearly all the ethnic rebellions have been ended by truces, but most of the former ethnic rebels are still in place, with their weapons and considerable distrust of outsiders. In some remote areas there is still fighting.

Ethnic Minorities

The country is divided into seven Divisions (*taìn*, တိုင်း) which are in the centre of the country, and seven States (*pye-neh*, ပြည်နယ်) which are around the borders. Each State is designated according to the largest minority group living there. The large minorities are the following:

Rakhine (Arakanese)	*răk'ain*	ရခိုင်
Chin	*c'ìn*	ချင်း
Kachin	*kăc'ìn*	ကချင်
Shan	*shàn*	ရှမ်း
Kayah (Karenni)	*kăyà*	ကယား
Karen	*kăyin*	ကရင်
Mon	*mun*	မွန်
national minority	*taìn-yìn-dhà-lu-myò*	တိုင်းရင်းသားလူမျိုး

There are more than a hundred other minorities, especially in the Shan and Kachin States. Many of these are also found in China, Thailand, Laos, India or Bangladesh.

Weather

cool season
(October to January)
s'aùn-ya-dhi
ဆောင်းရာသီ

hot season
(February to May)
nwe-ya-dhi
နွေရာသီ

rainy season
(June to September)
mò-dwìn
မိုးတွင်း

wind	*le*	လေ
cloud	*tein*	တိမ်
fog	*hnìn*	နှင်း
rain (v)	*mò-ywa-deh*	မိုးရွာတယ်
monsoon storm	*mò-theq-le-pyìn*	မိုးသက်လေပြင်း
season	*ya-dhi-ú-dú*	ရာသီဥတု
weather	*mò-le-wădhá*	မိုးလေဝသ

What will the weather be like today?

di-né mò-le-wădhá beh-lo-lèh? ဒီနေ့ မိုး‌လေဝသ ဘယ်လိုလဲ။

The weather is ...	*mò-le-wădhá ...*	မိုးလေဝသ ...
good	*kaùn-deh*	‌ကောင်းတယ်။
changeable	*pyaùn-nain-deh*	‌ပြောင်းနိုင်တယ်။
bad	*s'ò-deh*	ဆိုးတယ်။

It is very hot today.
   di-né theiq pu-deh ဒီနေ့ သိပ်ပူတယ်။
Will it rain tomorrow?
   măneq-p'yan mò-ywa-mălà? မနက်ဖြန် မိုးရွာမလား။
There is no wind.
   le-mătaiq-p'ù ‌လေမတိုက်ဘူး။
Are you cold?
   k'ămyà/shin c'àn-ne-là? ခင်ဗျား/ရှင် ချမ်းရဲ့လား။
The rain has stopped.
   mò-teiq-pi မိုး‌တိတ်ပြီ။

Placenames
Main Towns

Yangon (Rangoon)	*yan-goun*	ရန်ကုန်
Mandalay	*màn-dălè*	မန္တ‌လေး
Bagan (Pagan)	*băgan*	ပုဂံ
Taunggyi	*taun-jì*	‌တောင်ကြီး

Towns around Yangon (Rangoon)

Syriam	*tănyin*	သံလျင်
Bago (Pegu)	*băgo*	ပဲခူး

| Mawlamyine (Moulmein) | *maw-lămyaing* | မော်လမြိုင် |
| Pyay (Prome) | *pye* | ပြည် |

Towns around Mandalay

Sagaing	*zăgàin*	စစ်ကိုင်း
Mingun	*mìn-gùn*	မင်းကွန်း
Pyin-Oo-Lwin (Maymyo)	*pyin-ù-lwin* (*me-myó*)	ပြင်ဦးလွင် (မေမြို့)

Towns around Bagan (Pagan)

| Nyaung-oo | *nyaun-ù* | ညောင်ဦး |
| Kyaukpadaung | *cauq-pădaùn* | ကျောက်ပန်းတောင်း |

Towns around Taunggyi

Heho	*hèh-hò*	ဟဲဟိုး
Shwenyaung	*shwe-nyaun*	ရွှေညောင်
Inle Lake	*ìn-lè-kan*	အင်းလေးကန်

Further Afield

Tavoy	*dăweh*	ထားဝယ်
Mergui	*beiq*	မြိတ်
Lashio	*là-shò*	လားရှိုး
Kengtung	*càin-toun*	ကျိုင်းတုံ
Thandwe (Sandoway beach resort)	*than-dwèh*	သံတွဲ
Sittwe (Akyab)	*sit-twe*	စစ်တွေ
Pathein (Bassein)	*păthein*	ပုသိမ်
Bhamo	*bămaw*	ဗန်းမော်
Myitkyina	*myit-cì-nà*	မြစ်ကြီးနား

IN THE COUNTRY

Rivers

Ayeyarwadi (Irrawaddy)	*e-ya-wadi*	ဧရာဝတီ
Chindwin	*c'ìn-dwìn*	ချင်းတွင်း
Thanlwin (Salween)	*than-lwin*	သံလွင်

Along the Way

Please show me the way to ...
... ko làn pyá-pè-ba   ... ကို လမ်းပြပေးပါ။

How far is it to ...?
... ko beh-lauq-wè-dhǎlèh?   ... ကို ဘယ်လောက်ဝေးသလဲ။

How many hours will it take?
beh-hnǎna-yi ca-mǎlèh?   ဘယ်နှစ်နာရီကြာမလဲ။

Are there any road signs?
làn-hnyun-s'aìn-bouq shí-dhǎlà?   လမ်းညွှန်ဆိုင်းဘုတ်ရှိသလား။

Are there street signs/names?
làn-na-meh yè-t'à-dhălà? လမ်းနာမယ် ရေးထားသလား။
Which way?
beh-làn-lèh? ဘယ်လမ်းလဲ။
I don't think this is the right way.
di-làn măhman-bù t'in-deh ဒီလမ်းမမှန်ဘူး ထင်တယ်။
(I'm/We're) lost.
làn pyauq-thwà-bi လမ်းပျောက်သွားပြီ။
Please turn back.
pyan-hléh-ba ပြန်လှည့်ပါ။

beach	*kàn-byin*	ကမ်းပြင်
countryside	*tàw*	တော
field (irrigated)	*leh*	လယ်
hill	*taun/koùn*	တောင်/ကုန်း
island	*cùn*	ကျွန်း
lake	*ain*	အိုင်
lake (small/artificial)	*kan*	ကန်

USEFUL TIP

In formal situations and in cities, greet people with *min-găla-ba* .

'Are you well?', *ne-kàundhălà?* is fine for any informal encounter. You can reply with *ne-kàun-ba-deh*, 'I am well'.

map	*mye-boun*	မြေပုံ
sand	*thèh*	သဲ
sandbank	*thaun*	သောင်
town	*myó*	မြို့
track/trail	*làn-jaùn*	လမ်းကြောင်း
village	*ywa*	ရွာ
waterfall	*ye-dǎgun*	ရေတံခွန်
river	*myiq*	မြစ်
sea	*pin-leh*	ပင်လယ်

Fauna

bedbug	*jǎbò*	ကြမ်းပိုး
bee	*pyà*	ပျား
bird	*hngeq*	ငှက်
buffalo	*cwèh*	ကျွဲ
butterfly	*leiq-pya*	လိပ်ပြာ
cat	*caun*	ကြောင်
chicken	*ceq*	ကြက်
cockroach	*pò-haq*	ပိုးဟပ်
cow	*nwà*	နွား
crab	*gǎnàn*	ဂဏန်း
deer (barking)	*ji*	ချေ
deer (sambhar)	*s'aq*	ဆတ်
dog	*k'wè*	ခွေး
duck	*bèh*	ဘဲ
elephant	*s'in*	ဆင်
fish	*ngà*	ငါး
fly	*yin*	ယင်

frog	*p'à*	ဖါး
gecko	*tauq-téh*	တောက်တဲ့
goat	*s'eiq*	ဆိတ်
horse	*myìn*	မြင်း
insect	*pò-hmwà*	ပိုးမွှား
lizard	*p'uq*	ဖွတ်
mosquito	*c'in*	ခြင်
pig	*weq*	ဝက်
rat	*cweq*	ကြွက်
shark	*ngamàn*	ငါးမန်း
shrimp/prawn	*băzun*	ပုဇွန်
snake	*mwe*	မြွေ
tiger	*cà*	ကျား
turtle	*leiq*	လိပ်

Flora

bamboo	*wà*	ဝါး
bark (tree)	*thiq-k'auq*	သစ်ခေါက်
flower	*pàn*	ပန်း
flowering plant	*pàn-bin*	ပန်းပင်
leaf	*yweq*	ရွက်
lotus	*ca*	ကြာ
orchid	*thiq-k'wá-pàn*	သစ်ခွပန်း
pine	*t'ìn-yù-bin*	ထင်းရှူးပင်
rattan	*cein*	ကြိမ်
teak	*cùn-thiq*	ကျွန်းသစ်
tree	*thiq-pin*	သစ်ပင်
wood	*thiq-thà*	သစ်သား

Some Useful Phrases

What ... is that?	*da ba ... lèh?*	ဒါဘာ ... လဲ॥
animal	*dăreiq-s'an*	တိရစ္ဆာန်
flower	*pàn-pin*	ပန်းပင်
tree	*thiq-pin*	သစ်ပင်

Please could you write down
the name for me.

   na-meh yè-pè-ba   နာမယ်ရေးပေးပါ॥

Is it OK to swim here?

   di-hma ye-kù-ló-yádhălà?   ဒီမှာရေးကူးလို့ရသလား॥

Food

Most restaurants are privately run. Apart from Burmese food, various Shan dishes are popular. There are also good Chinese restaurants and Indian food stalls in most towns.

A full Burmese meal consists of a meat curry, some raw or cooked vegetables, a soup and rice — usually all served at once. The soup is eaten with a spoon, and everything else with the right hand. A snack could consist of a noodle dish or a curry. The food is not as overpoweringly hot as some Thai or Indian food, but chillies are used fairy liberally. Rice is the staple food.

A very large variety of deep-fried or grilled vegetable and meat snacks are sold by street vendors during the daytime. There are also many different kinds of sweet snacks, eaten especially in the evening and at festivals. A number of delicious cold drinks are also available, as well as seasonal fruits.

Where is the restaurant?
sà-thauq-s'ain
beh-hma-lèh?

စာသောက်ဆိုင်ဘယ်မှာလဲ။

Is there a ... near here?	... *di-nà-hma* *shí-dhǎlà?*	... ဒီနားမှာရှိသလား။
Shan noodle stall	*shàn-k'auk-swèh-zain*	ရှမ်းခေါက်ဆွဲဆိုင်
Chinese restaurant	*tǎyouq-s'ain*	တရုတ်ဆိုင်

Please bring ...	... yu-pè-ba	... ယူပေးပါ။
chopsticks	tu	တူ
fork	k'ăyìn	ခက်ရင်း
spoon	zùn	ဇွန်း
knife	dà	ဓါး
glass	p'an-gweq	ဖန်ခွက်
plate	băgan-byà	ပန်းကန်ပြား
bowl	băgan-loùn	ပန်းကန်လုံး
cup	k'weq	ခွက်

Do you have ...?	... shí-dhălà?	... ရှိသလား။
ice	ye-gèh	ရေခဲ
a chair	kălăt'ain	ကုလားထိုင်
a bigger table	po-jì-déh zăbwèh	ပိုကြီးတဲ့စားပွဲ

I can't eat ...	... măsà-nain-bù	... မစားနိုင်ဘူး။
meat	ăthà	အသား
chillies	ngăyouq-thì	ငရုပ်သီး
peanuts	mye-bèh	မြေပဲ
(chicken) eggs	ceq-ú	ကြက်ဥ

Meals

breakfast	măneq-sa	မနက်စာ
lunch	né-leh-za	နေ့လည်စာ
dinner	nyá-za	ညစာ
snack/small meal	móun/thăye-za	မုန့်/သရေစာ
food ('edibles')	sà-ya	စားစရာ
eat (v)	sà-deh	စားတယ်
drink (v)	thauq-teh	သောက်တယ်

Soups

clear soup	*hìn-jo*	ဟင်းချို
radish soup	*moun-la-ú-hìn-jo*	မုန်လာဥဟင်းချို
green soup	*hìn-nú-neh-hìn-jo*	ဟင်းနနယ်ဟင်းချို
sizzling rice soup	*s'an-hlaw-hìn-jo*	ဆန်လှော်ဟင်းချို
duck soup	*bèh-baun-hìn-jo*	ဘဲပေါင်ဟင်းချို
'12-taste' soup	*s'eh-hnǎmyò-hìn-jo*	ဆယ်နှစ်မျိုးဟင်းချို
'Thai soup' (sour, like Thai tom yam)	*yò-dǎyà-hìn-jo*	ယိုးဒယားဟင်းချို

Noodles

Noodles (*k'auq-s'wèh*, ခေါက်ဆွဲ) of all shapes and sizes are a popular breakfast dish in Myanmar. Mohinga is almost the national dish. The ingredients in the sauce vary according to the cook and the area of Myanmar. Stalls selling Shan noodles are found throughout Myanmar. Shan noodles tend to contain more tomatoes and less oil than mohinga, and may also contain meat.

mohinga (rice vermicelli in fish sauce)	*móun-hìn-gà*	မုန့်ဟင်းခါး
vermicelli with chicken	*ca-zan-hìn-gà*	ကြာဆန်ဟင်းခါး
Shan noodles	*shàn-k'auk-swèh*	ရှမ်းခေါက်ဆွဲ
Mandalay' moun-ti (spaghetti-like noodles with chicken or fish)	*móun-di*	မုန့်တီ
coconut noodles (with chicken and egg)	*oùn-nó-k'auk-swèh*	အုန်းနို့ခေါက်ဆွဲ

Rice

coconut rice	*oùn-t'ămìn*	အုန်းထမင်း
cooked rice	*t'ămìn*	ထမင်း
fried rice	*t'ămìn-gyaw*	ထမင်းကြော်
husked, uncooked rice	*s'an*	ဆန်
packet/bamboo section of sticky rice	*kauk-hnyìn-baùn*	ကောက်ညှင်းပေါင်း
rice gruel	*s'an-byouq*	ဆန်ပြုတ်
sticky rice	*kauk-hnyìn*	ကောက်ညှင်း
sticky rice, meat and garlic packed in leaves and pickled (Shan snack)	*shàn-t'ămìn-gyin*	ရှမ်းထမင်းချဉ်

Meat Dishes

meat dishes	*ăthà*	အသား
beef curry	*ămèh-dhà-hìn*	အမဲသားဟင်း
beef in gravy	*ămèh-hnaq*	အမဲနပ်
chicken curry	*ceq-thà-hìn*	ကြက်သားဟင်း
fried chicken	*ceq-thà-jaw*	ကြက်သားကြော်
fried spicy chicken	*ceq-thà-ăsaq-ceq*	ကြက်သားအစပ်ချက်
grilled chicken (satay)	*ceq-thà-gin*	ကြက်သားကင်
pork curry	*weq-thà-hìn*	ဝက်သားဟင်း
pork curry in thick sauce	*weq-thà s'i-byan*	ဝက်သားဆီပြန်
red pork	*weq-tha-ni*	ဝက်သားနီ
sweet chicken	*ceq-thà-ăc'o-jeq*	ကြက်သားအချိုချက်

Seafood

seafood	*pin-leh-za/*	ပင်လယ်စာ/
	ye-thaq-tăwa	ရေသတ္တဝါ
catfish	*ngăk'u*	ငါးခူ
eel	*ngăshín*	ငါးရှဉ့်
fish	*ngà*	ငါး
fish salad	*ngà-dhouq*	ငါးသုပ်
prawn salad	*băzun-thouq*	ပုစွန်သုပ်
shellfish	*k'ăyú*	ခရု
shrimp/prawn curry	*băzun-hìn*	ပုစွန်ဟင်း
squid	*pyi-jì-ngà*	ပြည်ကြီးငါး
steamed carp	*ngà-thălauq-paùn*	ငါးသလောက်ပေါင်း
steamed fish	*ngà-baùn*	ငါးပေါင်း
steamed fish in banana leaves	*ngà-baùn-douq*	ငါးပေါင်းထုပ်

Eggs

eggs	*ú*	ဥ
boiled (chicken) egg	*ceq-ú-byouq*	ကြက်ဥပြုတ်
chicken egg	*ceq-ú*	ကြက်ဥ
duck egg	*bèh-ú*	ဘဲဥ
fried (chicken) egg	*ceq-ú-jaw*	ကြက်ဥကြော်
omelette (with onions)	*ceq-ú-ceq-thun-jaw*	ကြက်ဥကြက်သွန်ကြော်

Vegetables

vegetables	*hìn-dhì-hìn-yweq*	ဟင်းသီးဟင်းရွက်
banana flower	*hngăpyàw-bù*	ငှက်ပျောဖူး
beans	*pèh-dhì*	ပဲသီး
cabbage	*gaw-bi-douq*	ဂေါ်ဖီထုပ်
carrot	*moun-la-ú-wa*	မုန်လာဥဝါ
cauliflower	*pàn-gaw-p'i*	ပန်းဂေါ်ဖီ
chick peas	*kălăbèh*	ကုလားပဲ
corn (cob)	*pyaùn-bù*	ပြောင်းဖူး
cucumber	*thăk'wà-dhì*	သခွါးသီး
eggplant/aubergine	*k'ăyàn-dhì*	ခရမ်းသီး
fried vegetables	*hìn-dhì-hìn-yweq-caw*	ဟင်းသီးဟင်းရွက်ကြော်
green beans	*pèh-dáun-sheh*	ပဲတောင့်ရှည်
lettuce	*s'ălaq-yweq*	ဆလတ်ရွက်
mushrooms	*hmo*	မှို
onion	*ceq-thun-ni*	ကြက်သွန်နီ
pickled salad	*thănaq*	သနပ်
pumpkin	*p'ăyoun-dhì*	ဖရုံသီး
salad	*ăthouq*	အသုပ်

tomato	k'ăyàn-jin-dhì	ခရမ်းချဉ်သီး
white radish	moun-la-ú-p'yu	မုန်လာဥဖြူ
vegetable curry	hìn-dhì-hìn-yweq-hìn/	ဟင်းသီးဟင်းရွက်ဟင်း/
	thì-zoun-hìn	သီးစုံဟင်း
zucchini/gourd	bù-dhì	ဘူးသီး

Sauces & Condiments

betel quid	kùn-ya	ကွမ်းယား
butter	t'àw-baq	ထောပတ်
cashews	thi-ho-zí	သီဟိုစေ့
chilli sauce	ngăyouq-yeh	ငရုတ်ရည်
coconut cream	oùn-nó	အုန်းနို့
fish/prawn paste	ngăpí	ငါးပိ
raw prawn fish	ngăpí-sein-zà	ငါးပိစိမ်းစား
fish paste sauce	ngăpí-yeh	ငါးပိရည်
fish sauce	ngan-pya-yeh	ငံပြာရည်
fried bananas	ngăpyàw-jaw	ငှက်ပျောကြော်
fried cicadas	păyiq-caw	ပုရစ်ကြော်
ghee	kalà t'àw-baq	ကုလားထောပတ်
ginger salad	jìn-dhouq	ဂျင်းသုပ်
honey	pyà-yeh	ပျားရည်
lime (for betel)	t'oùn	ထုံး
peanuts	mye-bèh	မြေပဲ
fried peanuts	mye-bèh-jaw	မြေပဲကြော်
pickled green tea	lăp'eq	လက်ဖက်
raisins	zăbyiq-thì-jauq	စပျစ်သီးခြောက်
sago/tapioca	tha-gu	သာဂူ

salt	*s'à*	ဆား
soy sauce	*pèh-ngan-pya-yeh*	ပဲငံပြာရည်
sugar	*thăjà*	သကြား
tofu/beancurd	*to-hù*	တိုဟူး
fried tofu squares	*to-hù-jaw*	တိုဟူးကြော်
tofu porridge	*to-hù-pyáw*	တိုဟူးပျော
tofu crackers	*to-hù-c'auq*	တိုဟူးခြောက်
vinegar	*sha-lăka-yeh*	ရှာလကာရည်
whole salted fish	*ngăpí-gaun*	ငါးပိကောင်

Fruit

fruit	*thiq-thì*	သစ်သီး
apple ('flower-fruit')	*pàn-dhì*	ပန်းသီး
avocado ('butter-fruit')	*t'àw-baq-thì*	ထောပတ်သီး
banana	*ngăpyàw-dhì*	ငှက်ပျောသီး
breadfruit	*paun-móun-dhì*	ပေါင်မုန့်သီး
coconut	*oùn-dhì*	အုန်းသီး
custard apple ('influence-fruit')	*àw-za-thì*	ဩဇာသီး
durian	*dù-yìn-dhì*	ဒူးရင်းသီး
lemon	*shauq-thì*	ရှောက်သီး
lime	*than-băya-dhì*	သံပရာသီး
lychee	*lain-c'ì-dhì*	လိုင်ချီးသီး
mango	*thăyeq-dhì*	သရက်သီး
orange	*lein-maw-dhì*	လိမ္မော်သီး
papaya ('boat-shaped fruit')	*thìn-bàw-dhì*	သင်္ဘောသီး

peach	*meq-mun-dhì*	မက်မွန်သီး
pear	*thiq-taw-dhì*	သစ်တော်သီး
pineapple	*na-naq-thì*	နာနတ်သီး
plum (damson)	*meq-màn-dhì*	မက်မန်သီး
jujube plum	*zì-dhì*	ဆီးသီး
pomelo	*cwèh-gàw-dhì*	ကျွဲကောသီး
rambutan ('cockscomb fruit')	*ceq-mauq-thì*	ကြက်မောက်သီး
tamarind	*măjì-dhì*	မန်ကျည်းသီး
watermelon	*p'ăyèh-dhì*	ပရဲသီး

Other Foods

biryani (rice with meat and spices, an Indian dish)	*dan-bauq*	ဒန်ပေါက်
dosa (potato-filled pancake, South Indian)	*to-she*	တိုရှေ
spring rolls/egg rolls	*kaw-pyán-jaw*	ကော်ပြန့်ကြော်
bread	*paun-móun*	ပေါင်မုန့်
toast	*paun-móun-gin*	ပေါင်မုန့်ကင်

USEFUL TIP

'I understand' is *nà-leh-ba-deh*;

'I don't understand' is *nà-măleh-ba-bù*.

Herbs & Spices

cardamon	*p'a-la-zé*	ဖါလာစေ့
chilli	*ngăyouq-thì*	ငရုတ်သီး
coriander	*nan-nan-bin*	နံနံပင်
galangal (white ginger-like root)	*meiq-thălin*	မိတ်သလင်
garlic	*ceq-thun-byu*	ကြက်သွန်ဖြူ
ginger	*gyìn*	ဂျင်း
lemongrass	*zăbălin*	စပါးလင်
rose syrup	*hnìn-yeh*	နှင်းရည်
sesame	*hnàn*	နှမ်း
turmeric	*s'ănwìn*	ဆနွင်း

Sweets & Cakes

When you sit down in a teashop, the waiter will usually put several plates of snacks in front of you without being asked. You will only be charged for what you eat.

agar-agar
(bright green or cream-coloured jelly sweet, can be drunk in a liquid)

cauk-càw
ကျောက်ကျော

biscuit/cookie	*bí-săkiq-móun*	ဘီစကစ်မုန့်
cake	*keiq-móun*	ကိတ်မုန့်
deep-fried dough-sticks (like Chinese 'you zha gui')	*i-ca-kwè*	အီကြာကွေး
durian cooked in jaggery	*dù-yìn-yo*	ဒူးရင်းယို
fried cake/snack	*móun-jaw*	မုန့်ကြော်
golden rice (sticky)	*shwe-t'ămìn*	ရွှေထမင်း
'husband & wife sweet' (hot circular rice sweet)	*móun-lin-măyà*	မုန့်လင်မယား
ice cream	*ye-gèh-móun*	ရေခဲမုန့်
jaggery (toddy candy)	*t'ănyeq*	ထန်းလျက်
jaggery, coconut milk and rice jelly (solid or drink)	*móun-leq-s'aùn*	မုန့်လက်ဆောင်း
jujube plums cooked in jaggery	*zì-yo*	ဆီးယို
sago/tapioca in syrup	*tha-gu-móun*	သာဂူမုန့်
semolina pudding	*s'ănwin-măkın*	ဆနွင်းမကင်း
steamed cake with shredded coconut	*móun-sein-baùn*	မုန့်စိမ်းပေါင်း
steamed rice dough pudding ('brain sweet')	*móun-ò-hnauq*	မုန့်ဦးနှောက်
steamed sticky rice	*kauk-hnyìn-baù*	ကောက်ညှင်းပေါင်း
sticky rice cake with jaggery	*móun-zàn*	မုန့်ဆန်း
sticky rice cake (purple)	*kauk-hnyìn-ngăjeiq*	ကောက်ညှင်းချိုပ်
sticky rice cake with jaggery and egg	*móun-ceq-ú*	မုန့်ကြက်အု
sticky rice pudding with sesamum (for Tabaung new moon)	*t'ămănèh*	ထမနဲ့
sticky rice wafer	*móun-le-bwe*	မုန့်လေပွေ

sugar candy	*dhǎjà-loùn*	သကြားလုံး
sweet fried rice pancakes	*móun-s'i-jaw*	မုန့်ဆီကြော်
toddy palm sugar cake	*t'àn-thì-móun*	ထန်းသီးမုန့်

Drinks
Cold Drinks

alcohol	*ǎyeq*	အရက်
beer	*bi-ya*	ဘီယာ
coconut juice	*oùn-yeh*	အုန်းရည်
lime juice	*than-bǎya-yeh*	သံပရာရည်
milk	*nwà-nó*	နွားနို့
orange juice	*lein-maw-yeh*	လိမ္မော်ရည်
soft drink	*bí-laq-yeh/p'yaw-yeh*	ဘီလပ်ရည်/ဖျော်ရည်
sugarcane juice	*can-yeh*	ကြံရည်
toddy	*t'àn-yeh*	ထန်းရည်
water	*ye*	ရေ
boiled cold water	*ye-jeq-è*	ရေချက်အေး
hot water	*ye-nwè*	ရေနွေး
cold water	*ye-è*	ရေအေး
bottled water	*thán-ye*	သန့်ရေ
('clean water')		
soda water	*s'o-da*	ဆိုဒါ
wine	*wain*	ဝိုင်

Hot Drinks

Plain green, Chinese (or Shan) tea comes free in all restaurants and teashops. A thermos of it sits on the table of most Myanmar homes. Other drinks (tea, coffee) tend to come pre-mixed in the cup with milk (or condensed milk) and plenty of sugar. If you ask for a black coffee, you may get local coffee (delicious black

with a wedge of lime) or instant coffee, known as 'Nes'.
Sachets of 'coffee-mix' (coffee, milk powder and sugar) are
becoming widespread.

plain green tea	*lăp'eq-yeh-jàn/*	လက်ဖက်ရည်ကြမ်း/
	ye-nwè-jàn	ရေနွေးကြမ်း
coffee	*kaw-fi*	ကော်ဖီ
Indian tea	*leq-p'eq-yeh*	လက်ဖက်ရည်
with milk	*nwà-nó-néh*	နွားနို့နဲ့
with condensed milk	*nó-s'ì-néh*	နို့ဆီနဲ့
with lime	*than-băya-dhì-néh*	သံပရာသီးနဲ့
with sugar	*dhăjà-néh*	သကြားနဲ့
Please don't add ...	*... măt'éh-ba-néh*	... မထဲ့ပါနဲ့
lime	*than-băya-dhì*	သံပရာသီး
sugar	*dhăjà*	သကြား
one bottle	*dăbălìn*	တစ်ပုလင်း
two cups	*hnăk'weq*	နှစ်ခွက်
waiter	*zăbwè-dò*	စားပွဲထိုး

Some Useful Words & Phrases

This is good to eat.
sà-kaùn-deh — စားကောင်းတယ်။

This is delicious.
di-ha ăya-dha theiq — ဒီဟာ အရသာ သိပ် ကောင်းတယ်။
kaùn-deh

(I am) hungry.
baiq-s'a-ne-deh — ဗိုက်ဆာနေတယ်။

(I'd) like something to drink.
tăkú-gú thauq-cin-deh — တစ်ခုခု သောက်ချင်တယ်။

Do you have any drinking water?
thauq-ye shí-dhălà? သောက်ရေရှိသလား။

Please bring two bottles of beer.
bi-ya hnăpălìn yu-pè-ba ဘီယာနှစ်ပုလင်းယူပေးပါ။

(We) like spicy food.
saq-téh ăsa caiq-teh စပ်တဲ့အစာ ကြိုက်တယ်။

(I) don't eat spicy food.
saq-téh ăsa măsàbù စပ်တဲ့အစာ မစားဘူး။

What is there to eat?
ba sà-zăya shí-dhălèh? ဘာစားစရာ ရှိသလဲ။

What's the best dish to eat today?
di-né ba-hìn ăkaùn-zoùn-lèh? ဒီနေ့ဘာဟင်းအကောင်းဆုံးလဲ။

Is it enough for three people?
thoùn-yauq sà-yin lauq-mălà? သုံးယောက်စားရင်လောက်မလား။

I didn't order this.
da măhma-bù ဒါ မမှာဘူး။

How much is it altogether?
à-loùn beh-lauq-lèh? အားလုံး ဘယ်လောက်လဲ။

It is sweet.	*c'o-deh*	ချိုတယ်။
It is sour.	*c'in-deh*	ချဉ်တယ်။
It is spicy.	*saq-teh*	စပ်တယ်။
It is bitter	*k'à-deh*	ခါးတယ်။

Shopping

With the legalisation of border trade with Thailand, China and India, a wide range of Western toiletries and medicines became available in the shops, often at prices lower than those in the West. However supplies and quality are erratic. If you have specific requirements, you should bring them with you.

Shopping means bargaining, except in government shops. Antiques must not be taken out of the country, but most of what you will be offered only looks old anyway. Various handicrafts are available; the country is also a major exporter of teak, gems and jade.

Where is the ...?	... beh-hma-lèh?	... ဘယ်မှာလဲ။
market	zè	ဈေး
shop	s'ain	ဆိုင်
bookshop	sa-ouq-s'ain	စာအုပ်ဆိုင်
medicine store	s'è-zain	ဆေးဆိုင်
factory	seq-youn	စက်ရုံ

Where can I buy ...?	... beh-hma?	... ဘယ်မှာဝယ်ရမလဲ။
	weh-yá-mǎlèh	
clothes	ǎwuq-ǎsà	အဝတ်အစား
books	sa-ouq	စာအုပ်
furniture	pǎrí-bàw-gá	ပရိဘောဂ
gems	cauq-myeq/yǎdǎna	ကျောက်မျက်/ရတနာ

96

lacquerware	*yùn-deh*	ယွန်းထည်
medicine	*s'è*	ဆေး

Do you have any ...?	*... shí-là?*	... ရှိလား။
matches	*mì-jiq*	မီးခြစ်
newspapers	*thădìn-za*	သတင်းစာ
soap	*s'aq-pya*	ဆပ်ပြာ
thread	*aq-c'i*	အပ်ချည်

Making a Purchase

How much is ...?	*... beh-lauq-lèh?*	... ဘယ်လောက်လဲ။
one shirt	*èin-ji tăt'eh*	အင်္ကျီတစ်ထည်
two sewing needles	*aq-hnăc'aùn*	အပ်နှစ်ချောင်း
four tickets	*leq-hmaq lè-zaun*	လက်မှတ်လေးစောင်
a pair of shoes	*p'ănaq tăyan*	ဖိနပ်တစ်ရန်

If you want to use a number, you must put a counter word after it. Although there are quite a lot of counters used in Burmese, you can get by with a few. In general *k'ú,* ခု can be used for counting anything but people. See the Numbers chapter, page 123, for more details on how to use counters.

two snacks	*móun hnăk'ú*	မုန့်နှစ်ခု
three tickets	*leq-hmaq thòun-zoùn*	လက်မှတ်သုံးစောင်
expensive	*zè-cì-deh*	ဈေးကြီးတယ်
cheap	*zè-pàw-deh*	ဈေးပေါတယ်

Please reduce the price.
zè-sháw-ba ဈေးလျှော့ပါ

Please give me a bigger one.
po-cì-déh tăk'ú pè-ba ပိုကြီးတဲ့တခုပေးပါ။

Please give me a little one.
ăthè tăk'u pè-ba အသေးတစ်ခု ပေးပါ။

It is very expensive.
zè theiq cì-deh ဈေးသိပ်ကြီးတယ်။

Do you have a cheaper one?
da-t'eq zèi po-pàw-dé tăk'ú shí-dhălà? ဒါထက် ဈေးပိုပေါတဲ့တစ်ခု ရှိသလား။

If I buy two, will you reduce the price?
hnăk'ú weh-yin, zè-sháw-pè-mălà? နှစ်ခုဝယ်ရင် ဈေးလျှော့ပေးမလား။

I will give you 100 (kyat).
tăya pè-meh တစ်ရာပေးမယ်။

That is not enough.
da mălauq-p'ù ဒါ မလောက်ဘူး။

I have only 200 kyat.
ngwe hnăya-bèh shí-deh ငွေနှစ်ရာဘဲ ရှိတယ်။

(You) have to give 300.
thoùn-ya pè-yá-meh သုံးရာ ပေးရမယ်။

OK (lit. 'good')
kaùn-ba-bi ကောင်းပါပြီ။

Clothing

broad-brimmed bamboo hat (electoral symbol of NLD)	k'ǎmauq	ခမောက်
button	ce-dhì	ကြယ်သီး
cloth	ǎt'eh	အထည်
clothing	ǎwuq-ǎsà	အဝတ်အစား
coat/jacket	taiq-poun	တိုက်ပုံ
cotton	c'i-deh	ချည်ထည်
hat	ouq-t'ouq	ဦးထုပ်
longyi (sarong)		
for man	pǎs'ò	ပုဆိုး
for woman	htǎmein	ထဘီ
shirt	èin-ji	အင်္ကျီ
shoelace	p'ǎnaq-cò	ဖိနပ်ကြိုး
shoes	p'ǎnaq	ဖိနပ်
silk	pò-deh	ပိုးထည်
thread	aq-c'i	အပ်ချည်
zipper	ziq	ဇစ်

Toiletries

comb	bì	ဘီး
lipstick	hnǎk'àn-ni	နှုတ်ခမ်းနီ
mirror	hman	မှန်
shampoo	gaùn-shaw-yeh	ခေါင်းလျှော်ရည်
soap	s'aq-pya	ဆပ်ပြာ
toothbrush	dhǎbuq-tan	သွားပွတ်တံ
toothpaste	thwà-taiq-s'è	သွားတိုက်ဆေး
toilet paper	ein-dha-thoùn-seq-ku	အိမ်သာသုံးစက္ကူ

SHOPPING

SHOPPING

Stationery & Books

book	*sa-ouq*	စာအုပ်
dictionary	*ăbí-dan*	အဘိဓာန်
envelope	*sa-eiq*	စာအိတ်
grammar	*tha̱da sa-ouq*	သဒ္ဒါစာအုပ်
guidebook	*làn-hnyun*	လမ်းညွှန်
map	*mye-boun*	မြေပုံ
notebook	*hmaq-sú-sa-ouq*	မှတ်စုစာအုပ်
paper	*seq-ku*	စက္ကူ
pencil	*k'èh-dan*	ခဲတံ
pen	*bàwpin*	ဘောပင်

Smoking

cigarette	*sì-găreq*	စီကရက်
cheroot	*s'è-byìn-leiq*	ဆေးပေါလိပ်
cheroot (stronger)	*s'è-bàw-leiq*	ဆေးပြင်းလိပ်
matches	*mì-jiq*	မီးခြစ်

No Smoking

s'è-leiq măthauq-yá ဆေးလိပ်မသောက်ရ

A packet of ...

... tăhtouq ... တစ်ထုပ်

Excuse me, do you have a light?

di-hma k'ămyá/shin mì ခင်ဗျား/ရှင် မီးရှိသလား။
shí-dhălà?

Please don't smoke.

s'è-leiq măthauq-pa-néh ဆေးလိပ်မသောက်ပါနဲ့ ။

I'm trying to give up.

s'è-leiq-p'yaq-p'ó ဆေးလိပ်ဖြတ်ဖို့ ကြိုးစားနေတယ်။
cò-zà-ne-deh

Do you mind if I smoke?
(lit: I'll smoke, is that OK?)
s'è-leiq thauq-meh
yá-deh-naw?

ဆေးလိပ်သောက်မယ် ရတယ်နော်။

Practical Items

camera	*kin-măra*	ကင်မရာ
fan (manual)	*yaq-taun*	ယပ်တောင်
hammer	*tu*	တူ
lightbulb	*mì-loùn*	မီးလုံး
microphone	*maiq-k'weq*	မိုက်ခွက်
radio	*re-di-yo*	ရေဒီယို
screwdriver	*weq-u-hlé*	ဝက်အူလှည့်
spanner/wrench	*gănàn-leq-má*	ဂဏန်းလက်မ
('crab's thumb')		

Precious Stones, Metals & Other Materials

amber	*păyìn*	ပယင်း
bronze/copper	*cè-ni*	ကြေးနီ

diamond	*sein*	စိန်
emerald	*myá*	မြ
gold (pure)	*shwe (ăsiq)*	ရွှေအစစ်
iron	*than*	သံ
jade ('green stone')	*cauq-sèin*	ကျောက်စိမ်း
ruby	*bădămya*	ပတ္တမြား
silver (pure)	*ngwe (ăsiq)*	ငွေအစစ်
wood	*thiq-thà*	သစ်သား

Souvenirs

bag	*eiq*	အိတ်
basket	*c'in-daùn*	ခြင်းတောင်း
betel box	*kun-iq*	ကွမ်းအစ်
bottle	*pălìn*	ပုလင်း
Burmese harp	*sàun*	စောင်း
chess	*siq-băyin*	စစ်တုရင်

cymbal	*lìn-gwìn*	လင်းကွင်း
earring	*năgaq*	နားကပ်
flute	*pălwe*	ပလွေ
lacquerware	*yùn-deh*	ယွန်းထည်
metal bowl	*p'ălà*	ဖလား
oboe	*hnèh*	နဲ
painting	*băji-kà*	ပန်းချီကား
plate	*băgan*	ပန်းကန်
ring	*leq-suq*	လက်စွပ်
shoulder bag	*lweh-eiq*	လွယ်အိတ်
small (pagoda) bell	*s'wèh-lèh*	ဆည်းလည်း
small cymbal-like bell	*sì*	စည်း
statue	*youq-tú*	ရုပ်တု
tray	*lin-bàn/byaq*	လင်ပန်း/ဗျပ်
umbrella	*htì*	ထီး
vase (for offerings to Buddha)	*nyaun-ye-ò*	ညောင်ရေအိုး
vase (for flowers)	*pàn-ò*	ပန်းအိုး
watercolour	*ye-s'è-baji-kà*	ရေဆေးပန်းချီကား

Colours

black	*ămèh*	အမဲ
blue	*ăpya*	အပြာ
brown	*ănyo*	အညို
green	*ăsèin*	အစိမ်း
orange	*lein-maw-yaun*	လိမ္မော်ရောင်
pink ('flower colour')	*pàn-yaun*	ပန်းရောင်
purple ('eggplant colour')	*k'ăyàn-yaun*	ခရမ်းရောင်
red	*ăni*	အနီ

| white | *ăp'yu* | အဖြူ |
| yellow | *ăwa* | အဝါ |

a white hat	*ouq-htouq-p'yu*	ဦးထုပ်ဖြူ
a black umbrella	*htì ămèh*	ထီးအမဲ
three red books	*sa-ouq-ni thòun-ouq*	စာအုပ်နီသုံးအုပ်

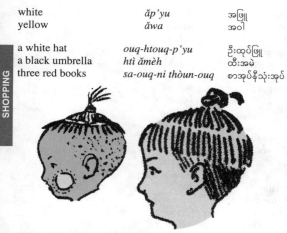

Weights & Measures

Weights and measures are like counters (see the Numbers & Amounts, page 123). They come after a number and when they are used there is no need for a separate counter.

inch ('thumb')	*leq-má*	လက်မ
foot	*pe*	ပေ
mile	*main*	မိုင်
acre	*e-ká*	ဧက
tical/kyat (16.5 grams or 2/5 oz. as a unit of weight)	*caq-thà*	ကျပ်သား
viss (1.65 kg, 3.65 lb)	*peiq-tha*	ပိဿာ

yard	*gaiq*	ကိုက်
half yard	*taun*	တောင်
cup	*k'weq*	ခွက်
two viss of sugar	*dhăjà hnăpeiq-tha*	သကြား၊နှစ်ပိဿာ
five miles	*ngà-main*	ငါး၊မိုင်
about two cups	*hnăk'weq-lauq*	နှစ်ခွက်လောက်

big	*cì-deh*	ကြီးတယ်
small	*thè-deh*	သေးတယ်
many	*myà-deh*	များတယ်
few	*nèh-deh*	နည်းတယ်
long	*sheh-deh*	ရှည်တယ်
short (length)	*to-deh*	တိုတယ်
high/tall	*myín-deh*	မြင့်တယ်
low/short (height)	*néin-deh*	နိမ့်တယ်
heavy	*lè-deh*	လေးတယ်
light (weight)	*páw-deh*	ပေါ့တယ်

SHOPPING

Health

Foreign residents of Myanmar who become seriously ill usually go overseas for treatment. However, if you do need some kind of medical treatment this chapter should be useful. Be aware that the incidence of infectious diseases is high, the standards of public hospitals are very low, and almost no medicines or other supplies are available from hospitals or government shops; most medicines, even the most basic, must be bought on the private market.

Where is the ... ?	... beh-hma-lèh?	... ဘယ်မှာလဲ။
ambulance	thăna-tin-yin/	သူနာတင်ယာဉ်/
	lu-na-tin-kà	လူနာတင်ကား
doctor	s'ăya-wun	ဆရာဝန်
dentist	thwà-s'ăya-wun	သွားဆရာဝန်
hospital	s'è-youn	ဆေးရုံ
medical superintendent	s'è-youn-ouq	ဆေးရုံအုပ်
(chief doctor of hospital)		
nurse	thu-na-byú	သူနာပြု
patient	lu-na	လူနာ
pharmacy/chemist	s'è-zain	ဆေးဆိုင်
private clinic	ăt'ù-s'è-gàn	အထူးဆေးခန်း
private generalist	ăpyin-s'è-gàn	အပြင်ဆေးခန်း
specialist	ăt'ù-gú	အထူးကုဆရာဝန်
	s'ăya-wun	

106

Please call a doctor.
s'ăya-wun kaw-pè-ba ဆရာဝန် ခေါ်ပေးပါ။

At the Doctor

HEALTH

My ... hurts
  cănáw/cămá ... na-deh ကျွန်တော်/ကျွန်မ ... နာတယ်။
I feel tired.
  pin-bàn-ne-bi ပင်ပန်းနေပြီ။
I'm not feeling very well.
  theiq ne-măkàun-bù သိပ် နေမကောင်းဘူး။
It hurts here.
  di-hma na-deh ဒီမှာ နာတယ်။
It itches here.
  di-hma yà-deh ဒီမှာ ယားတယ်။
I can't sleep.
  eiq-mă-pyaw-bù အိပ်မပျော်ဘူး။
I have chest pain.
  yin-baq áun-ne-deh ရင်ဘတ် အောင့်နေတယ်။
I vomit often.
  k'ăná-k'ăná an-deh ခဏခဏ အန်တယ်။
I feel faint.
  mù-lèh-deh မူးလဲတယ်။
Is it serious?
  theiq ăyè-gyi-dhălà? သိပ် အရေးကြီးသလား။
I don't want an injection.
  s'è măt'ò-ze-jin-ba-bù ဆေး မထိုးစေချင်ပါဘူး။

Parts of the Body

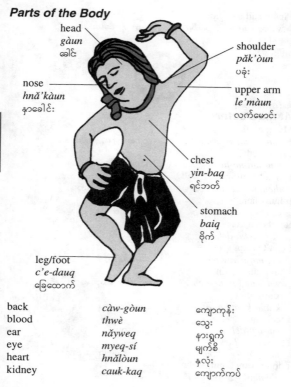

head
gàun
ခေါင်း

shoulder
păk'òun
ပခုံး

nose
hnă'kàun
နှာခေါင်း

upper arm
le'màun
လက်မောင်း

chest
yin-baq
ရင်ဘတ်

stomach
baiq
ဗိုက်

leg/foot
c'e-dauq
ခြေထောက်

HEALTH

back	*càw-gòun*	ကျောကုန်း
blood	*thwè*	သွေး
ear	*năyweq*	နားရွက်
eye	*myeq-sí*	မျက်စိ
heart	*hnălòun*	နှလုံး
kidney	*cauk-kaq*	ကျောက်ကပ်

liver	*ăthèh*	အသည်း
lungs	*ăs'ouq*	အဆုတ်
muscle	*cweq-thà*	ကြွက်သား
stomach	*ăsa-ein*	အစာအိမ်
teeth	*thwà*	သွား
throat	*leh-jàun*	လည်ချောင်း

Ailments

I/you have ... (disease)

| ... *shí-deh* | ... ရှိတယ်။ |
| ... *p'yiq-ne-deh* | ... ဖြစ်နေတယ်။ |

AIDS	*ko-k'an-à-cá-*	ကိုယ်ခံအား：
	s'ìn-déh-yàw-ga	ကျဆင်းတဲ့ရောဂါ
asthma	*(pàn-na-)yin-caq*	ပန်းနာရင်ကျပ်
cholera	*ka-lá-wùn-yàw-ga*	ကာလဝမ်းရောဂါ
dengue fever	*thwè-lun-touq-kwè*	သွေးလွန်တုပ်ကွေး
flu	*touq-kwè*	တုပ်ကွေး
malaria ('bird fever')	*hngeq-p'yà*	ငှက်ဖျား
rabies	*k'wè-yù-byan-*	ခွေးရူးပြန်ရောဂါ
	yàw-ga	
venereal disease	*ka-lá-dhà yàwga*	ကာလသားရောဂါ

The following diseases are expressed by adjectival verbs so you can use them on their own without *shí-deh/p'yiq-ne-deh*.

have anaemia	*thwè-à-nèh-deh*	သွေးအားနည်းတယ်
have a cold	*ăe mí-bi*	အအေးမိပြီ
have a cough	*c'àun s'ò-deh*	ချောင်းဆိုးတယ်
have cramps	*cweq teq-teh*	ကြွက်တက်တယ်

HEALTH

HEALTH

have diarrhoea	*wùn-shàw-deh/*	ဝမ်းလျှောတယ်/
	wùn-thwà-ne-deh	ဝမ်းသွားနေတယ်
have dysentery	*wùn kaiq-ne-deh*	ဝမ်းကိုက်နေတယ်
have a fever	*p'yà-deh*	ဖျားတယ်
have gonorrhea	*gǎno cá-deh*	ဂနိုကျတယ်
have a headache	*gàun kaiq-ne-deh*	ခေါင်းကိုက်နေတယ်
have pneumonia	*ǎs'ouq yaun-ne-deh*	အဆုတ်ရောင်နေတယ်
have a sore throat	*leh-jaùn-na-deh*	လည်ချောင်းနာတယ်
have a stomachache	*baiq na-deh*	ဗိုက်နာတယ်
have sunstroke	*ǎpu-shaq-teh*	အပူလျှပ်တယ်
have a toothache	*thwà kaiq-teh*	သွားကိုက်တယ်

Allergies & Conditions

I am allergic to penicillin.
   cǎnaw/cǎmá   ကျွန်တော်/ကျွန်မ
   pǎnǎsǎlin-né mǎtéh-bù   ပင်နီစလင်နဲ့, မတည့်ဘူး။
I am pregnant.
   baiq cì-deh/ko-wun shí-deh   ဗိုက်ကြီးတယ်/ကိုယ်ဝန်ရှိတယ်။

diabetes	*s'ì-jo-yàw-ga*	ဆီးချိုရောဂါ
hypertension	*thwè-do-yàw-ga*	သွေးထိုးရောဂါ

At the Dentist

Are you a dentist?
   hkǎmyà/shin   ခင်ဗျား;/ရှင် သွားဆရာဝန်ရဲ့လား။
   thwà-s'ǎya-wun-là?
My tooth hurts.
   cǎnáw/cǎmá thwà kaiq-teh   ကျွန်တော်/ကျွန်မ သွားကိုက်တယ်။
This tooth is broken.
   di-thwà cò-thwà-bi   ဒီသွားကျိုးသွားပြီ။

This tooth is chipped.
di-thwà péh-ne-deh ဒီသွားပဲ့နေတယ်။

Will you have take the tooth out?
thwà hnouq-săya lo-dhălà? သွားနှုတ်စရာ လိုသလား။

Please don't take it out.
mahnouq-pa-néh မနှုတ်ပါနဲ့ ။

Can the tooth be repaired?
thwà pyin-ló yá-là? သွားပြင်လို့ ရလား။

Can you fill the cavity?
thwà p'a-nain-dhălà သွားဖာနိုင်သလား။

USEFUL TIP

A good phrase to memorise, especially when you're looking things up in this book, is 'Just a minute', *k'ăná sáun-ne-ba.*

At the Chemist

See also page 99 in the Shopping chapter.

How many tablets a day?
tăné-ko beh-hnălòun-lèh? တစ်နေ့ကို ဘယ်နှလုံးလဲ။

What medicine is this?
di-s'è ba-s'è-lèh? ဒီဆေး ဘာဆေးလဲ။

prescription	*s'è-za*	ဆေးစာ
dosage directions	*s'è ăhnyùn*	ဆေးအညွှန်း

| Do you have ... ? | ... *shí-là* | ... ရှိလား။ |
| Where can I buy ...? | ... *beh-hma weh-yá-mălèh?* | ... ဘယ်မှာဝယ်ရမလဲ။ |

aspirin	*eq-săpărin*	အက်စပရင်
bandage (for sprain)	*paq-tì*	ပတ်တီး
gauze	*gauz/s'è-paq-tì*	ဂေါင်/ဆေးပတ်တီး
insulin	*in-s'u-lin*	အင်ဆူလင်
morphine	*maw-p'èin/ maw-p'ì-yà*	မော်ဖိန်း/မော်ဖီးယား
penicillin	*pănăsălin*	ပင်နီစလင်
pill	*s'è-lòun/s'è-byà*	ဆေးလုံး/ဆေးပြား
plaster	*păla-săta*	ပလာစတာ
sleeping pill	*eiq-s'è*	အိပ်ဆေး
syringe	*s'è-t'ò-aq*	ဆေးထိုးအပ်
thermometer	*bădà-dain*	ပြဒါးတိုင်
valium	*be-li-yan*	ဗေလီယံ
vitamin	*à-zè/bi-ta-min*	အားဆေး/ဗိတာမင်

HEALTH

Time, Dates & Festivals

The Buddhist lunar calendar is used for religious holidays, so these fall on different dates every year. Most other national holidays follow the Western calendar. The seven-day week, with Saturday and Sunday as non-working days, is used. Time is now reckoned by the Western 12-hour system.

What time is it?
beh-ăc'ein shí-bi-lèh?　　ဘယ်အချိန်ရှိပြီလဲ။
When (in the past)?
beh-dòun-gá-lèh?　　ဘယ်တုန်းကလဲ။
When (in the future)?
beh-dáw-lèh?　　ဘယ်တော့လဲ။
At what time?
beh-ăc'ein-hma-lèh?　　ဘယ်အချိန်မှာလဲ။

Time
The day is divided into four parts:

morning (6 am to midday)	*măneq*	မနက်
midday (midday to 3 pm)	*né-leh*	နေ့လည်
afternoon/evening (3 to 7 pm)	*nyá-ne*	ညနေ
night (7 pm to 6 am)	*nyá*	ည

113

There are also special words for midday and midnight:

midday	*mùn-déh*	မွန်းတည့်
midnight	*thăgaun*	သန်းခေါင်
hour	*na-yi*	နာရီ
minute	*măniq*	မိနစ်

7 am
  mǎneq k'únnǎna-yi　　မနက် ခုနစ်နာရီ
12 noon
  né-leh s'éh-hnǎna-yi/　　နေ့ လည်ဆယ့်နှစ်နာရီ/
  mùn-déh　　မွန်းတည့်
1 pm
  né-leh tǎna-yi　　နေ့ လည် တစ်နာရီ
4.30 pm
  nyá-ne lè-na-yi-gwèh　　ညနေ လေးနာရီခွဲ
9 pm
  nyá kò-na-yi　　ညကိုးနာရီ
10.15 pm
  nyá s'eh-na-yi s'éh-ngà-　　ည ဆယ်နာရီဆယ့်ငါးမိနစ်
  mǎniq
12 midnight
  nyá s'eh-hnǎna-yi/thǎgaun　　ညဆယ့်နှစ်နာရီ/သန်းခေါင်
3.25 am
  mǎneq thòun-na-yi　　မနက်သုံးနာရီနှစ်ဆယ့်ငါးမိနစ်
  hnǎs'éh-ngà-mǎniq

In some towns you may still hear the traditional three-hour watch bells, especially at night.

Some Useful Words & Phrases

What time is it?
  beh-ăc'ein shí-bi-lèh?   ဘယ်အချိန်ရှိပြီလဲ။

How long will it take?
  beh-lauq ca-mălèh?   ဘယ်လောက် ကြာမလဲ။

How many hours will it take?
  beh-hnăna-yi ca-mălèh?   ဘယ်နှစ်နာရီ ကြာမလဲ။

When will it get dark?
  beh-dáw mò-c'ouq-mălèh?   ဘယ်တော့မိုးချုပ်မလဲ။

It is late (of time).
  nauq-cá-deh   နောက်ကျတယ်။

What day (of the week) is it?
  di-né ba-né-lèh?   ဒီနေ့ ဘာနေ့ လဲ။

What is the date?
  di-né beh-hnăyeq-né-lèh?   ဒီနေ့ ဘယ်နှစ်ရက်နေ့လဲ။

today	*di-né*	ဒီနေ့
tomorrow	*măneq-p'yan*	မနက်ဖြန်
tomorrow morning	*măneq-p'yan-măneq*	မနက်ဖြန်မနက်
day after tomorrow	*dhăbeq-k'a*	သဘက်ခါ
next week	*nauq ăpaq*	နောက် အပတ်
yesterday	*măné-gá*	မနေ့ က
yesterday evening	*măné-nyá-gá*	မနေ့ ညက
last week	*lun-géh-déh-ăpaq-ká*	လွန်ခဲ့တဲ့ အပတ်က

USEFUL TIP

'When?' is (in past) *beh-dòun-gá*; (in future) *beh-dáw*
'What time is it?' is *be ăc'ein-shí-bi-lèh?*

Dates

The Burmese calendar, still used for some purposes, started with the lunar year corresponding to 638/639 AD. This is known as the Sakkaraj or Thagayit *(dhăgăyiq,* သက္ကရာဇ် *)* era. For most purposes the Christian era (Gregorian calendar) is now used instead.

Days of the Week

Sunday	*tănìn-gănwe-né*	တနင်္ဂနွေနေ့
Monday	*tănìn-la-né*	တနင်္လာနေ့
Tuesday	*in-ga-né*	အင်္ဂါနေ့
Wednesday	*bouq-dăhù-né*	ဗုဒ္ဓဟူးနေ့
Thursday	*ca-dhăbădè-né*	ကြာသပတေးနေ့
Friday	*thauq-ca-né*	သောကြာနေ့
Saturday	*săne-né*	စနေနေ့

Months

The lunar calendar does not correspond to the Western calendar: the following are approximate equivalents:

	Solar	Lunar
January	*zan-năwa-ri* ဇန်နဝါရီ	*pya-dho* ပြာသို
February	*p'e-băwa-ri* ဖေဖော်ဝါရီ	*tăbó-dwéh* တပို့တွဲ
March	*maq* မတ်	*tăbàun* တပေါင်း
April	*e-pyi* ဧပြီ	*dăgù* တန်ခူး
May	*me* မေ	*kăs'oun* ကဆုန်

June	*zun*	*năyoun*
	ဇွန်	နယုန်
July	*zu-lain*	*wa-zo*
	ဇူလိုင်	ဝါဆို
August	*àw-gouq*	*wa-gaun*
	ဩဂုတ်	ဝါခေါင်
September	*seq-tinba*	*taw-dhălìn*
	စက်တင်ဘာ	တော်သလင်း
October	*auq-to-ba*	*thădìn-juq*
	အောက်တိုဘာ	သီတင်းကျွတ်
November	*no-win-ba*	*tăzaun-mòun*
	နိုဝင်ဘာ	တန်ဆောင်မုန်း
December	*di-zin-ba*	*nădaw*
	ဒီဇင်ဘာ	နတ်တော်

The lunar year starts with *tăgù*, generally in early to mid April. Adjustments to bring the lunar year back into step with the seasons add a second month of Wazo approximately every four years (a *wa-t'aq* or leap year). In these years (eg 1996) there is First Wazo, *păt'ămá wa-zo*, ပထမဝါဆို and Second Wazo, *dú-tí-yá wa-zo*, ဒုတိယဝါဆို. Each lunar month begins with the day after the new moon, has 14 days of waxing moon, the full moon day (which is often a religious festival), then 13 or 14 days of waning moon and the last day of new moon.

waxing moon	*lá-zàn*	လဆန်း
full moon day	*lá-byé-né*	လပြည့်နေ့
waning moon	*lá-zouq*	လဆုတ်
new moon day	*lá-gweh-né*	လကွယ်နေ့
(no moon visible)		
year	*hniq*	နှစ်

month	*lá*	လ
week	*ăpaq*	အပတ်
day (daytime)	*né*	နေ့
day (24 hours)	*yeq*	ရက်
night	*nyá*	ည

Giving a date, you start with the year, then the month, day (or phase of moon day for the lunar calendar), and then sometimes the day of the week. Note the slightly different form (with *byé*, ပြည့် instead of *k'ú*, ခု) when the year ends in a zero.

(Friday) 10 May 1996
(tă)t'áun-kò-ya-kò-s'éh-c'auq-k'ú-hniq me-lá s'eh-yeq-né (thauq-ca-né)

၁၉၉၆ခုနှစ် မေလ(၁၀)ရက်နေ့ သောကြာနေ့

23 December 1997
(tă)t'áun-kò-ya-kò-s'éh-k'ú-hnăk'ú-hniq di-zin-ba-lá hnăs'eh-thòun-yeq-né

၁၉၉၇ခုနှစ် ဒီဇင်ဘာလာ(၂၃)ရက်နေ့

March 1990
(tă)t'áun-kò-ya-kò-s'eh-byé-hniq maq-lá

၁၉၉၀ပြည့်နှစ် မတ်လ

10th waning of Pyatho 1358 (= 1995)
(dhăgăyiq) t'áun-thòun-ya-ngà-zé-shiq-k'ú-hniq pyădho lá-zouq s'eh-yeq-né

သက္ကရာဇ်၁၃၅၈ခုနှစ်ပြာသိုလဆုတ်(၁၀)ရက်နေ့

Holidays & Festivals

Western calendar holidays are:

Independence Day   *luq-laq-yè-né*   လွတ်လပ်ရေးနေ့
(4 January, commemorating independence
in 1948)

Union Day   *pye-daun-zú-né*   ပြည်ထောင်စုနေ့
(12 February, commemorating the signing
of the Panglong Agreement)

Peasants Day   *taun-thu-leh-dhǎmà-*   တောင်သူလယ်သမားနေ့
(2 March)   *né*

Army Day   *taq-mǎdaw-né*   တပ်မတော်နေ့
(27 March)

Workers Day   *ǎlouq-thǎmà-né*   အလုပ်သမားနေ့
(1 May)

Martyrs Day   *a-za-ni-né*   အာဇာနည်နေ့
(19 July, commemorating the 1947 assassi-
nation of General Aung San and six other
leaders)

Christmas Day   *k'ǎriq-sǎmaq-pwèh-*   ခရစ္စမတ်ပွဲတော်နေ့
(25 December)   *daw-né*

Lunar calendar holidays are:

Karen New Year   *kǎyin-hniq-thiq-*   ကရင်နှစ်သစ်ကူးနေ့
(1st of *pyǎdho*)   *kù-né*

Tabaung Festival   *tǎbaun-pwèh-*   တပေါင်းပွဲတော်နေ့
(full moon of *tǎbaun*)   *daw-né*

ThingyanWater Festival   *thǎjan*   သင်္ကြန်
(four days in mid April)

TIME, DATES & FESTIVALS

Buddha Festival (full moon of *kǎs'oun*)	*nyaun-ye-thùn-pwèh-daw*	ညောင်ရေသွန်းပွဲတော်
Buddhist lent begins (full moon of *wa-zo*)	*dǎmǎseq-ca-né*	ဓမ္မစကြာနေ့
End of Lent (Thadingyut) (full moon of *thǎdìn-juq*)	*ǎbí-dǎma-né*	အဘိဓမ္မာနေ့
Festival of Lights (full moon of *tǎzaun-mòun*)	*tǎzaun-dain-pwèh-daw*	တန်ဆောင်တိုင်ပွဲတော်
National Day (10th waning of *tǎzaun-mòun*)	*ǎmyò-dhà-né*	အမျိုးသားနေ့

Other full moon days also have religious festivals. Buddhist observances and special events also take place on the eighth waxing, eighth waning and new moon days of each lunar month, particularly in Mandalay. These four days are known as *ú-bouq-né* (ဥပုသ်နေ့). The three months of Lent, at the peak of the rainy season, are the usual time for men and boys to enter the monastery. Marriages are put on hold and monks are not allowed to travel.

Many festivals or 'pwes' in Myanmar are religious, but not all are Buddhist. For example the spirits (*naq*, နတ်) are honoured at Taungbyone (*taun-byòun*, တောင်ပြွန်း), 30 km north of Mandalay, in the middle of Buddhist Lent. Individuals may also put on a festival; and some temple festivals may include drama, comedy, puppets or dancing. Most pwes are at night.

temple festival	*pwèh-daw*	ပွဲတော်
spirit festival	*naq-pwèh*	နတ်ပွဲ
dramatic performance	*zaq-pwèh*	ဇာတ်ပွဲ
dance/comedy	*ănyéin-pwèh*	အငြိမ့်ပွဲ
puppet show	*youq-thè-pwèh*	ရုပ်သေးပွဲ
dancing/singing chorus	*yèin*	ယိမ်း

Buddhism

abbot (head of monastery)	*săya-daw*	ဆရာတော်
authority	*àw-za*	ဩဇာ
Bodhisattva (future Buddha)	*p'ăyà-làun*	ဘုရားလောင်း
Buddhism	*bouq-dá ba-dha*	ဗုဒ္ဓဘာသာ
footprint of Buddha	*c'e-daw-ya*	ခြေတော်ရာ
good deed	*kàun-hmú*	ကောင်းမှု
ordination hall	*thein*	သိမ်
initiate a novice	*shin-pyú-deh*	ရှင်ပြုယ်
karma/fate	*kan*	က
merit	*kú-tho*	ကုသိုလ်
monastery/temple	*p'òun-jì-jàun*	ဘုန်းကြီးကျောင်း
pagoda trustee	*p'ăyà-lu-jì*	ဘုရားလူကြီး
monk (over 20)	*p'òun-jì*	ဘုန်းကြီး

nirvana/enlightenment	*neiq-ban*	နိဗ္ဗာန်
novice (young man)	*shin/ko-yin*	ရှင်/ကိုရင်
power/blessing	*p'òun*	ဘုန်း
rest house	*zăyaq*	ဇရပ်
stairway (up to a temple)	*zàun-dàn*	စောင်းတန်း
stupa/chedi	*ze-di*	စေတီ
virtue/prestige	*goun*	ဂုဏ်

Numbers & Amounts

Counters

Whenever you count things in Burmese, you must put in a counter (also known as a classifier) after the number. These always come after the noun counted. It's something like saying 'three items of clothing' or 'three slices of cheese'.

If you are giving a measure (miles, cups, etc — see Shopping) after the noun, then you don't need another counter; groups and round numbers work the same. And if all this seems too complicated, you may use the universal counter *k'ú* (ခု) for any inanimate noun; but not for monks, people or animals.

Buddha, temples	*s'u*	ဆူ
monks, royalty	*pà/bà*	ပါး
other high-status humans, and a formal, written form of *yauq*	*ù*	ဦး
people	*yauq*	ယောက်
animals	*kaun/gaun*	ကောင်
plants, rope, thread, hair	*pin/bin*	ပင်
round things, fruit, houses, furniture, machines	*lòun*	လုံး
flat things	*c'aq/jaq*	ချပ်

123

long things, teeth, fingers, toes, needles, legs, knives, pencils	*c'àun/jàun*	ချောင်း
clothing (cloth)	*t'eh/deh*	ထည်
written things, tickets, letters, newspapers	*saun/zaun*	စောင်
tools, instruments (hand)	*leq*	လက်
vehicles (large/small)	*sìn* or *sì/zì*	စင်း/စီး
books	*ouq*	အုပ်
rings, other ring-shaped things	*kwìn/gwìn*	ကွင်း
leaves (including paper)	*yweq*	ရွက်

USEFUL TIP

'How much?' is *beh-lauq-lèh?*
'How much is the room?' is *ăk'àn-gá beh-lauq-lèh?*
'How many?' is *beh-hnă* + counter + *lèh?*

Numbers

1	၁	*tiq / tă*	တစ်/တ
2	၂	*hniq / hnă*	နှစ်/နှ
3	၃	*thòun*	သုံး
4	၄	*lè*	လေး
5	၅	*ngà*	ငါး
6	၆	*c'auq*	ခြောက်
7	၇	*k'ú-hniq/k'ú-hnă*	ခုနှစ်/ခုနှ

8	၈	*shiq*	ရှစ်
9	၉	*kò*	ကိုး
10	၁၀	*(tă)s'eh*	တစ်ဆယ်

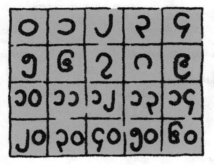

11	၁၁	*s'éh-tiq*	ဆယ့်တစ်
12	၁၂	*s'éh-hniq*	ဆယ့်နှစ်
20	၂၀	*hnăs'eh*	နှစ်ဆယ်
35	၃၅	*thòun-zéh-ngà*	သုံးဆယ့်ငါး
100	၁၀၀	*tăya*	တစ်ရာ
1000	၁၀၀၀	*(tă)t'aun*	တစ်ထောင်
10,000	၁၀၀၀၀	*(tă)thàun*	တစ်သောင်း
100,000	၁၀၀၀၀၀	*(tă)thèin*	တစ်သိန်း
million	၁၀၀၀၀၀၀	*(tă)thàn*	တစ်သန်း

One hundred thousand is often called one *lakh*.

NUMBERS & AMOUNTS

To put a number together, start from the highest number and work down.

144,285 (people)
tăthèin-lè-thàun-lè-daun-hnăyá-shiq-s'éh-ngà-(yauq)

တစ်သိန်းလေးသောင်းလေးထောင်နှစ်ရာ့ရှစ်ဆယ့်ငါးယောက်

21 (round things)
hnăs'éh-tă-lòun

နှစ်ဆယ့်တစ်လုံး

15 books
sa-ouq-s'éh-ngà-ouq

စာအုပ်ဆယ့်ငါးအုပ်

Ordinal Numbers

first	*păt'ămá*	ပထမ
second	*dú-tí-yá*	ဒုတိယ
third	*tá-tí-yá*	တတိယ
fourth	*sătouq-t'á*	စတုတ္ထ

Money

The currency is the kyat (*caq*, ကျပ်) which is divided into 100 (*pyà*, ပြား). As in most languages, there are special words for some coins as well; but coins have now disappeared from circulation. Note that for round amounts of money (10, 100, 1000 and so on) one should use *ngwe* (literally silver) before the round number, not *caq* after.

1 kyat note	*tăjaq-tan*	တစ်ကျပ်တန်
5 kyat note	*ngà-jaq-dan*	ငါးကျပ်တန်
10 kyat note	*ngwe tăs'eh-dan*	ငွေတစ်ဆယ်တန်
15 kyat note	*s'éh-ngà-jaq-tan*	ဆယ့်ငါးကျပ်တန်
20 kyat note	*hnăs'eh-jaq-tan*	နှစ်ဆယ်ကျပ်တန်

45 kyat note	*lè-zéh-ngà-jaq-tan*	လေးဆယ့်ငါးကျပ်တန်
50 kyat note	*ngà-zéh-jaq-tan*	ငါးဆယ့်ကျပ်တန်
90 kyat note	*kò-zéh-tan*	ကိုးဆယ်တန်
100 kyat note	*tǎya-dan*	တစ်ရာတန်
200 kyat note	*hnǎya-dan*	နှစ်ရာတန်
500 kyat note	*ngà-ya-dan*	ငါးရာတန်
1000 kyat	*ngwe tǎt'aun*	ငွေတစ်ထောင်

Foreign exchange certificates (FECs) were introduced in 1993. While officially called *nain-ngan-gyà-ngwe-lèh-leq-hmaq* (နိုင်ငံခြားငွေလဲလှယ်လက်မှတ်) they are more commonly known as FEC (အက်ဖ်အီးစီး) or 'Burma dollar' (ဗမာ ဒေါ်လာ).

Some Useful Words

half	*tǎweq*	တစ်ဝက်
a third	*thòun-bóun-tǎboun*	သုံးပုံတစ်ပုံ
a quarter	*lè-bóun-tǎboun/dǎzeiq*	လေးပုံတစ်ပုံ/တစ်စိတ်
five-eighths	*shiq-póun ngà-boun*	ရှစ်ပုံငါးပုံ
pair	*yan/soun/zoun*	ရန်/စုံ
dozen	*da-zin*	ဒါဇင်
count	*ye-deh*	ရေတွယ်
zero	*thoun-nyá*	သုည

Vocabulary

A

able, to be (can) (see also page 25)	... *nain* ...	... နိုင် ...
I can't do it.	*mălouq-nain-bù*	မလုပ်နိုင်ဘူး။
about (approx.)	... *lauq*	... လောက်
above (on top of)	*ăpaw-hma*	အပေါ်မှာ
abroad	*nain-ngan-jà-hma*	နိုင်ငံခြားမှာ
accept	*leq-k'an-deh*	လက်ခံတယ်
accidentally	*mătaw-tăs'á*	မတော်တဆ
accommodation	*ne-ya*	နေရာ
addict (drug)	*swèh-ne-déh-lu*	စွဲနေတဲ့လူ
addiction (drug)	*s'è-swèh-da*	ဆေးစွဲတာ
address	*leiq-sa*	လိပ်စာ
administration	*ouq-c'ouq-c'ìn*	အုပ်ချုပ်ခြင်း
admission charge	*win-cè*	ဝင်ကြေး
admit, let in	*win-gwín pè-deh*	ဝင်ခွင့်ပေးတယ်
advice	*ăcan*	အကြံ
advise (v)	*ăcan pèi-deh*	အကြံပေးတယ်
afraid, be	*cauq-teh*	ကြောက်တယ်
after (with n)	... *nauq*	... နောက်
after (with v)	... *pì-dáw*	... ပြီးတော့
again (with v)	*pyan* ...	ပြန် ...
again (another time)	*nauq-tăk'a*	နောက်တစ်ခါ

128

age	*ătheq*	အသက်
agree	*thăbàw-tu-deh*	သဘောတူတယ်
agriculture	*saiq-pyò-yè*	စိုက်ပျိုးရေး
ahead	*shé*	ရှေ့
aid (n)	*ăku-ănyi*	အကူအညီ
air-conditioned	*le-è-seq shí-deh*	လေအေးစက် ရှိတယ်
airline	*le-yin-byan koun-pǎni*	လေယာဉ်ပျံကုမ္ပဏီ
airmail	*le-jàun-za-pó*	လေကြောင်းစာပို့
airport	*le-zeiq*	လေဆိပ်
alarm clock	*hnò-seq-na-yi*	နှိုးစက်နာရီ
alcoholic	*ăyeq-thămà*	အရက်သမား
all	*à-lòun*	အားလုံး
allow	*k'wín-pè-deh*	ခွင့်ပေးတယ်
almost	*lú-nì-nì*	လုနီးနီး
alone (of person)	*tăyauq-t'èh*	တစ်ယောက်ထည်း
also	*... lèh*	လည်း
always	*ămyèh*	အမြဲ
amazing	*án-áw-săya kaùn-deh*	အံ့ဩစရာ ကောင်းတယ်
ambassador	*than-ămaq-cì*	သံအမတ်ကြီး
ambulance	*lu-na-din-gà*	လူနာတင်ကား
among	*ăleh-hma*	အလယ်မှာ
ancient	*shè-hàun-deh*	ရှေးဟောင်းတယ်
and (n + n)	*... néh*	noun + နဲ့
and (v + v)	*... lèh*	verb + လည်း
angry	*seiq-s'ò-deh*	စိတ်ဆိုးတယ်
animal	*dăreiq-s'an*	တိရစ္ဆာန်

answer (n)	ăp'ye	အဖြေ
answer (v)	p'ye-deh	ဖြေတယ်
ant	păyweq-s'eiq	ပရွက်ဆိတ်
antique	shè-hàun-pyiq-sì	ရှေးဟောင်း ပစ္စည်း
appointment	c'èin-t'à-da	ချိန်းထားတာ
approximately	... lauq	... လောက်
archaeology	shè-hàun-pyiq-sì lé-la-yè	ရှေဟောင်းပစ္စည်း လေ့လာရေး
argue	săgà-myà-deh	စကားများတယ်
army (Burmese)	taq-mădaw	တပ်မတော်
army (forces)	siq-taq	စစ်တပ်
arrest (v)	p'àn-deh	ဖမ်းတယ်
arrested	ăp'àn-k'an-yá-deh	အဖမ်းခံရတယ်
arrive	yauq-teh	ရောက်တယ်
art	ănú-pyin-nya	အနုပညာ
ashtray	s'è-leiq-pya-gweq	ဆေးလိပ်ပြာခွက်
ask	mè-deh	မေးတယ်
asleep	eiq-ne-deh	အိပ်နေတယ်
astrologer	bădin-s'ăya	ဗေဒင်ဆရာ
asylum (political)	k'o-hloun-gwín	ခိုလှုံ ခွင့်
at	... hma	... မှာ
aunt	ădaw	အဒေါ်
automatically	ălo-lo	အလိုလို

B

baby	kălè	ကလေး
babysitter, nanny	kălè-t'èin	ကလေးထိန်း
backpack	càw-pò-eiq	ကျောပိုး အိတ်

bad	s'ò-deh	ဆိုးတယ်
bag	eiq	အိတ်
baggage	tiq-ta/pyiq-sì	သေတ္တာ/ ပစ္စည်း
ball	bàw-lòun	ဘောလုံး
Bangladesh	bìngălà-desh	ဘင်္ဂလားဒက်ရှ်
Bangkok	ban-gauq	ဘန်ကောက်
bank	ban-daiq	ဘဏ်တိုက်
bar (place to drink)	ăyeq-s'ain	အရက်ဆိုင်
barbershop	zăbin-hnyaq-s'ain	ဆံပင်ညှပ်ဆိုင်
basket	chìn-dàun	ခြင်းတောင်း
bat (flying)	lìn-nó	လင်းနို့
battery	beq-t'ări	ဘက်ထရီ
be (see page 27)		
be born	mwè-deh	မွေးတယ်
beach	pin-leh-gàn-je	ပင်လယ်ကမ်းခြေ
beard	mouq-s'eiq	မုတ်ဆိတ်
beautiful	hlá-deh	လှတယ်
because (+ v)	... ló	... လို့
because (+ n)	... mó-ló	... မို့လို့
bed	eiq-ya/gădin	အိပ်ရာ/ ခုတင်
bedbug	jăbò	ကြမ်းပိုး
before (+ v)	mă ... k'in/gin	မ ... ခင်
beggar	dhădàun-sà	သူတောင်းစား
begging bowl (of monk)	dhă-beiq	သပိတ်
behind	... nauq	... နောက်
bell	k'aùn-laùn	ခေါင်းလောင်း
below	... auq	... အောက်
beside	năbè-hma	နံဘေးမှာ

best	*ăkàun-zòun*	အကောင်းဆုံး
bet	*làun-găsà-deh*	လောင်းကစားတယ်
better	*po-kàun-deh*	ပိုကောင်းတယ်
between	*... cà*	... ကြား
Bible	*k'ăriq-yan-thăma-càn*	ခရစ်ယာန်သမ္မာကျမ်း
bicycle	*seq-bèin*	စက်ဘီး
big	*cì-deh*	ကြီးတယ်
bill (account)	*ngwe-dàun-hlwa*	ငွေတောင်းလွှာ
bill (banknote)	*ngwe-seq-ku*	ငွေစက္ကူ
bird	*hngeq*	ငှက်
birthday	*mwè-né*	မွေးနေ့
bitter	*k'à-deh*	ခါးတယ်
bless (v)	*s'ú-pè-deh*	ဆုပေးတယ်
blind	*myeq-sí-kàn-ne-deh*	မျက်စိကန်းနေတယ်
boat (large)	*thin-bàw*	သင်္ဘော
boat (small)	*hle*	လှေ
body	*ko-k'an-da*	ကိုယ်ခန္ဓာ
bone	*ăyò*	အရိုး
bomb	*bòun*	ဗုံး
'Bon Appetit!'	*thòun-s'aun-ba*	သုံးဆောင်ပါ
book (n)	*sa-ouq*	စာအုပ်
bookshop	*sa-ouq-s'ain*	စာအုပ်ဆိုင်
bored, I'm	*pyìn-deh*	ပြင်းတယ်
borrow	*hngà-deh*	ငှါးတယ်
May I borrow this?	*èh-da hngà-ló yá-là?*	အဲဒါငှါးလို့ရလား။
boss (owner)	*ălouq-shin*	အလုပ်ရှင်
both	*hnă ... sălòun*	နှစ် ... စလုံး

bottle	*bălìn*	ပုလင်း
bottle opener	*bălìn p'auq-dan*	ပုလင်းဖေါက်တန်
box (container)	*tiq-ta/bù*	သေတ္တာ/ဘူး
boxing	*leq-hwé*	လက်ဝှေ့
boy	*kaun-lè*	ကောင်လေး
boyfriend	*yì-zà*	ရည်းစား
bracelet	*leq-kauq*	လက်ကောက်
brave	*yèh-deh*	ရဲတယ်
break (v; snap)	*cò-deh*	ကျိုးတယ်
break, rest (n)	*yaq-nà-jein*	ရပ်နားချိန်
breakfast	*mǎneq-sa*	မနက်စာ
breathe	*ǎtheq-shu-deh*	အသက်ရှူတယ်
bribe (v)	*laq-pè-deh*	လာဘ်ပေးတယ်
bridge	*dǎdà*	တံတား
bright (shiny)	*tauq-teh*	တောက်တယ်
bright (clever)	*t'eq-teh*	ထက်တယ်
bring	*yu-deh*	ယူတယ်
Can you bring it?	*èh-da yu-ló-yá-là?*	အဲဒါယူလို့ရလား။
We can bring one.	*tǎk'ú yu-nain-meh*	တစ်ခုယူနိုင်မယ်။
broken	*pyeq-thwà-bi*	ပျက်သွားပြီ
broom	*dǎbyeq-sì*	တံမျက်စည်း
bucket	*ye-bòun*	ရေပုံး
Buddha image	*p'ǎyà-s'ìn-dú-daw*	ဘုရားဆင်းတုတော်
building	*ǎs'auq-ǎ-oùn*	အဆောက်အအုံ
bull	*nǎthò*	နွားသိုး
burn (v)	*mì-tauq-laun-deh*	မီးတောက်လောင်တယ်
bus	*baq-sǎkà*	ဘတ်စ်ကား
bush	*c'oun-bouq*	ချုံပုတ်
business (company)	*louq-ngàn*	လုပ်ငန်း

business (trade)	sì-bwà-yè	စီးပွားရေး
busy	ălouq-myà-deh	အလုပ်များတယ်
but	da-be-méh	ဒါပေမဲ့
buy	weh-deh	ဝယ်တယ်

C

café	lăp'eq-yeh-zain	လက်ဖက်ရည်ဆိုင်
Calcutta	ka-la-kaq-tà	ကာလကတ္တား
camera	kin-măra	ကင်မရာ
camp (n)	săk'àn	စခန်း
camp (v)	săk'àn c'á-deh	စခန်းချတယ်
Can we camp here?	di-hma săk'àn c'á-ló-yá-là?	ဒီမှာ စခန်းချလို့ရလား။
can (v; physically able, see also pp 25 & 128)	... nain ...	... နိုင် ...
can (v; know)	... taq/daq...	... တတ် ...
Can you speak English?	ìn-găleiq-săgà pyàw-daq-thălà?	အင်္ဂလိပ်စကား ပြောတတ်သလား။
can (v; permissible)	yá-deh	ရတယ်
Can I take a photograph?	daq-poun yaiq-ló-yá-dhălà?	ဓါတ်ပုံရိုက်လို့ရသလား။
You can't do it.	măyá-bù	မရဘူး။
can (tin)	bù	ဘူး
can opener	bù-p'wín-seq	ဘူးဖွင့်စက်
candle	p'ăyàun-dain	ဖယောင်းတိုင်
capital city	myó-daw	မြို့တော်
capitalism	ăyìn-shin-săniq	အရင်းရှင်စနစ်

cards (playing)	*p'èh*	ဖဲ
care (about/for)	*gắyú saiq-teh*	ဂရုစိုက်တယ်
careful (v)	*dhădi t'à-deh*	သတိထားတယ်
carry	*theh-deh*	သယ်တယ်
I'll carry it for you.	*cănaw/cămá theh-pè-meh*	ကျွန်တော်/ကျွန်မ သယ်ပေးမယ်။
cashier	*ngwe-gain*	ငွေကိုင်
cave	*gu*	ဂူ
cemetery	*thìn-gyàin*	သင်္ချိုင်း
certain/sure	*the-ja-deh*	သေချာတယ်
Are you sure?	*the-ja-yéh-là*	သေချာရဲ့လား။
chance, by	*mătaw-tăs'á*	မတော်တဆ
chair	*kălăt'ain*	ကုလားထိုင်
change (money, clothes)	*lèh-deh*	လဲတယ်
change (trains, state)	*pyàun-deh*	ပြောင်းတယ်
cheap	*zè-pàw-deh*	ဈေးပေါတယ်
chemist (pharmacy)	*s'è-zain*	ဆေးဆိုင်
Chiangmai	*zìn-meh*	ဇင်းမယ်
child	*kălè*	ကလေး
choose	*ywè-deh*	ရွေးတယ်
Christmas	*k'ăriq-sămá pwèh-daw*	ခရစ္စမတ်ပွဲတော်
cigarettes	*sì-găreq*	စီးကရက်
citizen	*ămyò-dhà*	အမျိုးသား
city	*myó*	မြို့
clean	*thán-shìn-deh*	သန့်ရှင်းတယ်
close (nearby)	*di-nà-hma*	ဒီနားမှာ

close (shut)	*peiq-deh*	ပိတ်တယ်
It's shut.	*peiq-t'à-deh*	ပိတ်ထားတယ်॥
clothes	*ăwuq-ăsa*	အဝတ်အစား
cold (cool)	*è-deh*	အေးတယ်
colonel	*bo-hmù-jì*	ဗိုလ်မှူးကြီး
come	*la-deh*	လာတယ်
It's coming.	*la-ne-bi*	လာနေပြီ॥
Can we come	*măneq-p'yan*	မနက်ဖြန် လာရင်
tomorrow?	*la-yin yá-mălà?*	ရမလား॥
comfortably	*theq-táun-theq-tha*	သက်သောင့်သက်သာ
communism	*kun-myu-niq-săniq*	ကွန်မြူနစ်စနစ်
company	*koun-păni*	ကုမ္ပဏီ
complex (adj)	*shouq-teh*	ရှုပ်တယ်
compound (garden)	*wìn*	ဝင်း
computer	*kun-pyu-ta*	ကွန်ပျူတာ
condom	*kun-dun*	ကွန်ဒုန်
constipated	*wùn-c'ouq-teh*	ဝမ်းချုပ်တယ်
contact lens	*myeq-sí- kaq-*	မျက်စိကပ်မျက်မှန်
	myeq-hman	
contagious	*kù-seq-taq-teh*	ကူးစက်တတ်တယ်
contraceptive (pill)	*tà-s'è*	တားဆေး
convenient	*ăs'in pye-deh*	အဆင်ပြေတယ်
conversation	*săgà-pyàw-da*	စကားပြောတာ
cook (v)	*c'eq-teh*	ချက်တယ်
I like cooking.	*c'eq-yá-pyouq-*	ချက်ရပြုတ်ရတာ
	yá-da caiq-teh	ကြိုက်တယ်॥
copy	*kù-deh*	ကူးတယ်
corner	*t'áun/dáun*	ထောင့်
corrupt (adj)	*laq-sà-deh*	လာဘ်စားတယ်

corruption	*laq-pè-laq-yu*	လာဘ်ပေးလာဘ်ယူ
cost	*cá-deh*	ကျတယ်
How much does it cost?	*beh-lauq-cá-lèh?*	ဘယ်လောက်ကျလဲ။
count (v)	*ye-deh*	ရေတယ်
crazy	*yù-deh*	ရူးတယ်
credit card	*ngwe-t'ouq-kaq-pyà*	ငွေထုပ်ကပ်ပြား
crop	*kauq-pèh-thì-hnan*	ကောက်ပဲသီးနှံ
cross (angry)	*seiq-s'ò-deh*	စိတ်ဆိုးတယ်
culture	*yin-jè-hmú*	ယဉ်ကျေးမှု
curtain	*tìn-dein/kǎlǎga/ k'àn-zì*	တင်းတိမ်/ကုလားကာ/ ခန်းစည်း
customs (officials)	*ăkauq-k'un ăhmú-dàn*	အကောက်ခွန် အမှုထမ်း
cut (v; tree)	*k'ouq-teh*	ခုတ်တယ်
cut (v; paper)	*p'yaq-teh*	ဖြတ်တယ်

D

daily	*né-dàin*	နေ့တိုင်း
damp	*so-t'àin-deh*	စိုထိုင်းတယ်
dance	*ká-deh*	ကတယ်
dangerous	*an-dǎyeh shí-deh*	အန္တရာယ်ရှိတယ်
dark (sky)	*hmaun-deh*	မှောင်တယ်
date (time)	*yeq-swèh*	ရက်စွဲ
daughter	*thǎmì*	သမီး
dawn	*ăyoun*	အရုဏ်
day	*né*	နေ့
dead	*the-thwà-bi*	သေသွားပြီ

deaf	*nà pìn-deh*	နားပင်းတယ်
decide	*s'òun-p'yaq-teh*	ဆုံးဖြတ်တယ်
decision	*s'òun-p'yaq-c'eq*	ဆုံးဖြတ်ချက်
delicious	*ăyá-dha-shí-deh*	အရသာရှိတယ်
democracy	*di-mo-kăre-si*	ဒီမိုကရေစီ
demonstration	*s'an-dá-pyá-bwè*	ဆန္ဒပြပွဲ
depart (leave)	*t'weq-deh*	ထွက်တယ်
The plane departs at ...	*le-yin-byan ... hma t'weq-ba-deh*	လေယာဉ်ပျံ ... မှာ ထွက်ပါတယ်။
What time does it leave?	*beh-ăc'ein t'weq-dhălèh?*	ဘယ်အချိန် ထွက်သလဲ။
departure	*t'weq-ta*	ထွက်တာ
deposit (v)	*aq-t'à-deh*	အပ်ထားတယ်
destroy	*p'yeq-s'ì-deh*	ဖျက်ဆီးတယ်
development	*tò-teq-hmú*	တိုးတက်မှု
dictatorship	*a-na-shin săniq*	အာဏာရှင်စနစ်
dictionary	*ăbí-dan*	အဘိဓာန်
die	*the-thwà-deh*	သေသွားတယ်
different	*kwèh-deh*	ကွဲတယ်
It is different. (not the same)	*mătubù*	မတူဘူး
difficult	*k'eq-teh*	ခက်တယ်
dinner (evening)	*nyá-za*	ညစာ
diplomat	*than-tăman*	သံတမန်
dirt	*ănyiq-ăcè*	အညစ်အကြေး
dirty	*nyiq-paq-teh*	ညစ်ပတ်တယ်
disadvantage	*măkàun-déh-ăc'eq*	မကောင်းတဲ့အချက်
disagree	*thăbàw mătu-bù*	သဘောမတူဘူး
discount (v)	*zè-sháw-deh*	ဈေးလျှော့တယ်

discrimination	*k'wèh-c'à-da*	ခွဲခြားတာ
distant	*wè-deh*	ဝေးတယ်
divorce	*kwa-shìn-deh /*	ကွာရှင်းတယ်/
	pyaq-sèh-deh	ပြတ်စဲတယ်
do	*louq-teh*	လုပ်တယ်
I'll do it.	*cănaw/cămá*	ကျွန်တော်/ကျွန်မ
	louq-meh	လုပ်မယ်။
doctor	*s'ăya-wun*	ဆရာဝန်
doll	*kălè găzà-săya*	ကလေးကစားစရာ
	ăyouq	အရုပ်
down	*auq-ko*	အောက်ကို
downstairs	*auq-t'aq-hma*	အောက်ထပ်မှာ
downtown	*myó-leh-gaun*	မြို့လယ်ခေါင်
dream (v)	*eiq-meq-teh*	အိပ်မက်တယ်
dried/dry	*c'auq*	ခြောက်
drink (v)	*thauq-teh*	သောက်တယ်
drink (n)	*thauq-săya*	သောက်စရာ
drinkable water	*thauq-ye*	သောက်ရေ
drive (vehicle)	*màun-deh*	မောင်းတယ်
drought	*mò k'aun-deh*	မိုးခေါင်တယ်
drugs (medicine)	*băyá-s'è*	ပရဆေး
drugs (narcotics)	*mù-yiq-s'è-wà*	မူးယစ်ဆေးဝါး
drum	*boun*	ဗုံ
drums (round rack)	*s'àin-wain*	ဆိုင်းဝိုင်
drunk (inebriated)	*ăyeq-mù-deh*	အရက်မူးတယ်
dust	*p'oun*	ဖုံ
dustbin	*ăhmaiq-poun*	အမှိုက်ပုံ
duty (customs)	*ăkauq-k'un*	အကောက်ခွန်
duty (obligation)	*wuq-tăyà*	ဝတ္တရား

dye (v)	*s'ò-deh*	ဆိုးတယ်
dye (n)	*s'ò-s'è*	ဆိုးဆေး

E

each (thing)	*tăk'ú-zi*	တစ်ခုစီ
each (person)	*tăyauq-si*	တစ်ယောက်စီ
early (adv)	*sàw-zàw*	စောစော
earnings, income	*win-ngwe*	ဝင်ငွေ
Earth	*kăba-mye*	ကမ္ဘာမြေ
earthquake	*mye-ngălyin*	မြေငလျင်
easy	*lweh-deh*	လွယ်တယ်
eat	*sà-deh*	စားတယ်
economical	*zè-măcì-bù*	ဈေးမကြီးဘူး
economy	*sì-bwà-yè*	စီးပွားရေး
education	*pyin-nya-yè*	ပညာရေး
election	*ywè-kauq-pwèh*	ရွေးကောက်ပွဲ
electricity, electrical	*hlyaq-siq*	လျှပ်စစ်
elevator (lift)	*daq-hle-gà*	ဓာတ်လှေကား
embassy	*than-yòun*	သံရုံး
employer	*ălouq-shin*	အလုပ်ရှင်
empty (finished)	*koun-thwà-bi*	ကုန်သွားပြီ
end (v)	*pì-s'òun-deh*	ပြီးဆုံးတယ်
'The End'	*pì-bi*	ပြီးပြီ
energy	*sùn-à*	စွမ်းအား
English	*ìn-găleiq*	အင်္ဂလိပ်
enjoy (oneself)	*pyaw-deh*	ပျော်တယ်
enough	*lauq-teh*	လောက်တယ်
enter	*win-deh*	ဝင်တယ်

entrance	*win-bauq*	ဝင်ပေါက်
envelope	*sa-eiq*	စာအိတ်
equal	*tu-nyi-deh*	တူညီတယ်
especially	*ăt'ù-dhăp'yín*	အထူးသဖြင့်
ethnic minority	*tain-yìn-dhà-lu-myò*	တိုင်းရင်းသားလူမျိုး
evening	*nyá-ne*	ညနေ
event	*p'yiq-yaq*	ဖြစ်ရပ်
every	*... tàin/dàin*	... တိုင်း
every day	*né-dàin*	နေ့တိုင်း
everyone	*lu-dàin*	လူတိုင်း
everything	*à-lòun*	အားလုံး
exchange (v)	*lèh-hleh-deh*	လဲလှယ်တယ်
exhausted	*màw-deh*	မောတယ်
exile	*pye-pyè*	ပြည်ပြေး
exit	*t'weq-pauq*	ထွက်ပေါက်
expensive	*zè-cì-deh*	ဈေးကြီးတယ်
experience	*ătwéh-ăcoun*	အတွေ့အကြုံ
explain	*shìn-pyá-deh*	ရှင်းပြတယ်
export (v)	*nain-ngan-gyà-ko*	နိုင်ငံခြားကို
	tin-pó-deh	တင်ပို့ တယ်

F

false, wrong	*hmà-deh*	မှားတယ်
family	*mí-dhà-zú*	မိသားစု
fan (hand-held)	*yaq-taun*	ယပ်တောင်
fan (ceiling)	*pan-ka*	ပန်ကာ
far	*wè-deh*	ဝေးတယ်
farm (n; other than paddy)	*ya*	ယာ

farm (n; paddy)	*leh*	လယ်
farm (v)	*leh-louq-deh/*	လယ်လုပ်တယ်/
	ya-louq-deh	ယာလုပ်တယ်
fast (not eat)	*ú-bouq sáun-deh*	ဥပုသ်စောင့်တယ်
fast (quick)	*myan-deh*	မြန်တယ်
fat (adj)	*wá-deh*	ဝတယ်
fault	*ăpyiq*	အပြစ်
fee	*ăk'á-cè-ngwe*	အခကြေးငွေ
feel (v; touch)	*t'í-deh*	ထိတယ်
feeling (sentiment)	*k'an-zà-hmú*	ခံစားမှု
ferry	*gădó*	ကူးတို့
festival	*pwèh*	ပွဲ
fever, to have a	*p'yà-deh*	ဖျားတယ်
few	*nèh-deh*	နည်းတယ်
fiancé/ée	*sé-saq-t'à-déh-lu*	စေ့စပ်ထားတဲ့လူ
film (movie)	*youq-shin-kà*	ရုပ်ရှင်ကား
film (roll of)	*daq-poun p'ălin*	ဓာတ်ပုံဖလင်
fine (penalty)	*dan-ngwe*	ဒဏ်ငွေ
finger	*leq-c'àun*	လက်ချောင်း
fingernail	*leq-thèh*	လက်သည်း
finish	*pì-deh*	ပြီးတယ်
fire	*mì*	မီး
firewood	*t'in*	ထင်း
flag	*ălan*	အလံ
flashlight (torch)	*leq-hneiq-daq-mì*	လက်နှိပ်ဓာတ်မီး
flat (apartment)	*ein-gàn*	အိမ်ခန်း
flat (level)	*pyà-deh*	ပြားတယ်
flavour	*ăyădha*	အရသာ
flea, louse	*thàn*	သန်း

flip-flops	*pănaq*	ဘိနပ်
flood (v)	*ye-jì-deh*	ရေကြီးတယ်
floor (1st, 2nd)	*ăt'aq*	အထပ်
floor	*càn-byin*	ကြမ်းပြင်
flour (wheat)	*joun-móun*	ဂျုံမုန့်
flower	*pàn*	ပန်း
fly (bird)	*pyan-deh*	ပျံတယ်
fly (go by plane)	*le-yin-byan-néh*	လေယာဉ်ပျံနဲ့သွားတယ်
	thwà-deh	
fly (insect)	*yin-kaun*	ယင်ကောင်
follow	*laiq-teh*	လိုက်တယ်
food	*ăsà-ăsa*	အစားအစာ
food poisoning	*ăsa-ăs'eiq-thín-deh*	အစာအဆိပ်သင့်တယ်
foreign	*nain-ngan-jà*	နိုင်ငံခြား
foreigner	*nain-ngan-jà-thà*	နိုင်ငံခြားသား
forever	*ăsin*	အစဉ်
forget (v)	*mé-deh*	မေ့တယ်
I've forgotten.	*cănaw/cămá*	ကျွန်တော်/ကျွန်မ
	mé-thwà-bi	မေ့သွားပြီ။
forgive	*k'wín-hluq-teh*	ခွင့်လွှတ်တယ်
formal	*t'òun-zan ătàin*	ထုံးစံအတိုင်း
fragile (things)	*kwèh-lweh-deh*	ကွဲလွယ်တယ်
free (of charge)	*ălăgà/ăk'á-méh*	အလကား/အခမဲ့
free (not bound)	*luq-laq-teh*	လွတ်လပ်တယ်
free (release)	*hluq-teh*	လွှတ်တယ်
freeze	*k'èh-deh*	ခဲတယ်
fresh (not stale)	*laq-teh*	လတ်တယ်
friend	*thăngeh-jìn*	သူငယ်ချင်း
friendly	*k'in-daq-teh*	ခင်တတ်တယ်

full	*pyé-deh*	ပြည့်တယ်
fun	*ăpyaw-ăpà*	အပျော်အပါး
funny	*yi-zăya kàun-deh*	ရယ်စရာ ကောင်းတယ်

G

game	*găzà-bwèh*	ကစားပွဲ
garbage	*ăhmaiq*	အမှိုက်
garden	*ú-yin*	ဥယျာဉ်
gas	*daq-ngwé*	ဓါတ်ငွေ့
gas cylinder	*daq-ngwé-ò*	ဓါတ်ငွေ့ အိုး
gate	*dăgà-bauq*	တံခါးပေါက်
generous	*yeq-yàw-deh*	ရက်ရောတယ်
genuine, real	*siq-teh*	စစ်တယ်
girl	*mèin-kălè*	မိန်းကလေး
girlfriend	*yì-zà*	ရည်းစား
give	*pè-deh*	ပေးတယ်
Give me ...	*cănaw/cămá-go*	ကျွန်တော်/ကျွန်မကို
	... pè-ba	... ပေးပါ။
glass (of water)	*ye-p'an-gweq*	ရေဖန်ခွက်
glasses	*myeq-hman*	မျက်မှန်
go	*thwà-deh*	သွားတယ်
Are you going there?	*ho-beq thwà-mălà?*	ဟိုဘက် သွားမလား။
I won't go today.	*di-né măthwà-bù*	ဒီနေ့.မသွားဘူး။
God	*p'ăyà thăk'in*	ဘုရားသခင်
good	*kàun-deh*	ကောင်းတယ်
government	*ăsò-yá*	အစိုးရ

grandchild	*myè*	မြေး
grandfather	*ăp'ò*	အဘိုး
grandmother	*ăp'wà*	အဘွား
greedy	*làw-bá cì-deh*	လောဘကြီးတယ်
grow up (v)	*cì-t'wà-deh*	ကြီးထွားတယ်
guard (v)	*sáun-deh*	စောင့်တယ်
guard (n)	*ăsáun*	အစောင့်
guess (v)	*hmàn-s'á-deh*	မှန်းဆတယ်
guest	*éh-dheh*	ဧည့်သည်
guide (n)	*làn-hnyun*	လမ်းညွှန်
guidebook	*làn-hnyun sa-ouq*	လမ်းညွှန်စာအုပ်
guilty	*ăpyiq shí-deh*	အပြစ်ရှိတယ်
guitar	*giq-ta*	ဂစ်တာ
gun	*thănaq*	သေနတ်

H

hair (of body)/fur	*ămwè*	အမွေး
hair (of head)	*zăbin*	ဆံပင်
half	*tăweq*	တစ်ဝက်
hand	*leq*	လက်
handbag	*leq-s'wèh-eiq*	လက်ဆွဲအိတ်
handicrafts	*leq-hmú-pyiq-sì*	လက်မှုပစ္စည်း
handsome	*c'àw-màw-deh*	ချောမောတယ်
happy	*pyaw-deh*	ပျော်တယ်
hard (not soft)	*k'ain-ma-deh*	ခိုင်မာတယ်
hard (not easy)	*k'eq-teh*	ခက်တယ်
hat	*ouq-t'ouq*	ဦးထုပ်

hate (v)	*mòun-tì-deh*	မုန်းတီးတယ်
have (see pg 28)	*shí-deh*	ရှိတယ်
I have ...	*... shí-ba-deh*	... ရှိပါတယ်
Have you (got) ... ?	*... shí-dhǎlà?*	... ရှိသလား။
health	*càn-ma-yè*	ကျန်းမာရေး
hear	*cà-deh*	ကြားတယ်
heat	*pu-da*	ပူတာ
heater	*ǎpu-pè-seq*	အပူပေးစက်
heavy	*lè-deh*	လေးတယ်
Hello!	*min-gǎla-ba*	မင်္ဂလာပါ။
help (v)	*ku-nyi-deh*	ကူညီတယ်
Can I help?	*ku-nyi-ba-ze?*	ကူညီပါစေ
Help!	*keh-ba*	ကယ်ပါ။
here	*di-hma*	ဒီမှာ
heroin	*bein-byu/'Number 4'*	ဘိန်းဖြူ/နံဘတ်ဖိုး
high	*myín-deh*	မြင့်တယ်
hill	*taun-gòun*	တောင်ကုန်း
hire	*hngà-deh*	ငှါးတယ်
I'd like to hire ...	*... hngà-jin-deh*	... ငှါးချင်တယ်။
history	*thǎmàin*	သမိုင်း
historical	*thǎmàin-win-deh*	သမိုင်းဝင်တယ်
hit	*yaiq-teh*	ရိုက်တယ်
hitchhike	*ǎk'á-méh kà-coun-sì-deh*	အခမဲ့ ကားကြီးစီးတယ်
holiday (day off)	*à-laq-yeq*	အားလပ်ရက်
holy	*myín-myaq-teh*	မြင့်မြတ်တယ်
home	*ein*	အိမ်
homeland	*mí-mí-tàin-pye*	မိမိတိုင်းပြည်

homosexual	*lein-tu chiq-téh-lu /*	လိင်တူချစ်တဲ့လူ/
	mèin-má-sha	မိန်းမရှာ
honest	*yò-thà-deh*	ရိုးသားတယ်
hope (v)	*hmyaw-lín-deh*	မျှော်လင့်တယ်
hope (n)	*hmyaw-lín-jeq*	မျှော်လင့်ချက်
horse	*myìn*	မြင်း
hospitality	*éh-wuq*	ဧည့်ဝတ်
hospital	*s'è-youn*	ဆေးရုံ
hot (temperature)	*pu-deh*	ပူတယ်
hot (spicy)	*saq-deh*	စပ်တယ်
hotel	*haw-teh*	ဟော်တယ်
hour	*na-yi*	နာရီ
house	*ein*	အိမ်
housework	*ein ălouq*	အိမ်အလုပ်
how	*beh-lo*	ဘယ်လို
How do I get to ...?	*... go beh-lo thwà-yá-mălèh?*	... ကို ဘယ်လို သွားရမလဲ။
How much is ...?	*... beh-lauq-lèh?*	... ဘယ်လောက်လဲ။
How are you?	*ne-kàun-yéh-là?*	နေကောင်းရဲ့လား။
How? (in what way?)	*beh-lo-lèh?*	ဘယ်လိုလဲ။
humanity	*lu-dhà*	လူသား
human rights	*lu-ăk'wín-ăyè*	လူ့အခွင့်အရေး
hungry	*baiq s'a-deh*	ဗိုက်ဆာတယ်
I'm hungry.	*cănaw/cămá baiq s'a-ba-deh*	ကျွန်တော်/ကျွန်မ ဗိုက်ဆာပါတယ်
Are you hungry?	*baiq s'a-yéh-là?*	ဗိုက်ဆာရဲ့လား။
hurriedly	*ăyin-zălo*	အလျင်စလို
hurt (pain)	*na-deh*	နာတယ်
husband	*yauq-cà*	ယောကျ်ား

I

ice	ye-gèh	ရေခဲ
idea	seiq-kù	စိတ်ကူး
identity card	hmaq-poun-tin	မှတ်ပုံတင်
if	... yin	... ရင်
ill	ne-măkaùn-bù	နေမကောင်းဘူး
illegal	ú-băde-néh mănyi-bù	ဥပဒေနဲ့မညီဘူး
imagine	seiq-kù-deh	စိတ်ကူးတာ
immediately	c'eq-c'ìn	ချက်ချင်း
imitate	tú-pá-deh	တုပတယ်
import (v)	tin-thwìn-deh	တင်သွင်းတယ်
important	ăyè-jì-deh	အရေးကြီးတယ်
impossible (no chance)	măp'yiq-nain-bù	မဖြစ်နိုင်ဘူး။
imprisonment	t'aun-c'á-da	ထောင်ချတာ
in	... hma	... မှာ
included, be	pa-deh	ပါတယ်
inconvenient	ăs'in măthín-bù	အဆင်မသင့်ဘူး
industry	seq-hmú-louq-ngàn	စက်မှုလုပ်ငန်း
infectious	kù-seq-taq-teh	ကူးစက်တတ်တယ်
informal	sì-kàn-măcì-bù	စည်းကမ်းမကြီးဘူး။
information	dhădìn	သတင်း
inject (medicine)	s'è t'ò-deh	ဆေးထိုးတယ်
injury	dan	ဒဏ်
insecticide	pò thaq-s'è	ပိုးသတ်ဆေး
inside	ătwìn	အတွင်း
insurance	a-má-k'an	အာမခံ
It's insured.	a-má-k'an shí-deh	အာမခံရှိတယ်

intelligent	*ăthi-nyan shí-deh*	အသိဉာဏ်ရှိတယ်
interested, be	*seiq-win-sà-deh*	စိတ်ဝင်စားတယ်
interesting	*seiq-win-sà-săya kaùn-deh*	စိတ်ဝင်စားစရာ ကောင်းတယ်
international	*nain-ngan-dăga*	နိုင်ငံတကာ
interpreter	*zăgăbyan*	စကားပြန်
introduce	*meiq-s'eq pè-deh*	မိတ်ဆက်ပေးတယ်
invite (v)	*p'eiq-teh/k'aw-deh*	ဖိတ်တယ်/ခေါ်တယ်
iron (metal)	*than*	သံ
iron (for clothes)	*mì-bu*	မီးပူ
iron (v)	*mì-bu taiq-deh*	မီးပူတိုက်တယ်
island	*cùn*	ကျွန်း
itchy	*yà-deh*	ယားတယ်

J

jail	*ăcìn-daun*	အကျဉ်းထောင်
jazz	*jaz gi-tá*	ဂျတ်ဇီကီတ
jeans	*jìn-bàun-bi*	ဂျင်းဘောင်းဘီ
jewellery	*leq-wuq-leq-sà*	လက်ဝတ်လက်စား
job	*ălouq*	အလုပ်
joke (n)	*yi-săya*	ရယ်စရာ
joke (v)	*yi-săya pyàw-deh*	ရယ်စရာ ပြောတယ်
jump (v)	*k'oun-deh*	ခုန်တယ်
just (fair)	*tăyà-pa-deh*	တရားပါတယ်
justice/law	*tăyà-ú-băde*	တရားဥပဒေ

K

key	*tháw*	သော့
kill	*thaq-teh*	သတ်တယ်

kind, be	*cin-na-deh*	ကြင်နာတယ်
kind (type)	*ămyò-ăsà*	အမျိုးအစား
king	*băyin / mìn*	ဘုရင်/မင်း
kiss (v)	*nàn-deh*	နမ်းတယ်
kitchen	*mì-bo-jaun*	မီးဖိုချောင်
kite	*le-dăgun*	လေတံခွန်
knapsack	*càw-pò-eiq*	ကျောပိုးအိတ်
knee	*dù*	ဒူး
knife	*dà*	ဓါး
know	*thí-deh*	သိတယ်
I know him.	*thu-go thí-deh*	သူ့ကို သိတယ်။
I know that.	*èh-da thí-deh*	အဲဒါသိတယ်။
know (how to)	*... taq/daq ...*	... တတ် ...
I know how to dance.	*ká-taq-teh*	ကတတ်တယ်။

L

lake	*ain/kan*	အိုင်/ကန်
land	*mye*	မြေ
land (v; plane etc)	*s'aiq-teh*	ဆိုက်တယ်
language	*zăgà*	စကား
last, latest (adj)	*nauq-s'òun*	နောက်ဆုံး
late	*nauq-cá-deh*	နောက်ကျတယ်
laugh	*yi-deh*	ရယ်တယ်
laundry (shop)	*pìn-mìn-s'ain*	ပင်မင်းဆိုင်
law	*ú-bădeh*	ဥပဒေ
lawyer	*shé-ne*	ရှေ့နေ
laxative	*wùn-nouq-s'è*	ဝမ်းနုတ်ဆေး

lazy	*pyìn-deh*	ပျင်းတယ်
learn	*thin-deh*	သင်တယ်
leather	*thăye*	သားရေ
leave/depart	*t'weq-teh*	ထွက်တယ်
leave (behind)	*c'an-deh*	ချန်တယ်
left (not right)	*beh-beq*	ဘယ်ဘက်
leg/foot	*c'e-dauq*	ခြေထောက်
legal	*ú-băde-néh nyi-deh*	ဥပဒေနဲ့ ညီတယ်
less	*po-nèh-deh*	ပိုနည်းတယ်
letter	*sa*	စာ
letter (ABC etc)	*eq-k'ăya*	အက္ခရာ
library	*sa-cí-daiq*	စာကြည့်တိုက်
lie (not tell the truth)	*lein-nya-deh*	လိမ်ညာတယ်
lice	*thàn*	သန်း
lid	*ăp'oùn*	အဖုံး
life	*ătheq/băwá*	အသက်/ဘဝ
lift (elevator)	*daq-hle-gà*	ဓာတ်လှေကား
light (weight)	*páw-deh*	ပေါ့တယ်
light (colour)	*p'yáw-deh*	ဖျော့တယ်
light switch	*mì-k'ălouq*	မီးခလုပ်
lightning	*mò-jò*	မိုးကြိုး
like/similar	*tu-deh*	တူတယ်
like (v)	*caiq-teh*	ကြိုက်တယ်
line	*myìn-jàun*	မျဉ်းကြောင်း
lip	*hnouq-k'àn*	နှုတ်ခမ်း
listen	*nà-t'aun-deh*	နားထောင်တယ်
little (adj)	*ngeh-deh*	ငယ်တယ်
live (v)	*ne-deh*	နေတယ်

VOCABULARY

lock (n)	*tháw-gǎlauq*	သော့ခလောက်
long (adj)	*sheh-deh*	ရှည်တယ်
long ago (adv)	*shè-dòun-gá*	ရှေးတုန်းက
look at (v)	*cí-deh*	ကြည့်တယ်
look for (v)	*sha-deh*	ရှာတယ်
lose (item)	*pyauq-deh*	ပျောက်တယ်
lose (fail)	*shòun-deh*	ရှုံးတယ်
lost, It is	*pyauq-thwà-bi*	ပျောက်သွားပြီ
loud	*ceh-deh*	ကျယ်တယ်
love (v)	*c'iq-teh*	ချစ်တယ်
I love you.	*k'ǎmya/shin-go*	ခင်ဗျား/ရှင်ကို
	c'iq-teh	ချစ်တယ်။
lucky	*kan kàun-deh*	ကံကောင်းတယ်
lunch	*ne-leh-za*	နေ့လည်စာ

M

machine	*seq*	စက်
mad (crazy)	*yù-deh*	ရူးတယ်
major (army)	*bo-hmù*	ဗိုလ်မှူး
majority	*lu-myà-zú*	လူများစု
make	*louq-teh*	လုပ်တယ်
Did you make it	*ko-dain*	ကိုယ်တိုင်
yourself?	*louq-thǎlà?*	လုပ်သလား။
make a bed	*eiq-ya pyin-deh*	အိပ်ရာပြင်တယ်။
many	*ǎmyà-jì*	အများကြီး
map	*mye-boun*	မြေပုံ
marijuana	*s'è-c'auq*	ဆေးခြောက်
market	*zè*	ဈေး

marry	*leq-taq-teh*	လက်ထပ်တယ်
marriage	*ein-daun-yè*	အိမ်ထောင်ရေး
marriage ceremony	*min-găla s'aun*	မင်္ဂလာဆောင်
married	*ein-daun shí-bi*	အိမ်ထောင် ရှိပြီ
massage	*hneiq-deh*	နှိပ်တယ်
matches	*mì-jiq*	မီးခြစ်
matter, issue	*keiq-sá*	ကိစ္စ
It doesn't matter.	*keiq-sá-măshí-ba-bù*	ကိစ္စမရှိပါဘူး။
maybe	*p'yiq-léin-meh*	ဖြစ်လိမ့်မယ်
meet	*twéh-deh*	တွေ့တယ်
I'll meet you.	*k'ămyà/shin-néh*	ခင်ဗျား/ရှင်နဲ့
	twéh-meh	တွေ့မယ်။
mend	*pyin-deh*	ပြင်တယ်
message	*ăhma-zăgà*	အမှာစကား
middle, in the	*ăleh-hma*	အလယ်မှာ
mind (n)	*seiq*	စိတ်
minister (government)	*wun-jì*	ဝန်ကြီး
minority	*lu-nèh-zú*	လူနည်းစု
minute (time)	*măniq*	မိနစ်
miss (long for)	*lùn-deh /lwàn-deh*	လွမ်းတယ်
mistake, make a	*hmà-deh*	မှားတယ်
mix (v)	*yàw-deh*	ရောတယ်
modern	*kiq-paw-deh*	ခေတ်ပေါ်တယ်
monastery	*p'oun-jì-caùn*	ဘုန်းကြီးကျောင်း
money	*paiq-s'an*	ပိုက်ဆံ
monkey	*myauq*	မျောက်
monument	*ăt'èin-ăhmaq*	အထိမ်းအမှတ်
	cauq-tain	ကျောက်တိုင်
more (pl)	*po-myà-deh*	ပိုများတယ်

morning	*măneq*	မနက်
mosque	*băli*	ဗလီ
mosquito	*c'in*	ခြင်
mountain	*taun*	တောင်
mountaineering	*taun teq-ta*	တောင်တက်တာ
mouth	*băzaq*	ပါးစပ်
movie	*youq-shin-kà*	ရုပ်ရှင်ကား
mud	*shún*	ရွှံ့
museum	*pyá-daiq*	ပြတိုက်
music	*thăc'in*	သီချင်း

N

nail	*than-jaùn*	သံချောင်း
name (n)	*na-meh*	နာမည်
name, give a	*kin-mun taq-teh*	ကင်ပွန်းတပ်တယ်
narrow	*cìn-deh*	ကျဉ်းတယ်
national park	*ămyò-dhà-ú-yin*	အမျိုးသားဥယျာဉ်
nature/natural	*dhăba-wá*	သဘာဝ
near (adj)	*nà-deh*	နားတယ်
nearby (close)	*di-nà-hma*	ဒီနားမှာ
necessary (adj)	*măshí-măp'yiq-téh*	မရှိမဖြစ်တဲ့
need	*lo-jin-deh*	လိုချင်တယ်
neighbour	*ein-nì-jìn*	အိမ်နီးချင်း
neighbourhood	*yaq-kweq*	ရပ်ကွက်
never (in the past)	*tăk'a-hmá*	တစ်ခါမှ
never (in the future)	*beh-dáw-hmá*	ဘယ်တော့မှ
new	*thiq-teh*	သစ်တယ်
news	*thădìn*	သတင်း

newspaper	*thădìnza*	သတင်းစာ
next time	*nauq-tăk'a*	နောက်တစ်ခါ
nice (person)	*thăbàw kaùn-deh*	သဘော ကောင်းတယ်
night	*nyá*	ည
No.	*măhouq-pa-bù*	မဟုတ်ပါဘူး။
noise	*ăthan*	အသံ
noisy	*s'u-nyan-deh*	ဆူညံတယ်
none	*tăk'ú-hmá*	တစ်ခုမှ
normal	*poun-hman p'yiq-teh*	ပုံမှန် ဖြစ်တယ်
nothing	*ba-hmá*	ဘာမှ
not any more	*măp'yiq-táw-bù*	မဖြစ်တော့ဘူး။
not yet	*măp'yiq-thè-bù*	မဖြစ်သေးဘူး။
now	*ăk'ú*	အခု
nuclear energy	*ănú-myu daq-à*	အဏုမြူဓါတ်အား
nun	*thi-lá-shin*	သီလရှင်
nurse (n)	*thu-na-byú*	သူနာပြု
nut	*thiq-sí*	သစ်စေ့

O

obvious	*t'in-shà-deh*	ထင်ရှားတယ်
occasionally	*tăk'a-tăk'a*	တစ်ခါတစ်ခါ
occupation	*ălouq*	အလုပ်
ocean, sea	*pin-leh*	ပင်လယ်
offer (v; religious)	*hlu-deh*	လှူတယ်
office	*yòun*	ရုံး
officer (military)	*siq-bo*	စစ်ဗိုလ်
official	*ăya-shí*	အရာရှိ
often	*k'ăná-k'ăná*	ခဏခဏ
oil (cooking)	*s'i*	ဆီ

oil (petroleum)	*ye-nan*	ရေနံ
oily	*s'i myà-deh*	ဆီများတယ်
old (of person)	*ătheq-cì-deh*	အသက်ကြီးတယ်
old (of thing)	*hàun-deh*	ဟောင်းတယ်
on	*... hma*	... မှာ
once	*tăk'a*	တစ်ခါ
one	*tiq*	တစ်
open, be	*pwín-deh*	ပွင့်တယ်
open (something)	*p'wín-deh*	ဖွင့်တယ်
opinion	*ăyu-ăs'á*	အယူအဆ
opium	*bèin*	ဘိန်း
opportunity	*ăk'wín*	အခွင့်
opposite (adv)	*myeq-hnăjìn-s'ain*	မျက်နှာချင်းဆိုင်
opposition	*s'án-cin-beq*	ဆန့်ကျင်ဘက်
or	*da-hmá măhouq-yin*	ဒါမှ မဟုတ်ရင်
order (v: eg army)	*ăméin pè-deh*	အမိန့်ပေးတယ်
order (v; food etc)	*hma-deh*	မှာတယ်
order (n)	*ăméin*	အမိန့်
ordinary	*tha-man*	သာမန်
organisation	*ăs'ì-ăyòun*	အစည်းအရုံး
organise (v)	*si-zin-deh*	စီစဉ်တယ်
original	*năgo*	နဂို
orphan	*mí-pá-méh kălè*	မဘမဲ့ကလေး
other	*ăc'à*	အခြား
outside	*ăpyin-beq*	အပြင်ဘက်
overnight (v)	*nyá eiq-teh*	ညအိပ်တယ်
overseas	*pin-leh yaq-c'à*	ပင်လယ်ရပ်ခြား
owe (v)	*ăcwè tin-deh*	အကြွေးတင်တယ်
owner	*pain-shin*	ပိုင်ရှင်

P

package/packet	*ăt'ouq*	အထုပ်
pack of cigarettes	*sì-găreq tăt'ouq*	စီးကရက်တစ်ထုပ်
paddy (rice)	*zăbà*	စပါး
paddy (field)	*leh*	လယ်
padlock	*tháw-gălauq*	သော့ခလောက်
page	*sa-myeq-hna*	စာမျက်နှာ
painful	*na-ze-deh*	နာစေတယ်
painting	*păjì-kà*	ပန်းချီကား
pair	*tăyan/tăsoun*	တစ်ရန်/တစ်စုံ
palace	*nàn-daw*	နန်းတော်
paper	*seq-ku*	စက္ကူ
parade (v)	*tàn-si shauq-teh*	တန်းစီလျှောက်တယ်
parcel	*pa-s'el*	ပါဆယ်
parents	*mí-bá*	မိဘ
park	*pàn-jan*	ပန်းခြံ
parliament	*hluq-taw*	လွှတ်တော်
parrot	*ceq-tu-ywè*	ကြက်တူရွေး
part (piece)	*tăzeiq-/tăk'àn*	တစ်စိတ်/တခန်း
participate (v)	*pa-win-deh*	ပါဝင်တယ်
party (social)	*pyaw-bwèh*	ပျော်ပွဲ
party (political)	*pa-ti*	ပါတီ
party member	*pa-ti ăp'wéh-win*	ပါတီအဖွဲ့ဝင်
pass (mountain)	*taun-jà-làn*	တောင်ကြားလမ်း
passenger	*k'ăyì-dhi*	ခရီးသည်
passport	*nain-ngan-gù-leq-hmaq*	နိုင်ငံကူးလက်မှတ်
path	*làn*	လမ်း
patriotism	*myò-c'iq-seiq*	မျိုးချစ်စိတ်
pay (v)	*pè-deh*	ပေးတယ်

VOCABULARY

pay (n; monthly)	*lá-gá*	လခ
peace	*nyèin-jàn-yè*	ငြိမ်းချမ်းရေး
pearl	*pălèh*	ပုလဲ
pen	*baw-pin/kălaun*	ဘောပင်/ကလောင်
people (in general)	*lu-myà*	လူများ
People, The	*lu-dú*	လူထု
percentage	*ya-k'ain-hnoùn*	ရာခိုင်နှုန်း
period (time)	*kiq-ka-lá*	ခေတ်ကာလ
period, to have a	*ya-thi-thwè-cá-deh*	ရာသီသွေးလ ကျတယ်
permanent	*ămyèh-dàn*	အမြဲတမ်း
permission	*ăk'win*	အခွင့်
permit (v)	*k'win-pè-deh*	ခွင့်ပေးတယ်
permit (n)	*k'win-pyú-jeq*	ခွင့်ပြုချက်
persecute	*hnyin-s'eh-deh*	ညှင်းဆဲတယ်
person	*pouq-go*	ပုဂ္ဂိုလ်
personal, private	*pouq-gălí-ká*	ပုဂ္ဂလိက
personality, nature	*săyaiq*	စရိုက်
petrol (gasoline)	*daq-s'i*	ဓါတ်ဆီ
pharmacy	*s'è-zain*	ဆေးဆိုင်
photograph (n)	*daq-poun*	ဓါတ်ပုံ
photograph (v)	*daq-poun yaiq-teh*	ဓါတ်ပုံရိုက်တယ်
Can I take a	*daq-poun*	ဓါတ်ပုံရိုက်လို့
photograph?	*yaiq-ló yá-dhălà*	ရသလား။
piece	*ăseiq-ăpàin*	အစိတ်အပိုင်း
pilgrim	*p'ăyà-p'ù-dhi*	ဘုရားဖူးသည်
pilgrimage, go on a	*p'ăyà-p'ù-thwà-deh*	ဘုရားဖူးသွားတယ်
pill	*s'è-loùn*	ဆေးလုံး
pillow	*gaùn-oùn*	ခေါင်းအုံး
pipe (tobacco)	*s'è-dan*	ဆေးတံ

place	*ne-ya*	နေရာ
plane	*le-yin-byan*	လေယာဉ်ပျံ
plant (n)	*ăpin*	အပင်
plant(n)	*saiq-teh*	စိုက်တယ်
plate	*păgan*	ပန်းကန်
play (v)	*găza-deh*	ကစားတယ်
plug	*ăs'ó*	အဆို့
poem	*kăbya*	ကဗျာ
point (v)	*hnyun-deh*	ညွှန်တယ်
poison	*ăs'eiq*	အဆိပ်
police	*yè*	ရဲ
politics	*nain-ngan-yè*	နိုင်ငံရေး
pollution	*nyiq-nyàn-ze-da*	ညစ်ညမ်းစေတာ
pool (swimming)	*ye-kù-gan*	ရေကူးကန်
poor	*s'ìn-yèh-deh*	ဆင်းရဲတယ်
post office	*sa-daiq*	စာတိုက်
pot	*ò*	အိုး
poverty	*s'ìn-yèh-da*	ဆင်းရဲတာ
power (influence)	*àw-za*	ဩဇာ
practical	*leq-twéh-cá-deh*	လက်တွေ့ကျတယ်
pray	*s'ú-t'àun-deh*	ဆုတောင်းတယ်
prefer	*po-caiq-teh*	ပိုကြိုက်တယ်
pregnant	*ko-wun shí-deh*	ကိုယ်ဝန်ရှိတယ်
prepare	*pyin-zin-deh*	ပြင်ဆင်တယ်
present (time)	*ăk'ú ăk'a*	အခုအခါ
present (gift)	*leq-s'aun*	လက်ဆောင်
president	*thămădá*	သမ္မတ
pretty	*hlá-deh*	လှတယ်
prevent	*tà-s'ì-deh*	တားဆီးတယ်

VOCABULARY

price	zè-hnoùn	ဈေးနှုန်း
pride	ma-ná	မာန
prime minister	wun-jì-jouq	ဝန်ကြီးချုပ်
prison	ăcìn-daun	အကျဉ်းထောင်
prison sentence	t'aun-dan	ထောင်ဒဏ်
prisoner (m)	ăcìn-dhà	အကျဉ်းသား
prisoner (f)	ăcìn-dhu	အကျဉ်းသူ
prisoner of war	siq-thoún-bàn	စစ်သုံ့ပန်း
private (army)	siq-thà	စစ်သား
private possession	ko-bain pyiq-sì	ကိုယ်ပိုင်ပစ္စည်း
problem	pyaq-dhăna	ပြဿနာ
profit	ămyaq	အမြတ်
programme	ăsi-ăsin	အစီအစဉ်
promise (n)	gădí	ကတိ
promise (v)	gădí pyú-deh	ကတိပြုတယ်
prostitute	pyé-dăza	ပြည့်တန်ဆာ
protect	ka-kweh-deh	ကာကွယ်တယ်
protest (n; march)	s'an-dá pyá-bwèh	ဆန္ဒပြပွဲ
public	ămyà pye-dhu	အများပြည်သူ
pull	s'wèh-deh	ဆွဲတယ်
push	tùn-deh	တွန်းတယ်
pun	zăgà-lein	စကားလိမ်

Q

quality	ăyi-ăthwè	အရည်အသွေး
quarter (fourth)	ăseiq/	အစိတ်/လေးပုံတစ်ပုံ
	lè-poún-tăpoun	
quarter (town)	yaq-kweq	ရပ်ကွက်
queen	băyin-má	ဘုရင်မ

question (n)	*mè-gùn*	မေးခွန်း
queue (v)	*tàn-si-deh*	တန်းစီတယ်
quick	*myan-deh*	မြန်တယ်
quiet	*nyein-theq-teh*	ငြိမ်သက်တယ်

R

race (contest)	*ăpyè-pyàin-bwè*	အပြေးပြိုင်းပွဲ
railway (line)	*mì-yăt'à-làn*	မီးရထားလမ်း
rain (v)	*mò*	မိုး
It's raining.	*mò ywa-ne-deh*	မိုးရွာနေတယ်။
rape (n)	*mú-dèin*	မုဒိမ်း
rape (v)	*mú-dèin cín-deh*	မုဒိမ်းကျင့်တယ်
rare	*shà-pà-deh*	ရှားပါးတယ်
rat	*cweq*	ကြွက်
raw	*ăsèin*	အစိမ်း
read	*p'aq-teh*	ဖတ်တယ်
ready	*ăthín-shí-deh*	အသင့်ရှိတယ်
reason	*ăcò-ăcàun*	အကျိုးအကြောင်း
receipt	*pye-za*	ပြေစာ
recently	*măca-gin-gá*	မကြာခင်က
recommend	*ăcan pè-deh*	အကြံပေးတယ်
refugee	*douq-k'á-dhi*	ဒုက္ခသည်
refund (v)	*pyan-àn-deh*	ပြန်အမ်းတယ်
refuse (v)	*leq-măk'an-bù*	လက်မခံဘူး
region	*de-thá*	ဒေသ
regulation	*nì-ú-băde*	နည်းဥပဒေ
relatives	*swe-myò-dwe*	ဆွေမျိုးတွေ
relationship	*ăs'weq-ăsaq*	အဆက်အစပ်
relax, rest (v)	*ănà-yu-deh*	အနားယူတယ်

religion	*ba-dha-yè*	ဘာသာရေး
remember (recognise)	*hmaq-mí-deh*	မှတ်မိတယ်
remember (think of)	*dhǎdí-yá-deh*	သတိရတယ်
remote	*theiq-wè-deh*	သိပ်ဝေးတယ်
rent (n)	*hngà-gá*	ငှါးခ
rent (v)	*hngà-deh*	ငှါးတယ်
repeat	*pyan ...*	ပြန် ...
Please repeat that.	*pyan-pyàw-ba-oùn*	ပြန်ပြောပါအုံး။
representative	*ko-zà-hleh*	ကိုယ်စားလှယ်
republic	*thǎmǎdá nain-ngan*	သမ္မတနိုင်ငံ
reserve (v)	*co-tin-si-sin-t'à-deh*	ကြိုတင်စီစဉ်ထားတယ်
respect (n)	*yo-the-deh*	ရိုသေတယ်
responsibility	*ta-wun*	တာဝန်
restaurant	*sa-thauq-s'ain*	စားသောက်ဆိုင်
return (v)	*pyan-deh*	ပြန်တယ်
We'll return on ...	*... pyan-la-meh*	... ပြန်လာမယ်။
return ticket	*ǎthwà-ǎpyan leq-hmaq*	အသွားအပြန်လက်မှတ်
revolution	*taw-hlan-yè*	တော်လှန်ရေး
rich	*càn-tha-deh*	ချမ်းသာတယ်
rich person	*thǎt'è*	သူဌေး
right (not left)	*nya-beq*	ညာဘက်
right (correct)	*hman-deh*	မှန်တယ်
ripe	*hméh-deh*	မှည့်တယ်
risky	*bèh-myà-deh*	ဘေးများတယ်
river	*myiq*	မြစ်
road	*làn*	လမ်း

robber ('dacoit')	*dămyá*	ဓါးပြ
robe	*thin-gàn*	သင်္ကန်း
roof	*ămò*	အမိုး
room	*ăk'àn*	အခန်း
root	*ămyiq*	အမြစ်
rope	*cò*	ကြိုး
rotten	*pouq-teh*	ပုပ်တယ်
round (adj)	*wàin-deh*	ဝိုင်းတယ်
rubber	*ceq-paun-zè*	ကြက်ပေါင်ဆေး
rubbish	*ăhmaiq*	အမှိုက်
rude	*yàin-deh*	ရိုင်းတယ်
ruins	*ăpyeq- ăsì*	အပျက်အစီး
rule (n; regulation)	*sì-kàn*	စည်းကမ်း
rule (v; govern)	*ouq-c'ouq-teh*	အုပ်ချုပ်တယ်
run	*pyè-deh*	ပြေးတယ်

S

sad	*wùn-nèh-deh*	ဝမ်းနည်းတယ်
safe (n)	*mì-k'an-tiq-ta*	မီးခံသေတ္တာ
safe (adj)	*bè-kin-deh*	ဘေးကင်းတယ်
salary (monthly)	*lá-sa*	လစာ
salty	*s'à-ngan-deh*	ဆားငန်တယ်
same	*ătu-du*	အတူတူ
sand	*thèh*	သဲ
sandbank	*thaun*	သောင်
sardine	*ngà-tiq-ta*	ငါးသေတ္တာ
satellite	*jo-dú*	ဂြိုဟ်တု

say	*pyàw-deh /s'o-deh*	ပြောတယ်/ဆိုတယ်
I said ...	*... ló s'o-deh*	... လို့ ဆိုတယ်။
Can you say that again?	*pyan-pyàw-ba?*	ပြန်ပြောပါ။
scenery	*shú-hmyaw-kìn*	ရှုမျှော်ခင်း
schedule	*ăsi-ăsin*	အစီအစဉ်
school	*caùn*	ကျောင်း
scissors	*kaq-cì*	ကတ်ကြေး
scorpion	*kìn-mì-gauk*	ကင်းမြီးကောက်
seasickness	*hlàin-mù-deh*	လှိုင်းမူးတယ်
secret (adj)	*shó-hweq-teh*	လျှို့ဝှက်တယ်
see	*myin-deh*	မြင်တယ်
I see. (understand)	*nà-leh-deh*	နားလည်တယ်။
I see. (it)	*ho-ha myin-deh*	ဟိုဟာ မြင်တယ်။
selfish	*kó-ăcò cí-deh*	ကိုယ့်အကျိုးကြည့်တယ်။
sell	*yàun-deh*	ရောင်းတယ်
send	*pó-deh*	ပို့တယ်
sentence (words)	*weq-cá*	ဝါကျ
serious	*lè-neq-teh*	လေးနက်တယ်
several	*ătaw-ătan*	အတော်အတန်
sex (n)	*lein*	လိင်
shade (n)	*ăyeiq*	အရိပ်
share (v)	*we-zú-deh*	ဝေစုတယ်
share (n)	*we-zú*	ဝေစု
shave	*yeiq-teh*	ရိတ်တယ်
sheet (bed)	*eiq-ya-k'ìn*	အိပ်ရာခင်း
shop	*s'ain*	ဆိုင်
shoot (gun)	*pyiq-teh*	ပစ်တယ်
shoot (movie)	*yaiq-teh*	ရိုက်တယ်

short (height)	*pú-deh*	ပုတယ်
shortage	*pyaq-laq-hmú*	ပြတ်လပ်မှု
shout (v)	*aw-deh*	အော်တယ်
show (v)	*pyá-deh*	ပြတယ်
Show me.	*cǎnaw/cǎmá-go pyá-ba*	ကျွန်တော်/ကျွန်မကို ပြပါ။
shut (closed)	*peiq-teh*	ပိတ်တယ်
shy	*sheq-teh*	ရှက်တယ်
sick (unwell)	*ne-mǎkaùn-bù*	နေမကောင်းဘူး
sign (n)	*ǎhmaq-ǎthà*	အမှတ်အသား
sign (v; one's name)	*leq-hmaq t'ò-deh*	လက်မှတ်ထိုးတယ်
similar	*tu-nyi-deh*	တူညီတယ်
since	*... gǎdèh-gá*	... ကထည်းက
sing	*dhǎjìn-s'o-deh*	သီချင်းဆိုတယ်
single (unmarried)	*ein-daun mǎcá-thè-bù*	အိမ်ထောင်မကျသေးဘူး။
sink (n)	*leq-s'è-gan/be-sin*	လက်ဆေးကန်/ဘေစင်
sit	*t'ain-deh*	ထိုင်တယ်
situation	*ǎc'e-ǎne*	အခြေအနေ
size	*ǎyweh*	အရွယ်
skin	*ǎye*	အရေ
sky	*kaùn-gin*	ကောင်းကင်
sleep (v)	*eiq-teh*	အိပ်တယ်
sleepy (to be)	*eiq-c'in-deh*	အိပ်ချင်တယ်
slow (retarded)	*hnè-deh*	နှေးတယ်
Please drive slowly.	*pyè-pyè maùn-ba*	ပြည်းပြည်းမောင်းပါ။
small	*ngeh-deh*	ငယ်တယ်
smell (good)	*hmwè-deh*	မွှေးတယ်
smell (bad)	*nan-deh*	နံတယ်

smile	*pyoùn-deh*	ပြုံးတယ်
snake	*hmwe*	မြွေ
socialism	*s'o-sheh-liq-sániq*	ဆိုရှယ်လစ်စနစ်
soft	*nú-deh*	နုတယ်
soldier	*siq-thà*	စစ်သား
sole (of foot)	*c'e-p'ăwà*	ခြေဖဝါး
solid (sturdy)	*k'ain-deh*	ခိုင်တယ်
some	*tăc'ó*	တချို့
somebody	*tăsoun-tăyauq*	တစ်စုံတယောက်
something	*tăk'ú-gú*	တစ်ခုခု
sometimes	*tăk'a-tăle*	တစ်ခါတလေ
son	*thà*	သား
song	*tè/dhăjìn*	တေး/သီချင်း
soon	*măca-gin*	မကြာခင်
sorry, I'm	*wùn-nèh-ba-deh*	ဝမ်းနည်းပါတယ်။
souvenir	*ăhmaq-tăyá*	အမှတ်တရ
spa	*ye-pu-sàn*	ရေပူစမ်း
speak	*zăgà-pyaw-deh*	စကားပြောတယ်
special	*ăt'ù săpeh-sheh*	အထူးစပယ်ရှယ်
spider	*pín-gu*	ပင့်ကူ
spirit shrine	*naq-kùn*	နတ်ကွန်း
spoon	*zùn*	ဇွန်း
sport	*à-găzà*	အားကစား
stairs/ladder	*hle-gà*	လှေခါး
stamp	*tăzeiq-k'aùn*	တံဆိပ်ခေါင်း
standard, level	*ăs'ín-ătàn*	အဆင့်အတန်း
star (in sky)	*kyeh*	ကြယ်
state (nation)	*nain-ngan*	နိုင်ငံ

station	*bu-da-youn*	ဘူတာရဲ့
stay (v; lodge with)	*tèh-deh*	တည်းတယ်
stay (v; remain)	*ne-deh*	နေတယ်
steal	*k'ò-deh*	ခိုးတယ်
sting (v)	*touq-teh*	တုပ်တယ်
stone	*cauq-tòun*	ကျောက်တုံး
stop (v)	*yaq-teh*	ရပ်တယ်
storm	*moun-dàin*	မုန်တိုင်း
story (tale)	*wuq-t'ú*	ဝတ္ထု
straight	*téh-déh*	တည့်တည့်
strange	*t'ù-s'àn-deh*	ထူးဆန်းတယ်
stranger	*lu-zèin*	လူစိမ်း
street	*làn*	လမ်း
strike (on)	*thăbeiq-hmauq-teh*	သပိတ်မှောက်တယ်
string	*cò*	ကြိုး
strong (person)	*à-shí-deh*	အားရှိတယ်
study (v)	*thin-deh*	သင်တယ်
student (f)	*caùn-thu*	ကျောင်းသူ
student (m)	*caùn-thà*	ကျောင်းသား
stupid	*maiq-teh*	မိုက်တယ်
successful	*aun-myin-deh*	အောင်မြင်တယ်
suddenly	*youq-tăyeq*	ရုတ်တရက်
sun	*ne*	နေ
sunglasses	*ne-ga myeq-hman*	နေကာမျက်မှန်
sunrise	*ne-t'weq-c'ein*	နေထွက်ချိန်
sunset	*ne-win-c'ein*	နေဝင်ချိန်
sure	*the-ja-deh*	သေချာတယ်
Are you sure?	*the-ja-yéh-là?*	သေချာရဲ့လား။

VOCABULARY

surprised	*án-áw-deh*	အံ့ဩတယ်
swear (v; curse)	*s'èh-deh*	ဆဲတယ်
sweat (v)	*c'wè-t'weq-teh*	ချွေးထွက်တယ်
sweat (n)	*c'wè*	ချွေး
sweet (adj)	*c'o-deh*	ချိုတယ်
swim (v)	*ye kù-deh*	ရေ ကူးတယ်

T

table	*zăbwèh*	စားပွဲ
tail	*ămì*	အမြီး
tailor	*aq-c'ouq-dhămà*	အပ်ချုပ်သမား
take	*yu-deh*	ယူတယ်
I'll take one.	*tăk'ú yu-meh*	တစ်ခု ယူမယ်။
Can I take this?	*di-tăk'ú*	ဒီတစ်ခု
	yu-ló-yá-là?	ယူလို့ရလား။
talk (v)	*pyàw-deh /s'o-deh*	ပြောတယ်/ဆိုတယ်
tall	*ăyaq myín-deh*	အရပ်မြင့်တယ်
tasty	*ăyá-tha shí-deh*	အရသာရှိတယ်
tax	*ăk'un*	အခွန်
teacher (f)	*caùn-s'ăya-má*	ကျောင်းဆရာမ
telephone (n)	*(teh-li-)p'òun*	(တယ်လီ)ဖုန်း
telephone (v)	*p'òun s'eq-deh*	ဖုန်းဆက်တယ်
telephone book	*p'òun làn-hnyun*	ဖုန်းလမ်းညွှန်
temperature (weather)	*ăpu-c'ein*	အပူချိန်
temperature, have (fever)	*p'yà-deh*	ဖျားတယ်
tent	*mò-ga-tèh*	မိုးကာတဲ

thank (v)	*cè-zù-tin-zăgà*	ကျေးဇူးတင်စကား
	pyàw-deh	ပြောတယ်
Thanks.	*cè-zù-bèh*	ကျေးဇူးပဲ။
Thank you.	*cè-zù-tin-ba-deh*	ကျေးဇူးတင်ပါတယ်။
then (at that time)	*ho ăc'ein-gá*	ဟိုအချိန်က
then (next)	*eh-di nauq*	အဲဒီနောက်
there	*ho-hma*	ဟိုမှာ
thermos	*daq-bù*	ဓါတ်ဘူး
thick	*t'u-deh*	ထူတယ်
thief	*thăk'ò*	သူခိုး
thin (thing)	*pà-deh*	ပါးတယ်
thin (person)	*pein-deh*	ပိန်တယ်
thing	*pyiq-sì*	ပစ္စည်း
think	*t'in-deh*	ထင်တယ်
thirsty (to be)	*ye ngaq-teh*	ရေ ငတ်တယ်
throw	*pyiq-teh*	ပစ်တယ်
thumb	*leq-má*	လက်မ
thunder (v)	*mò-jein-deh*	မိုးခြိမ်းတယ်
ticket	*leq-hmaq*	လက်မှတ်
tight/crowded (adj)	*caq-teh*	ကျပ်တယ်
time	*ăc'ein*	အချိန်
What time is it?	*beh ăc'ein shí-bi-lèh?*	ဘယ်အချိန်ရှိပြီလဲ။
timetable	*ăcein-săyìn*	အချိန်စာရင်း
tin can	*bù*	ဘူး
tin can opener	*bù-p'wín-seq*	ဘူးဖွင့်စက်
tip ('donation')	*dhădą-jè*	သဒ္ဒါကြေး
tired, I'm	*nùn-deh/màw-deh*	နွမ်းတယ်/မောတယ်
tobacco	*s'è-yweq-cì*	ဆေးရွက်ကြီး

today	*di-né*	ဒီနေ့
together	*ătu-du*	အတူတူ
toilet	*ein-dha*	အိမ်သာ
toilet paper	*ein-dha seq-ku*	အိမ်သာစက္ကူ
tomorrow	*mǎneq-p'yan*	မနက်ဖြန်
tonight	*di-né-nyá*	ဒီနေ့ည
tongue	*sha*	လျှာ
too	*... lèh*	... လည်း
toothbrush	*thǎpuq-tan*	သွားပွတ်တံ
toothpaste	*thwà-taiq-s'è*	သွားတိုက်ဆေး
toothpick	*thwà-jà-t'ò-dan*	သွားကြားထိုးတံ
torch (flashlight)	*leq-hneiq-daq-mì*	လက်နှိပ်ဓါတ်မီး
touch (feel) (v)	*t'í-deh*	ထိတယ်
tour (v)	*k'ǎyì-thwà-deh*	ခရီးသွားတယ်
tourist	*k'ǎyì-dhi*	ခရီးသည်
toward	*... beq-go*	... ဘက်ကို
towel	*myeq-hnǎthouq-pǎwa*	မျက်နှာသုတ်ပုဝါ
town	*myó*	မြို့
toy	*gǎzà-sǎya*	ကစားစရာ
trade	*koun-thweh-yè*	ကုန်သွယ်ရေး
trade union	*thá-meq-gá*	သမဂ္ဂ
tradition	*dǎlé*	ဓလေ့
traditional	*yò-ya*	ရိုးရာ
translate (spoken)	*sǎgà pyan-deh*	စကားပြန်တယ်
translate (written)	*ba-dha pyan-deh*	ဘာသာပြန်တယ်
travel agency	*k'ǎyì-thwà-louq-ngan*	ခရီးသွားလုပ်ငန်း
tree	*thiq-pin*	သစ်ပင်
trek ('walk')	*làn shauq-teh*	လမ်းလျှောက်တယ်
trip	*k'ǎyì*	ခရီး

truck (lorry)	*koun-tin-kà*	ကုန်တင်ကား
true	*hman-deh*	မှန်တယ်
trust	*youn-ci-deh*	ယုံကြည်တယ်
try (+ v)	*... cí-deh*	... ကြည့်တယ်
Try it! (food)	*sà-jí-ba*	စားကြည့်ပါ။
turtle	*leiq*	လိပ်
twice	*hnăk'a/hnăs'a*	နှစ်ခါ/နှစ်ဆ
typewriter	*leq-hneiq-seq*	လက်နှိပ်စက်

U

ugly	*ăyouq s'ò-deh*	အရုပ်ဆိုးတယ်
umbrella	*t'ì*	ထီး
uncle	*ù-jì/ù-lè*	ဦးကြီး/ဦးလေး
under	*auq-hma*	အောက်မှာ
understand	*nà-leh-deh*	နားလည်တယ်
I don't understand.	*nà-măleh-ba-bù*	နားမလည်ပါဘူး။
unemployed (adj)	*ălouq-méh*	အလုပ်မဲ့
United Nations	*kú-lá thá-meq-gá*	ကုလသမဂ္ဂ
university	*teq-kătho*	တက္ကသိုလ်
unsafe	*măloun-joun-bù*	မလုံခြုံဘူး
until	*ăt'í*	အထိ
up	*ăt'eq-ko*	အထက်ကို
upstairs	*ăpaw-daq-hma*	အပေါ်ထပ်မှာ
urinate	*s'ì-thwà-deh*	ဆီးသွားတယ်
useful	*ăthòun cá-deh*	အသုံးကျတယ်

V

vaccinate	*cauq-s'è t'ò-deh*	ကျောက်ဆေးထိုးတယ်
vaccine	*cauq-s'è-yeh*	ကျောက်ဆေးရည်

valley	*taun-jà*	တောင်ကြား
valuable	*ăp'ò cì-deh*	အဖိုးကြီးတယ်
value (price)	*ăp'ò*	အဖိုး
vegetable	*hìn-dhì-hìn-yweq*	ဟင်းသီးဟင်းရွက်
vegetarian (adj/n)	*theq-thaq-luq*	သက်သတ်လွတ်
very	*theiq/ăyàn*	သိပ်/အရမ်း
veteran	*siq-pyan*	စစ်ပြန်
view (n)	*myin-kwìn*	မြင်ကွင်း
village	*ywa*	ရွာ
visa	*bi-za*	ဗီဇာ
visit (v)	*thwà-leh-deh*	သွားလည်တယ်
vitamin	*bi-ta-min*	ဗီတာမင်
voice	*ăthan*	အသံ
vomit	*an-deh*	အန်တယ်
vote (v)	*mèh-s'an-dá pè-deh*	မဲဆန္ဒပေးတယ်

W

waist	*k'à*	ခါး
wait	*sáun-ne-deh*	စောင့်နေတယ်
Wait a moment!	*k'ăná sáun-ne-ba!*	ခဏစောင့်နေပါ။
wake (someone)	*hnò-deh*	နှိုးတယ်
walk	*làn shauq-teh*	လမ်းလျှောက်တယ်
wall	*nan-yan*	နံရံ
wallet	*paiq-s'an-eiq*	ပိုက်ဆံအိတ်
want (see pg 26)	*lo-jin-deh*	လိုချင်တယ်
I want ...	*cănaw/cămá ...*	ကျွန်တော်/ကျွန်မ ...
	lo-jin-deh	လိုချင်တယ်။
Do you want ...?	*... lo-jin-dhălà*	... လိုချင်သလား။

war	*siq*	စစ်
warm	*nwè-deh*	နွေးတယ်
wash (oneself)	*ye-c'ò-deh*	ရေချိုးတယ်
I want to bathe.	*ye-c'ò-jin-ba-deh*	ရေချိုးချင်ပါတယ်။
wash (clothes, hair)	*shaw-deh*	လျှော်တယ်
The clothes need to be washed.	*ăwuq shaw-yà-meh*	အဝတ်လျှော်ရမယ်။
watch (v)	*cí-deh*	ကြည့်တယ်
watch (timepiece)	*leq-paq-na-yi*	လက်ပတ်နာရီ
water	*ye*	ရေ
waterfall	*ye-dăgun*	ရေတံခွန်
wax	*p'ăyàun*	ဖယောင်း
way/manner (n)	*nì*	နည်း
weak	*ìn-à măshí-bù*	အင်းအားမရှိဘူး
wear	*wuq-teh*	ဝတ်တယ်
weather	*mò-le-wá-dhá*	မိုးလေဝသ
weave	*yeq-teh*	ရက်တယ်
week	*ăpaq*	အပတ်
weight	*ălè-c'ein*	အလေးချိန်
well (n)	*ye-dwìn*	ရေတွင်း
wet	*so-deh*	စိုတယ်
what	*ba ...*	ဘာ
What time is it?	*beh ăc'ein shí-bi-lèh?*	ဘယ်အချိန်ရှိပြီလဲ။
What did you say?	*ba pyàw-dhălèh?*	ဘာပြောသလဲ။
wheel	*bèin*	ဘီး
when (in past)	*beh-dòun-gá*	ဘယ်တုန်းက
When did you arrive in Myanmar?	*Myăma-pye beh-dòun-gá yauq-thălèh?*	မြန်မာပြည် ဘယ်တုန်းက ရောက်သလဲ။

when (in future)	*beh-dáw*	ဘယ်တော့
When is the next	*nauq-thin-bàw*	နောက်သဘော
boat?	*beh-dàw-lèh?*	ဘယ်တော့လဲ။
where	*beh-hma*	ဘယ်မှာ
Where is ... ?	*... beh-hma-lèh?*	... ဘယ်မှာလဲ။
who	*bădhu*	ဘယ်သူ
Who do I ask?	*bădhú-go*	ဘယ်သူ့ကို
	mè-yá-dhălèh?	မေးရသလဲ။
wide	*ceh-deh*	ကျယ်တယ်
wife	*zănì/măyà*	ဇနီး/မယား
win	*nain-deh*	နိုင်တယ်
wing	*ătaun-ban*	အတောင်ပံ
wise	*pyin-nya shí-deh*	ပညာ ရှိတယ်
wish (n)	*s'ú*	ဆု
wish (v)	*s'ú taùn-deh*	ဆုတောင်းတယ်
with	*... néh*	... နဲ့
within	*ăt'èh-hma*	အထဲမှာ
wood	*thiq-thà*	သစ်သား
wool	*thò-mwè*	သိုးမွေး
work (v)	*ălouq-louq-teh*	အလုပ်လုပ်တယ်
work (n)	*ălouq*	အလုပ်
world	*kăba*	ကမ္ဘာ
worse	*po-s'ò-deh*	ပိုဆိုးတယ်
write	*yè-deh*	ရေးတယ်
wrong	*hmà-deh*	မှားတယ်

Y

yawn (v)	*thàn-deh*	သမ်းတယ်
year	*hniq*	နှစ်

Yes.	*houq-kéh*	ဟုတ်ကဲ့။
yesterday	*măné-gá*	မနေ့က
young	*ngeh-deh*	ငယ်တယ်

Z

zero	*thoun-nyá*	သုည
zone	*ăpàin*	အပိုင်း
zoo	*dăreiq-s'an-youn*	တိရစ္ဆာန်ရုံ

Emergencies

Help!	*keh-ba*	ကယ်ပါ။
Watch out!	*dhădí t'à-ba*	သတိထားပါ။
Go away!	*thwà-zàn*	သွားဆန်း။
Stop!	*yaq*	ရပ်။
Don't do it!	*mălouq-néh*	မလုပ်နဲ့။
Thief!	*thăk'ò*	သူခိုး။
Pickpocket!	*găbaiq-hnaiq*	ခါးပိုက်နှိုက်။

Call a doctor!
  s'ăya-wun-go k'aw-pè-ba   ဆရာဝန်ကို ခေါ်ပေးပါ။
Call an ambulance!
  lu-na-din-gà k'aw-pè-ba   လူနာတင်ကားခေါ်ပေးပါ။
I am ill.
  ne-măkàun-bù   နေမကောင်းဘူး။

I am lost.
  làn pyauq-thwà-bi   လမ်းပျောက်သွားပြီ။
I've been raped.
  mú-dèin cín-k'an-yá-deh   မုဒိမ်းကျင့်ခံရတယ်။
I've been robbed.
  ăk'ò-k'an-yá-deh   အခိုးခံရတယ်။

176

My pocket was picked.
găbaiq-hnaiq k'an-yá-deh ခါးပိုက်နှိုက်ခံရတယ်။

My camera was stolen.
cănáw/cămá kin-măra ကျွန်တော်/ ကျွန်မ
k'ò-k'an-yá-deh ကင်မရာခိုးခံရတယ်။

I've lost … *cănaw/cămá …* ကျွန်တော်/ ကျွန်မ
  pyauq-thwà-deh ပျောက်သွားတယ်။

my bag	*tiq-ta*	သေတ္တာ
my money	*paiq-s'an*	ပိုက်ဆံ
my passport	*nain-ngan-kù-*	နိုင်ငံကူးလက်မှတ်
	leq-hmaq	
my travellers' cheques	*k'ăyì c'eq-leq-hmaq*	ခရီးချက်လက်မှတ်

Could I use the telephone?
teh-li-p'òun k'ăná တယ်လီဖုန်း ခဏ ဆက်လို့ရသလား။
s'eq-ló-yá-dhălà?

I have (medical) insurance.
cănaw/cămá (s'è) a-má-gan ကျွန်တော်/ ကျွန်မ (ဆေး)
shí-ba-deh အာမခံ ရှိပါတယ်။

Index

LONELY PLANET PHRASEBOOKS

Complete your travel experience with a Lonely Planet phrasebook. Developed for the independent traveller, the phrasebooks enable you to communicate confidently in any practical situation – and get to know the local people and their culture.

Skipping lengthy details on where to get your drycleaning ironed, information in the phrasebooks covers bargaining, customs and protocol, how to address people and introduce yourself, explanations of local ways of telling the time, dealing with bureaucracy and bargaining, plus plenty of ways to share your interests and learn from locals.

Arabic (Egyptian)
Arabic (Moroccan)
Australian
  *Introduction to Australian English,
  Aboriginal and Torres Strait languages.*
Baltic States
  *Covers Estonian, Latvian and
  Lithuanian.*
Bengali
Brazilian
Burmese
Cantonese
Central Europe
  *Covers Czech, French, German,
  Hungarian, Italian and Slovak.*
Eastern Europe
  *Covers Bulgarian, Czech, Hungarian,
  Polish, Romanian and Slovak.*
Ethiopian (Amharic)
Fijian
Greek
Hindi/Urdu
Indonesian
Japanese
Korean
Lao
Latin American (Spanish)
Mandarin

Mediterranean Europe
  *Covers Albanian, Greek, Italian,
  Macedonian, Maltese, Serbian &
  Croatian and Slovene.*
Mongolian
Nepali
Papua New Guinea (Pidgin)
Pilipino
Quechua
Russian
Scandinavian Europe
  *Covers Danish, Finnish, Icelandic,
  Norwegian and Swedish.*
Sri Lanka
Swahili
Thai
Thai Hill Tribes
Tibetan
Turkish
USA
  *Introduction to US English,
  Vernacular Talk, Native American
  languages and Hawaiian.*
Vietnamese
Western Europe
  *Useful words and phrases in Basque,
  Catalan, Dutch, French, German, Irish,
  Portuguese and Spanish (Castilian).*

LONELY PLANET AUDIO PACKS

Audio packs are an innovative combination of a cassette/CD and phrasebook presented in an attractive cloth wallet made from indigenous textiles by local communities.

The cassette/CD presents each language in an interactive format. A number of successful language teaching techniques are used, enabling listeners to remember useful words and phrases with little effort and in an enjoyable way.

Travellers will learn essential words and phrases – and their correct pronunciation – by participating in a realistic story. The scripts have been developed in the belief that the best way to learn a new language is to hear it, then to practise it in the context in which you will use it. The emphasis is on effective communication.

The cassette/CD complements the relevant phrasebook, and the cloth wallet makes the pack an attractive and convenient package – easy to display in shops and useful and practical for travellers.

Cassettes & CDs
* complement phrasebooks
* realistic storylines explore situations that will be useful for all travellers
* languages are spoken by native speakers
* listeners learn key words and phrases in repetition exercises, then hear them used in context
* realistic sound effects and indigenous music used throughout
* length: 80 minutes

Cloth Pack
* ticket-wallet size – suitable for airline tickets, notes etc
* made from traditional textiles woven and sewn by local communities
* cardboard reinforced and sealed in plastic for easy display
* size: 140 x 260 mm

Available now: Indonesian audio pack; Japanese audio pack; Thai audio pack

PLANET TALK

Lonely Planet's FREE quarterly newsletter

Every issue is packed with up-to-date travel news
and advice including:

- a letter from Lonely Planet co-founders Tony and
  Maureen Wheeler
- go behind the scenes on the road with a Lonely
  Planet author
- feature article on an important and topical travel
  issue
- a selection of recent letters from travellers
- details on forthcoming Lonely planet promotions
- complete list of Lonely Planet products

To join our mailing list contact any Lonely Planet office.

LONELY PLANET PUBLICATIONS

AUSTRALIA
PO Box 617, Hawthorn 3122, Victoria
tel: (03) 9819 1877 fax: (03) 9819 6459
e-mail: talk2us@lonelyplanet.com.au

USA
Embarcadero West,
155 Filbert St, Suite 251,
Oakland, CA 94607
tel: (510) 893 8555
TOLL FREE: 800 275-8555
fax: (510) 893 8563
e-mail: info@lonelyplanet.com

UK
10 Barley Mow Passage, Chiswick,
London W4 4PH
tel: (0181) 742 3161 fax: (0181) 742 2772
e-mail: 100413.3551@compuserve.com

FRANCE:
71 bis rue du Cardinal Lemoine, 75005
Paris
tel: 1 44 32 06 20 fax: 1 46 34 72 55
e-mail: 100560.415@compuserve.com

World Wide Web: http://www.lonelyplanet.com